THE EPIC HERO IN CAMPŪ KĀVYA

(A Study of the Campūrāmāyaṇa)

INDIRA SAIKIA
Department of Sanskrit
Pragjyotish College, Guwahati-9
Kamrup (Assam)

PUNTHI PUSTAK
KOLKATA - 700004
INDIA

Published by
P. K. Bhattacharjee
PUNTHI PUSTAK
Publishers, Booksellers & Exporters
136/4B, Bidhan Sarani
P. O. Box-16602
Kolkata - 700004
Fax - 91-33-25555573
Tex : 2555-5573
E-mail : punthipustak@hotmail.com
info@punthipustak.com
Website www.punthipustak.com

First Published
2004

ISBN : 81-86791-47-7

Price : Rs. 450

Printed at
ARUNIMA PRINTING WORKS
81, Simla Street
Kolkata - 700006

Dedicated to
The sacred memory of
Late lamented brother-in-law
G.K. Bora with affection and respect

Author

FOREWORD

I consider it my privilege to forward Dr. Indira Saikia's *Epic Hero in Campūkāvya :* a critical assessment of the *Campūrāmāyaṇa,* to the literary circle. Campū is a mixed literary composition in which prose and verse are blended for a single purpose. The art was cultured by Indians since very ancient times. It been clearly noticed in the *Ādiparvan* of the *Mahābhārata* itself in the beginning of classical Sanskrit literature. Campū, however, emerged as a distinct class of ornamental literature since the 10th century A.D. when Trivikramabhaṭṭa wrote his famous *Nalacampū* on the love story of Nala and Damayantī of the *Mahābhārata.* As centuries rolled on, Campū writers employed many new techniques in their writing in order to impart novelty to the particular type of Kāvya literature. Dr. Indira Saikia has discussed these features appropriately in the introduction to her book.

King Bhoja of Dhārā, the author of his single Campūkāvya, was a prolific writer and a profound scholar. He was a master in almost all branches of Sanskrit literature right from poetics to vāstuśātra, horse-lore, veterinary science, lexicography, grammar, astrology and the Śaiva philosophy.

Dr. Saikia has rendered a very useful service to the academic circle by writing an eleborate and exhaustive critical work on the *Campūrāmāyaṇa* which will immensely benefit the common readers and scholars alike. She has not only adequately discussed the poetic merits of the *Campūrāmāyaṇa,* but also has put forth an excellent-introduction to the extensive literary activities of Bhoja. The introduction displays the great scholarship and critical insight of the author. The *Epic Hero in the Campūkāvya* is truly relishable to the connoisseurs of poetry.

May 30, 2004 **Apurba Chandra Borthakuria**

PREFACE

This book is based on a part of my thesis entitled "The *Campūrāmāyaṇa* – A study" which was presented and approved for the Degree of Doctor of philosophy in the University of Gauhati in 1993. A few amendments have been made in it. The importance of the *Campūrāmāyaṇa* lies in the fact that it was responsible for changing the sentimental appeal of the mixed Kāvya to that of the intellectual and hence began a new approach in the history of sanskrit literature. Embellished expressions are not rare in sanskrit literature from the very remote period.

I always found a deep interest in the study of the Campū literature which by itself is a distinct class of poetic composition. Though some Campū Kāvyas are greatly mechanical and cumberous, I was attracted by the style of writing and the other literary beauties of the *Campūrāmāyaṇa*.

I had an opportunity of studing the *Campūrāmāyaṇa* of Bhoja and Lakṣmaṇsūri in M.A. class in sanskrit in Gauhati University. The melodious tunes of its poems, the diversity of the style, effective characterization and the set of images presented the book are always the source of delight for readers. This is one reason for which I decided to publish the Ph.D. thesis in the form of a book in the interest of the academic circle. Though the *Campūrāmāyaṇa* is a popular work, I have found that no adequate, critical work on the book has been published so far. Therefore, I have considered it proper to published the present book, which, I hope, will render some service to scholars and researchers.

I have no words to express my deep gratitude to my revered teacher Dr. Apurba Chandra Borthakuria M.A. Ph.D. (Cal) veda Sāhitya-Śāstri, formerly Professor and Head of the Department of Sanskrit, Gauhati University, for his valuable guidance, inspiration and kind help rendered to me in accomplishment of my task and I am highly grateful to him, who was kind enough to write a foreword.

I can not forget the useful advices and love received from all the honourable teachers of the Sanskrit Department of Gauhati University who constantly advised me to publish the present work. I express my sincere gratitude to them all.

I am also grateful to the staff of the National Library Calcutta, the staff of the Oriental Research Institute of Mysore, the Govt. Oriental Manuscript Library of Madras and the staff of the Gauhati University Library, Librarian and Staff of Darrang College, Tezpur, for their kind co-operation and immense help which were rendered to me in different ways for collection of materials for publishing this book and I expresses my deep gratitude to Sri P.K. Bhattacharya of Punthi-Pustak for his kind consent to publish this book from his farm.

At this occasion, I express my deepest sense of gratitude towards my brother-in-law late revered Ghana Kanta Bora B.E., who left us, for his word of affection and inspiration still ring in my ears as an evergreen memory. As a token of affection and admiration this minor work is dedicated to him.

In the end, I express my heartful gratitude to my husband Sri Tapan Kr. Bora who helped me and co-operated with me with his heart and soul in accomplishing the present task.

Date : June 5, 2004 **Indira Saikia**

CONTENTS

CHAPTER I

CHAPTER II

Chapter III

Chapter IV

Chapter V

Chapter VI

Chapter VII

SCHEME OF TRANSLITERATION

अ = a
आ = ā
इ = i
ई = ī
उ = u
ऊ = ū
ऋ = ṛ
ए = e
ऐ = ei
ओ = o
औ = ou
ं = ṁ
: = ḥ
क् = k
ख् = kh
ग् = g
घ् = gh
ङ् = ṅ
च् = c
छ् = ch
ज् = j
झ् = jh
ञ् = ñ
ट् = ṭ
ठ् = ṭh
ड् = ḍ
ढ् = ḍh
ण् = ṇ
त् = t
थ् = th
द् = d
ध् = dh
न् = n
प् = p
फ् = ph
ब् = b
भ् = bh
म् = m
य् = y
र् = r
ल् = l
व् = v
श् = ś
ष् = ṣ
स् = s
ह् = h
क्ष = kṣ

ABBREVIATION

AB	=	Aitareya Brāhmaṇa
Abh	=	Abhijñanaśākuntalam
Ac	=	Aśvacikitsita
Ādyar skt. Mss. Cata	=	Ādyar Sanskrit Manuscript Catalogue
Ak	=	Amarakoṣa
Ap	=	Agnipurāṇa
AV	=	Aśvavaidyaka
AVC	=	Ānandavṛnāvanacampū
BC	=	Bhāgavatacampū
Bhā	=	Bhāgavata
Bha. p.	=	Bhāgavata Purāṇa
Bhaṭṭi	=	Bhaṭṭikāvya
Bhoja. pra	=	Bhojaprabandha
BHP	=	Bhāvaprakāśa
BP	=	Bhāgavatpurāṇa
Bra. Purāṇa	=	Brahmāṇḍapurāṇa
BS	=	Bṛhatsaṁhitā
BSŚ	=	Brahmasūtrasāṅkarabhāsya
Cāru	=	Cārucaryā
CC	=	Colacampū
CCampū	=	Citracampū
CIH	=	The Chronology of Indian History
CKA	=	Campū Kāvya kā Ālocanatmaka Evaṁ Aitihāsika Adhyayana
CKT	=	Cikitsātilaka
CM	=	Chandomañjarī
CR	=	Campūrāmāyaṇa ed. by Pt. Rāmānāth Tripāthi
CR (R)	=	Campūrāmāyaṇa with Commentary of Rāmacandra Budhendra
DB	=	Devī Bhāgavata
DC	=	Descriptive Sanskrit Manuscript Catalogue, Mysore
DK	=	Daśakumāracarita

DR	=	Daśarupaka
DV	=	Dhvanyāloka
FDAI	=	Food and drinks in Ancient India
G. Campū	=	Gopālcampū
GT	=	Gaṇakataraṅginī
GVC	=	Gaṅgāvataranacampū
HC	=	Harṣacarita
HCSL	=	History of Classical Sanskrit Literature
HGAI	=	Historical Geography of Ancient India.
HIL	=	History of Literature
HR	=	Reports of Sanskrit Manuscripts in S. India, by E. Hultzsch. Madras
HSL	=	History of Sanskrit Literature
HV	=	Harivaṁśa
HV Campū	=	Hanūmatvijaya capmū
Ind. Off. Cata	=	India Office Catalogue
IW	=	Indian Wildlife
JM	=	Jātakamālā
JVC	=	Jivandharacampū
Kāma	=	Kāmandakīyanītisāra
KD	=	Kāvyādarśa
KP	=	Kathopaniṣad
KPŚ	=	Kāvyaprakāśa
KŚ	=	Kāvyānuśāsana
KTS	=	Kathāsaritsāgara
KUP	=	Kūrmapurāṇa
Manu	=	Manusaṁhitā
Mārgacampū	=	Mārgasahāyacampū
Mbh.	=	Mahābhārata
MD	=	Meghadūta
Mitra cata.	=	Mitra Catalogue or Notice of the Sanskrit Manuscripts, Vol. I. II. Calcutta, Ed. by Rajendralal Mitra.
MM. Campū	=	Mandāramaranda Campū
MNS	=	Mānasollāsa
MUP	=	Mundakopaniṣad
Nāma	=	Nāmamālikā
Nai. Car	=	Naiṣadhacarita
NC	=	Nalacampū
NP	=	Nāradapurāṇa

N. R. Campū	=	Nṛsiṁhacampū
NŚ	=	Nātyaśāstra
Ori. Lib.	=	Oriental Library, Madras
Pañca	=	Pañcatantra
Pra. cin.	=	Prabandhacintāmoṇi
Pra. carita	=	Prabhvāvakacarita
Prā p.	=	Prākṛtprakāśa
Purāṇic Ency.	=	Purāṇic Encyclopaedia
Raghū	=	Raghūvaṁśa
Rāja (A)	=	Rājamārtaṇḍa (Astrology)
Rāja (M)	=	Rājamārtaṇḍa (Medicine)
Raja (Yoga)	=	Rājamārtaṇḍa (Yogasūtra)
Rāmā	=	Rāmāyaṇa
RJT	=	Rājataraṅginī
Ṛs	=	Ṛtusaṁhāra
Ṛv	=	Ṛgveda
Sad. DS	=	Saddarśanasaṁgraha
Śāli	=	Śālihotra
Samarā	=	Samarāṅgaṇasūtradhāra
SD	=	Sāhityadarpaṇa
SDS	=	Sarvadarśanasaṃgraha
SDT	=	Siṁhāsanadvātriṃśikā
Śiśu	=	Śiśupālavadha
SKB	=	Sarasvatīkaṇṭhābharaṇa
SKD	=	Śabdakalpadruma
SKP	=	Sanskritpoetics
Sṛ. pra	=	Sṛṇgāraprakāśa
ŚŚ	=	Śabdanuśāsana
SS	=	Saṁkṣiptasāra
Śuklayaju	=	Śuklayajurveda
Śukra	=	Śukranīti
Tattva	=	Tattvaprakāśa
Tattacampū	=	Tattvaguṇādarśacampū
TC	=	Triennal Catalogue of Sanskrit Manuscript Library, Madras
T. cata.	=	Tanjore catalogue
TM	=	Tāmbulamañjarī
TS	=	Taittīriya Saṁhitā
URC	=	Uttararāmacarita
Vaija.	=	Vaijayantīkoṣa of Jādavaprakāśa

Vāl. Rāmā	=	Vālmīki Rāmāyaṇa
Vara. campu	=	Varadāmbikāpariṇayacampū
VDC	=	Vikramāṅkadevacarita
Vid. Campū	=	Vidanmodataraṅginīcampū
Viś. Campū	=	Viśaguṇādarśacampū
VP	=	Viṣṇupurāṇa
Vyācampū	=	Vyāghraleśaaṣṭamīmahotsavacampū
YC	=	Yaśastilakacampū
YPcampū	=	Yātrāprabandhacampū
Yukti	=	Yuktikalpataru

Chapter 1

INTRODUCTION

1. (a) A brief idea of the book and its author

The *Campūrāmāyaṇa* of Bhoja is a very popular work among the Campūkāvyas in Sanskrit literature. Though Bhoja is described as its author, he wrote up to the Sundarakāṇḍa only. Thc rcmaining portion of the book was completed by Lakṣmaṇasūri who also proves his ability to compose excellent prose and poetry. Bhoja was a poet, a prose writer and a erudite scholar who composes the Campū work in a sonorous language which appeals deeply to all its readers.

A Campūkāvya is a mixed Kāvya in which prose and verse are blended indiscriminately for the same purpose. The definition of Campū is found in the *Kāvyādarśa* of Daṇḍin for the first time, in which the literary composition written partly in prose and partly in verse is called a 'Campū'.[1] There are some special features of the *Campūrāmāyaṇa*. It has been written in a musical style. The author himself praises the beauty of a musical Campūkāvya in following manner in the Bālakāṇḍa of his work :

'gadyānubandharasamiśritapadyasūktir
hṛdyā hi vādyakalayā kaliteva gītiḥ/
tasmāddadhātu kavimārgajuṣāṃ sukhāya
campūprabandharacanāṃ rasanā madīyā//[2]

Though every Campūkāvya does not bear a musical quality, the *Campūrāmāyaṇa* surely is an exception to this.

The author rewrites the narrative of the *Rāmāyaṇa* of Vālmīki in prose and verse in this work in a melodious and lucid language.[3] Even in the description of the demoness Tāḍakā which creates awe in the minds of the readers, the poet mixes a touch of melody in order to make the description a delightful one. Thus, he writes :

> *'tatkāle piśitāśanāśapiśunā sandhyeva kācinmune*
> *radhvānaṁ tarasā rurodha rudhirakṣodāruṇā dāruṇā*
> *svādhīne hanane purīṁ vidadhatī mṛtyoḥ svakṛtyātyaya*
> *krīḍatkiṁkarasaṁghasaṁkaṭamahāśṛṅgātakāṁ*
> *tāḍakā..*[4]

(b) The author of the Campūrāmāyaṇa, his life, date and place of birth

Bhoja the author of the *Campūrāmāyaṇa* has established himself as a prolific writer and an erudite scholar. He wrote a large number of books on different subjects including poetics, grammar, philosophy, astrology, rhetorics, medicinal science, architecture and lexicography.[5]

The name 'Bhoja' is famous in Sanskrit literature. There were several kings by the same name in different times in this country.[6] Kālidāsa refers to one Bhoja who was a contemporary of king Raghū of the 'Solar dynasty'.[7]

The author of the *Campūrāmāyaṇa* was a king of Mālava. He belonged to the Paramāra dynasty.[8] Many authors including Abul-Fazal, the author of the *'Āini Ākbari'* have referred to this poet as a scholar monarch. According to the *Prabandhacintāmaṇi* of 'Merutuṅgācārya, Bhoja was the paramount ruler of Mālavaka Maṇḍala.[9]

Ballālasena, the author of the *Bhojaprabandha* narrates that king Muñja of Dhārā, was the paternal uncle of Bhoja.[10] He was afraid by a prediction of astrologers that Bhoja would rule for fifty five (55) years, seven (7) months and three (3) days over a vast part of India comprising the country of Gauḍa and Dakṣiṇāpatha.[11] Muñja tried to assassinate him through private agents, but the plot did not materialise. We learn from the different sections of the *Bhojaprabandha* that

Bhoja who ascended the throne after Muñja showed immense interest in academic and intellactual activities. Though, Bhoja is described as the kings of Mālava, his fame spread far and wide in the country.

The eminent writers like Bilhaṇa, the author of the *Vikramāṅkadevacarita*,[12] Kalhaṇa the author of the *Rājataraṅginī*[13] and Mammaṭa the author of the *Kāvyaprakāśa*[14] refer to this great king of India. M. Winternitz expresses this view regarding the date of Bhoja.[15] Dr. S. K. Dey opines that 'all this' however, will justify us in fixing Bhoja's date with a great porbability between 1010 A.D. to 1055 A. D. roughly covering a part of the first and whole of the second quarter of the 11th century, and he may have lived into the third quarter of same century. The exact dates of his succession and death are unknown but he fought with Bhīma' king of Gujrāt and Kalacūri Karṇa of Tripurī.[16]

Kedār Nāth Śāstrī and Vāsudeva Śāstrī render a valuable service to the readers by furnishing a genealogy of the Paramāra kings of Mālava in which Bhojadeva is shown as a successor of king Sindhurāja, the hero of the *Navasāhasāṁkacarita* of Padmagupta, and a contemporary of Bhīmadeva of Gujrāt. According to this genealogy, Bhīmadeva flourished between 1010–1055 A.D.[17]

According to Dr. V. Rāghavan, 'Bhoja might have assumed reigns of government about or somewhat later. His 'Rājamṛgāṅka' is dated 1042 or 1043 A.D. He died sometime after 1062 A. D.'[18]. It has been discussed above that Bhoja was the cousin of king Muñja of Dhārā. According to a prediction of astrologers he was destined to be a paramount ruler of a vast territory. But actual details of his achievements as a king and a warrior are found in the Udaipur inscription of the writings of Bilhaṇa.[19]

According to the 'Udaipur inscription' Bhoja defeated the king of Cedī, king of Toggala and king Bhīma, who ruled the countries of Karṇāṭa, Lāṭa, Gurjara and Turkīsthāna. These descriptions clearly show that Bhoja extended his territory to the far north and the far west of India.[20] However, according to Bilhaṇa Bhoja was challenged by Somesvara of Kāśmīr in a grim battle.[21] Bhoja was a ruler of Ujjayinī also as described in the *Siṁhāsanadvātriṁśikā*. It is narrated in this work that Bhoja excavated a mound and recovered the lost throne of King Vikramāditya of Ujjayinī who has earned reputation as a great monarch of India.[22]

Bhoja himself says in his colophone of the work *Campūrāmāyaṇa* that he was a king of Vidarbha.[23] The ancient Vidarbhadeśa is a part of Modern Andhra Pradesh. It indicates that Bhoja's Kingdom stretched up to a part of modern Andhrapradesh. Thus, Bhoja was a master of a vast kingdom. Bhoja was not only a warrior but also he was poet and a erudite scholar and also a great lover of scholars and beneficial social activities. According to the *Bhojaprabandha*, there were many poets in the court of Bhoja though some of these accounts are imaginary.[24] It can be easily understood from the critical study of the work that he was a great lover of learning. He established a school called 'Sarasvatī-kaṇṭhābharaṇa' in Dhāra.[25] He prepared a sacrificial Kuṇḍa in Kapaṭeśvara,[26] which shows his great love for religion. He also donated lands to the Brāhmaṇas through selfsigned copperplate, three of which have been recovered by the scholars.[27] The Udaipur inscription of the kings of Mālava describes Bhoja's achievements in a single verse :

> '*sādhitaṁ vihitaṁ dattaṁ Jñataṁ tad yanna kenacit/*
> *kimanyatkavirājasya śrībhojasya praśasyate//*'[28]

(c) Erudition of Bhoja

It has been stated above that Bhoja was a prolific writer. Candraprabhasūri, the author of the *Prabhāvakacarita* offers the most adequate complement of Bhoja in the following poem.

> '*bhojavyākaraṇaṁ hyetat śabdaśāstraṁ pravartate//*
> *asau hi mālavādhīśo vidvaccakraśiromaṇiḥ/*
> *śabdālaṁkāra-daivajña-tarkaśāstrāṇi nirmame//*
> *cikitsā-rājasiddhānta-taru-vāstudayāni ca/*
> *aṁka-śākunakādhyātma-svapna-sāmudrikāṇyapi//*

granthānnimittavyākhyāna-praśnacūḍāmaṇīnīha/
vivṛttiṁ cāyasadbhāve'arthaśāstraṁ meghamālayā//[29]

According to above poems, scholar Bhoja was the author of many eminent texts on a wide variety of subjects like grammar, poetics, medicinal science, symbolical literature, architecture, dream theories, philosophy and astrology.

Let us now give a detailed account of the books written by Bhoja.

Sarasvatīkaṇṭhābharaṇa

Bhoja was a great authority on Sanskrit grammar. His *Sarasvatīkaṇṭhābharaṇa* is at the same time a work on poetics and grammar.[30] This work is popularly known as '*Bhojavyākaraṇa*'.[31] *Sarasvatīkaṇṭhābharaṇa* is mainly based on the '*Aṣṭādhyāyī*' of Pāṇini[32]. Bhoja also wrote a short commentary on Uṇādisūtras of Śākaṭāyana which bears the stamp of Bhoja's original approach to the science of grammar. He presents new sūtras in order to explain such rare words as 'campū'[33] and 'murmura'.[34]

Bhoja differs from his predeessors like Pāṇini. The treatment of grammatical matters which display his originality as a grammarian. Pāṇini presents the sūtra 'ajādyataṣṭāp' in the section of feminine gender in his grammar. The Pāṇinian Sūtra 'ajādyataṣṭāp' in split by Bhoja into many sūtras. After giving a sūtra ataṣṭāp (3.4.2) he gives ten more sūtras where all the words of 'ajādi (has probably known as *Śabdānuśāsana*). In the preface of his commentary on the '*Yogasūtra*' of Patañjali, Bhoja presents the following śloka :

'Śabdānuśāsanaṃ vidadhatā pātañjale kurvatā/
vṛtti Rājamṛgāṃkasaṃgakaṃapi
vyātanvatāvaidhyake//

The commentator on the *Sarasvatīkaṇṭhābharaṇa* goes by the name of Daṇḍanātha Nārāyaṇa. But the identity of this author is not known to us from available records. It is not unlikely that Daṇḍanātha was Bhoja himself.[37]

Apart from grammatical matters, Bhoja discusses Rīti, Rasa, Guṇa and poetic blemishes and different types of *Śabdālaṁkāras* and Arthālaṁkāras in an exhaustive manner in the *Sarasvatīkaṇṭhābharaṇa*. While doing so, he exhibits his great originality as a writer. Bhoja recognises six different Rītis which include Māgadhī and Āvantikā Rīti.[38] In the course of his discussion on poetic blemishes the author refers to a discourse between a king and palanquin-bearer. While the king uses verb 'bādhati' which is grammatically incorrect, the palanquin bearer replies in a tone of mild reprimand that the verb 'bādhate' and not 'bādhati' is correct.[39] This discourse is suggestive of the fact that persons without a proper knowledge of grammar may sometimes commit mistakes in using verbs, but it is the grammarian's duty to try to show them the correct use.

Śṛṇgāraprakāśa

Besides his well known *Sarasvatīkaṇṭhābharaṇa*, Bhoja also worte another book called *Śṛṇgāraprakāśa* which deals mainly with Sanskrit poetics and dramaturgy. The first eight chapters are devoted to the study of grammar, and also the theories of Vṛtti. The ninth and tenth chapters describe the blemishes and excellence of expression i.e. doṣas and guṇas, while the eleventh and twelfth chapters deal respectively with the Mahākāvya and drama. The next twenty-four chapters treat Rasas. In the discussion śṛṇgārarasa with all its different aspects occupies a prominent place.[40] He recognises a special variety of it called Abhimāna Śṛṇgāra[41]. His treatment of Śṛṇgāra rasa is related to the four puruṣārthas or goals of life viz. Dharma,[42] Artha,[43] Kāma,[44] and Mokṣa.[45] Thus, he discusses four new kinds of Śṛṇgāra rasa.

Rājamārtaṇḍa Medicinal text

Bhoja writes three books of the same name viz. *Rājamārtaṇḍa*. One of them is an astrological text, while two other books are written on philosophy and medicine.

The *Rājamārtaṇḍa* which is a work on Indian medicine

contains several sections on many important topics of medicine.[46] The *Rājamārtaṇḍa* consists of thirty-four chapters where Bhoja deals with various diseases of the human body and their methods of treatment.[47] There is an interesting and useful discussion on the science of rearing pigeons. Bhoja writes that the breeding of multicoloured pigeons is possible by feeding them with lentils.[48]

Aufrecht gives a long list of Bhoja's works in his *Catalogus Catalogorum*[49], but many of them are not available at present. Bhoja was an eminent authority on Indian astrology. He wrote at least two books viz. *Rājamṛgāṅka* and *Rājamārtaṇḍa* on the astrogical science. The *Rājamṛgāṅka* is not available to scholars at present. It has been written by Rāmachandra Ghosa, that some scholars from Jasalmere presented a copy of the book to Dr. Bhāudājī, but Bhāudājī could not trace the book after some time.[50]

Rājamārtaṇḍa Astrological text

This *Rājamārtaṇḍa*[51] contains a large number of topics related to the science of astrology. It deals with planets and constellations, their movements and their influence on man's life. It is said in the beginning of the work that, a king rising from his bed should have a sight of the royal astrologers, ministers and the priest,[52] In one section of the *Rājamārtaṇḍa* the author deals with the science of architecture. He shows how the residential houses should be constructed in different manner according to the shape of the plot of the land.[53] He offers a detailed account of different Tithis, Vratas and Festivals. In this connection he gives several interpretations of Mahājeṣṭhi tithi[54] and Sāvitrīvrata.[55]

Bhoja was an authority on Indian philosophy also and particularly on Śaivism. He may be described as an authority on Śaiva philosophy and Pātañjala yoga philosophy. These two philosophical systems are treated by Bhoja in the *Tattvaprakāśa* and the *Rājamārtaṇḍa*.

Tattvaprakāśa

The *Tattaprakāśa* of Bhoja is an exhaustive work on Śaiva philosophy which occupies an independent position among the philosophical systems of India. Bhoja was a great authority on the subject and atleast one passage from the book has been quoted in Mādhava's *Sarvadarśana-saṃgrah.*[56] Traditionally Śiva or Maheśvara is described as the propounder of this philosophy. Sāṅkarācārya discusses the basic tenets of the Śaiva philosophical system in the *Sāṅkarabhāsya* on the *Brahmasūtra* of Vādarāyaṇa.[57] The doctrines of pati,paśu and pāśa play a pivotal role in this system.[58] The *Mṛgendratantra* presents all the basic views of Śaiva philosophy.[59] Bhoja presents in his *Tattvaprakāśa* the cardinal doctrines of the Śaiva system in a lucid and easily intelligible language. Similarly, Bhoja had a first hand knowledge of the Yoga philosophy of Patañjali. He wrote philosophical text on this subject called *Rājamārtaṇḍa.*

Rājamārtaṇḍa

We have described above that the *Rājamārtaṇḍa* is a philosophical text. This work has been divided into four parts viz. Samādhi, Sādhana, Vibhūti and Kaivalya. It deals with the nature of self-concentration and yogic methods[60] including kaivalya. Kaivalya[61] means the result attained from self-concentration in yogic sādhanā. The relation of the individual spirit to God is treated as part of the ethic yoga or Kriyāyoga in the book.[62]

Cārucaryā

The *Cārucaryā* of Bhoja is another scholastic and informative book dealing primarily with the principles of healthy living.

The book contains about twenty-two subjects. The author discusses in this book the daily activities associated with the hygienic living such as the cleaning of mouth,[63] bathing,[64] decoration of the body[65], dietics[66] and other habits including moral code for healthy living.

The *Cārucaryā* is also a metrical composition, in which the author presents in details the utility of chewing betelnuts[67] and merits and demerits of different kinds of eating and drinking vessels,[68] the unhygienic effect of enjoying old women[69] and other miscellaneous topics.[70] He gives his readers an elaborate idea of chewing betel-nuts mixed with different articles. He shows that when khadira powder is mixed with betel-nuts it produces a hygienic effect on the teeth.[71]

In one passage of the *Cārucaryā*, Bhoja writes about the malefic effect of taking betel-leafs without proper care. He warns that stalk of a betel-leaf creates diseases, the tip of a betel-leaf is full of dangerous germs, a dry leaf consumes longevity, while the spine of the leaf destroys one's intellect.[72] In this context we can refer to the *Bhāvaprakāśa* of Bhāvamiśra where a detail description of chewing betel-nuts is given.[73] A similar account is found in the *Tāmbulamañjarī*[74] and *Mānasollāsa*[75] of Someśvara. It is clear from Bhoja's scholastic discussion that golden[76], silver[77], copper[78], iron[79] and different types of other utensils[80] always produce different types of effect on the human body. Similarly, the plaintain leaf and the lotus leaf also produce similar effect when used as eating vessels.[81] It may be mentioned here that the *Cikitsātilaka* also offers a similar discussion on this subject.[82]

Yuktikalpataru

The *Yuktikalpataru* of Bhoja is another extensive work of varied interest, relating to polity,[83] construction of building[84], selection of sites,[85] use of articles of furniture[86] precious stones, ornaments,[87] weapons[88] ships and vehicles drawn by arrivals.[89]

In one section of the *Yuktikalpataru* Bhoja discusses the science of city building most adequately.[90] It may be mentioned here that Śukrācārya author of the *Śukranīti*[91] and *Kāmandakīyanītisāra*[92] also offer similar discussion on this very important topic.

Samarāngaṇasūtradhāra

The *Samarāngaṇasūtradhāra* of Bhoja is an encyclopaedic work of mediavel Indian architecture. The author has divided the work into eighty-three chapters. The subject-matter of the *Samarāngaṇasūtradhāra* is partly confined to 'Vāstuśāstra' or the science of architecture. He deals in it with the construction of buildings,[93] palaces[94] and also the art of painting and image making.[95] In the work he discusses in details the art of making different types of image of gods and goddesses, the materials used for preparing images and also describes the various poses (saṃsthānas) of the images and their measurements.[96] We learn from this work that the same deity worshipped in the town and the villages should be made differently.[97] In the last chapter of the book the author gives a critical analysis on the Rasa (sentiment) theory of Indian poetics.[98] The author also gives the patākās or postures of the hands which include Tripatākā,[99] Kartarīmukhaḥ[100] and Śukatuṇḍa[101] etc.

We wonder to think about how a king and a warlord like Bhoja could devote so much of his busy time in academic activities which entrance innumerable topics of varied interest.

Śālihotra

The horse-lore has been cultured in ancient India by the several authors. The '*Aśvacikitsa*' of Nakula and the *Śālihotraśāstra* of sage Śālihotra are two famous texts on Aśvavaidyā.

The *Pañcatantra* quotes one important passage from the *Śālihotra* śāstra which describes that the oil extracted from monkeys can cure burnsores of horses.[102] Bhoja also wrote a book named *Śālihotra* which is certainly different from the earlier *Śālihotra*. In the *Yuktikalpataru* of Bhoja we find a section on Aśvayukti and many verses of the Aśvayukti are similar with those of his *Śālihotra*.[103]

In the commentary of Jayadattasūri on the *Aśvavaidyaka*, we find a few verses quoted from Bhoja's *Śālihotra* or work on horse-lore.[104] Incidentally, the contents of the *Śālihotra* of Bhoja are remarkably indentical to very great extent with the text of the *Aśvacikitsita* of Nakula.[105]

The *Śālihotra* of Bhoja consists of eleven chapters. However, it is not a work on veterinary science proper, but it deals with the different kinds of horses and their auspicious and inauspicious signs.[106] According to him when the feet,[107] the tails [108] , the chest,[109] the head and the forehead[110] of a horse are white, such a horse or horses are considered as auspicious. In the *Śālihotra* the author Bhoja discusses the different kinds of 'āvartas' possessed by a horse. Those horses having two 'āvartas' or circles are called 'candra' and Āditya.[111] Further, the author says that Aśvaśāla should be erected to the east of the palace by a king, according to the rules laid down in the works on architecture.[112] To speak precisely, the *Śālihotra* of Bhoja may be termed a work on *Sāmudrikaśāstra* written upon horses.

Nāmamālikā

It is Bhoja's next significant contribution to the science of lexicography. In India, the science of lexicography has been cultured by many eminent authors like Amarasiṁha and the authors of the *Vaijayantī* and the *Medinīkoṣa* with great ardour. In fact, lexicography is a very important science the need of which is felt more keenly in modern times by the linguists.

The *Nāmamālikā* of Bhoja is a very useful lexicon. The book is divided into three chapters, viz. Svargādinā-madheyaprakaraṇa, Gaganādināmadheyaprakaraṇa and Bhūmyādināmadheyaprakaraṇa. The author appears to have been very much influenced by the *Vaijayantī Koṣa* of *Yādavaprakāśa* as many passages have been quoted from these lexicons in the *Nāmamālikā*.[113]

The work *Nāmamālikā* is also called Bhoja's Nighaṇṭu.[114]

Bhoja deals the topics included in the three vargas of his *Nāmamālikā* in a systematic manner, when we read the Svargādi varga we find that in this section, Bhoja discusses the different names of Svarga or heaven, the names of Lord Indra, the ruler of heaven and all other matters concerning the Hindu concept of heavenly life.[115] In the second chapter of the book Bhoja discusses the different names of gagana or sky,[116] day[117] and night[118] and various names of stars.[119]

In the Bhūmyādināmadheyaprakarṇa the author mentions the different terms which express the sense of earth,[120] the animals,[121] gems and stones[122] , seasons.[123] and the castes[124] in the Hindu society.

Apart from these books mentioned above, Bhoja was author of many other works written on a wide variety of subjects. Aufrecht, in his *Catalogus Catalogrum* part I, attributes the authorship of the books also to Bhoja :

1. Ādityapratāpasiddhānta
2. Āyurvedasarvasva
3. Cāṇakyanīti
4. Vidyāvinodakāvyam
5. Vidvajjanavallabha (Praśnajñāna)
6. Viśrāntavidyāvinoda (Medicine)
7. Vyavahārasamuccaya (Dharmaśāstra)
8. Siddhāntasaṁgraha (Śaivaśāstra)
9. Subhāṣitaprabandha
10. Bhojarājavārtika
11. Rājamṛgāṅka (Jyotiṣa and Medicine)
12. Śabdānuśāsana
13. Śivatattvaratnakalikā
14. Bhujavala (Astronomy)
15. Hanumannāṭaka.[125]

Among these books *Hanumannāṭaka* is available to us at present. It is also called *Mahānāṭaka* or *Chāyānāṭaka or Shadowplay*. It is said that Hanumān composed this work, but this work was lost in the sea. On hearing this Vālmīki recomposed this work. Later Bhoja of Dhārā recovered this play in a rackedict and recast it into the form of a work in the middle of 11th Century. This is available in two recensions. One is prepared by Madhusūdhana in nine Acts and the other by Dāmodara in fourteen Acts.[126]

C. M. Duff says in his work '*The Chronology of Indian history*' that the *Śṛṅgāramañjrīkathā* was written by Bhoja[127] and two Prākṛt poems lately discovered at Dharā[128]. The Commentator of *Śarasvatīkaṇṭhābharaṇa* Ājada says that the number of Bhoja's works was eighty-four (84). According to him, Bhoja had written these works under the nickname Biruda.[129]

A large number of works written by a single scholar shows how industrious this ancient Indian scholar had been. In ancient India the great scholars were not proficient in one or two branches of literature only, but they studied and cultured a wide variety of subjects.

(d) The life, date, place of birth of Lakṣmaṇasūri

Lakṣmaṇa was the son of Gaṅgādhara and Gaṅgāmbikā. He lived in a village named Śanagara.[130] It has been already stated that the *Campūrāmāyaṇa* of Bhoja is an incomplete work as the author wrote up to the end of the Sundarakāṇḍa only.[131] Ghanaśyāma, in his comentary on the *Campūrāmāyaṇa* says that only five kāṇḍas of the *Campūrāmāyaṇa* were written by Bhoja. The subsequent kāṇḍa i. e. the Yuddhakāṇḍa has been supplimented by Lakṣmaṇasūri, which Lakṣmaṇa himself admits in the beginning of the Yuddhakāṇḍa.[132]

Veṇkaṭādhvarin the author of the *Uttaracampūrāmāyaṇa* says that the story of the Yuddhakāṇḍa was made up by Lakṣmaṇasūri later on.[133] Likewise Nārāyaṇa also mentions in the commentary of Padayojanā that the Yuddhakāṇḍa of the *Campūrāmāyaṇa* was written by Lakṣmaṇasūri.[134] Kāmeśvarasūri in his commentary on Yuddhakāṇḍa says that the sixth kāṇḍa of the *Campūrāmāyaṇa* was written by Lakṣmaṇasūri in a lucid and elegant style.[135] Thus, there is hardly any doubt about the authorship of the Yuddhakāṇḍa of the *Campūrāmāyaṇa*. Regarding the date of Lakṣmaṇasūri scholars are silent. Probably he lived in the 11th century

A.D. According to M. Krishnamāchāriar the story of the Yuddhakāṇḍa was written by Rājacūḍāmaṇi Dīkṣita,[136] by Ghanaśyāma[137] and by Ekāmbara Nātha[138] also besides Lakṣmaṇasūri. Thus, it is a later composition.

(e) A brief note of the meaning of Campū, with special reference to Daṇḍin, Bhoja and Viśvanātha

The 'Campū' is a literary type of composition in which prose and verse are blended by the author without any discrimination for the same purpose.

A brief note of the meaning of 'Campū' with special reference of Daṇḍin Bhoja and Sāhityadarpaṇa will be discussed in the second chapter of this dissertation.

However, we present briefly the definitions of Campū as given by Daṇḍin and other authors. According to Daṇḍin, a Campū is a 'gadyapadyamayībhāṣā'[139] Hemacandra and Vāgbhaṭa think that a 'Campū' must be divided into Aṅkas and Ucchvāsas.[140] Bhoja defines Campū as a literary composition meant for giving pleasure to the readers.[141] Viśvanātha, the author of the *Sāhityadarpaṇa* follows Daṇḍin in defining Campū.[142]

2. (a) The Hero of the Campūrāmāyaṇa : a critical study

Sanskrit rhetoricians discuss in detail the hero of a drama. But there is no discussion in any alaṁkāra śāstra about the hero of a Campūkāvya. Still we can examine the question and determine the hero of the Campūrāmāyaṇa, in the light of the treatment made by *ālaṁkārikas* regarding the hero of a Sanskrit play.

According to Sanskrit poeticians the hero of a drama must possess certain important qualities. He must be a young man born in a noble family. He must be powerful, active and steady in his pursuit. He must be humble and gentle. The spirit of self-sacrifice is one of the essential other good qualities like the purity of character, righteousness and firmness in his cause.[143]

Bharata and other eminent authors of Kāvya works classify the heroes of Sanskrit kāvyas into four distinct types viz. (i) Dhīrodātta, (ii) Dhīroddhatta, (iii) Dhīralalita and (iv) Dhīraprasānta.[144] This classification is made according to certain specific qualities possessed by these four types of Character.

A critical examination of the character of the *Campūrāmāyaṇa* clearly shows that Rāma belongs to the Dhīrodātta type of hero.[145] This type of hero never praises himself. He always conceals his pride. He is always very grave and steady. He also possesses the quality of forgiveness (Kṣamāvān).

Coming to the *Campūrāmāyaṇa* we see that Rāma is the hero of the *Campūrāmāyaṇa*. He is a Dīrodātta hero and the prince of Ayodhyā who possesses many great qualities. He is a dignified and exalted young prince and he forgives the audacity of the adversary Paraśurāma.[146] He is polite, and never boasts of his meritorious and chivalrous deeds.

It has been already discussed that a Ḍhīrodātta hero possesses the spirit of forgiveness. Viśvanātha corroborates this view.[147] The quality of forgiveness is found in the character of Jīmūtavāhana, the hero of the *Nāgānanda* of Śrīharṣa But Rāma does not forgive their wicked enemies. He fights against Rāvaṇa, king of Laṇkā and destroys his army completely, Thus, there is a striking distinction between Rāma and Jīmūtavāhana. While Rāma is a Dhīrodātta nāyaka. Jīmutavāhana is a Dhīraprasānta Nāyaka according to poetic standard.[148]

(b) The Heroine of the Capūrāmāyaṇa

According to Sanskrit rhetoricians the heroine must possesses certain important qualities like purity, chastity and other good qualities. There are three types of heroine (i) Svīyā, (ii) Anyā, (iii) Sāmānyā.[149]

Now a 'Svīyā type of heroine is one who possesses some very important qualities. She should be active in the household works, gentle in behaviour. and purity in character.

In the *Campūrāmāyaṇa* Śitā is the heorine of the work. We see that she is a Svīyā type of heroine. She is the true heroine in all the senses. She is the princess of Mithilā daughter of king Janaka and wife of Rāma, the prince of Ayodhyā, Bhoja has given her the highest pinnacle of being by making her self born and describing her as the adopted child of Janaka who was the abode of the highest spiritual wisdom. Rāma says to her

> *'jajñe tadatrabhavatī janakasya yajñe*
> *devyāścirāya dharaṇerraṇeḥ śikheva/*
> *vaṃśe manorapi vadhūrbhvatkimanya*
> *drāmastathāpi vidhinā racito virāmaḥ*[150]

The author has lavished as much art in the delineation of Sītā as on the delineation of Rāma. Vālmīki says in his *Rāmāyaṇa* :

> *'iyaṁ sītā mama sutā sahadharmacaritvā/*
> *Praticca caināṃ bhadraṃ pāṇimgṛhisvo pāṇināṃ/*
> *pativratā mahābhāgā chāyevānugatā sadā//*[151]

In the Sundarakaṇḍa we find her moral greatness. The author of the *Campūrāmāyaṇa* refers to various sweet and charming traits of her character such as her sweetness and splendour of speech.[152] Hanumān is transported by her noble forgiveness and says that she is eminently fit to be the dharmapatnī of Rāma.[153] Mandodarī wife of Rāvaṇa feels that Rāvaṇa's glory burnt up by the fire of Sītā's chastity.[154] Her loyality to Rāma is unmatched in literature and her greatness as a pativratā (devoted wife) is unique.

3. The theme of the Campūrāmāyaṇa

The *Compūrāmāyaṇa* of Bhoja is a prose and poetical composition narrating the story of Rāma as described in detail by Vālmīki in his *Rāmāyaṇa*. The *Compūrāmāyaṇa* of Bhoja is an incomplete work, as the author wrote up to the end of the Sundarakāṇḍa only. The subsequent kāṇḍa (Yuddhakāṇḍa) has been supplemented by Lakṣmaṇasūri.

The story of the *Campūrāmāyaṇa* starts with a description of Daśaratha of the solar dynasty who ruled Kosala with Ayodhyā as his capital. Sage Vasiṣṭha was his family preceptor. King Daśaratha ruled his country in peace and prosperity. He married three wives but still for many years he had no son. So on the advice of Vasiṣṭha, Daśaratha invited Ṛṣyaśṛṇga for performing the 'Putrakāmeṣṭi' yajña. In due course his queens delivered four sons, Kausalyā gave birth to Rāma, Kaikeyī begot Bharata and Sumitrā gave birth to Lakṣmaṇa and Śatrughna.[155] The four sons of Daśaratha grew up in Ayodhyā under proper royal care.

Once sage Viśvāmitra decided to conduct a sacrifice for the happiness and contentment of all people but the Rākṣasas tried to spoil it. Mārīca and Subāhu sons of Tāḍakā were the leaders of the obstructionists. Viśvāmitra knew that Rāma was the most effective weapon against the Rākṣasas and requested king Daśaratha to send Rāma for his help.[156] Daśaratha felt sad about it and Viśvāmitra was getting excited over the former's attitude. Later on the advice of Vasiṣṭha, Daśaratha sent Rāma and Lakṣmaṇa along with Viśvāmitra to the hermitage of Viśvāmitra.[157] While walking in the forest. Viśvāmitra told many old stories to Rāma and Lakṣmaṇa. They crossed the river Sarayū, passed by many āśramas of sages.[158] Here Viśvāmitra imparted to Rāma and Lakṣmaṇa two mantras 'Balā' and Atibalā[159] He also taught them the use of divine missiles called Jṛmbhakāstra.[160] Accordingly they killed Tāḍakā, Subāhu, Mārīca and drove away the other Rākṣasas.[161]

Next, Viśvāmitra, hearing about the Svayamvara of Sītā, daughter of king Janaka started for his palace with Rāma and Lakṣamaṇa.[162] In the Svayamvara assembly Rāma was given a bow by Janaka which was given by Lord Śiva to Janaka. It was broken by Rāma and Sītā was married to Rāma as per Janaka's promise.[163] While returing from Mithilā Rāma defeated Paraśurāma who challenged him.[164]

The theme of the Ayodhyākāṇḍa is the same as that of the Rāmāyaṇa. King Daśaratha decided to install Śri Rāma as crown prince. But Kaikeyī being instigated by Mantharā demanded that Rāma should be banished in the forest and Bharata be made crown prince, she reminded the old king two boons which he had promised to her.[165] On hearing the propensity of Kaikeyī, Daśaratha fell fainted. But to keep the word of his father Rāma started for the forest followed by Sītā and Lakṣmaṇa. Daśaratha died after some time under the torment of grief for his son.[166]

Bharata and Śatrughna were brought to Ayodhyā from the Kekaya country where they lived with their maternal uncle Yudhājit, at the time of these incidents.[167] After arriving in the capital Bharata learnt from his mother the sad episode.[168] Bharata went to the forest and met Rāma at Citrakūṭa, and informed about the death of their father. He requested Rāma to return to Ayodhyā and ascend the throne.[169] Rāma broke into tears on hearing the news of the death of their father, but refused to return.[170] At last Bharata yielded to Rāma's injunction and returned to Ayodhyā with the sacred footwears of Rāma. He did not enter the palace. Instead he built an āśrama at Nandīgrāma and started to rule the country from there.[171] Meanwhile Rāma, Sītā and Lakṣmaṇa left their abode in Citrakūṭa and proceeded further into the jungle.[172]

In the Araṇyakāṇḍa a sad and freightening incident is narrated by the poet which is borrowed from the *Rāmāyaṇa*. A wicked Rākṣasa named Virādha tried to kidnap Sītā. But Rāma killed Virādha and salvation Sītā.[173] In their journey in the forest they visited several āśramas of sages.[174] One day a Rākṣasī named Śurpaṇakhā assuming the form of a beautiful damsel came to Lakṣmaṇa and proposed to marry him. But Lakṣmaṇa chopped off her nose and turned her back disappointed and angry.[175] The Śūrpaṇakhā informed Khara and Duṣaṇa of the incident. They fought with Rāma and Lakṣmaṇa. In the battle fourteen thousand Rākṣasas were killed.[176] Then Śūrpaṇakhā went to the court of Rāvaṇa and instigated him against Rāma. Rāvaṇa consoled her and discussed the shameful affair with Mārīca. Mārīca advised him not to fight against Rāma.[177] Rāvaṇa rebuked him and made him to accept his proposal by threatening with death-penalty. Mārīca appeared in the form of a golden deer and aroused curiosity in the heart of Sītā.[178] In order to capture the deer Rāma entrusted Sītā to Lakṣmaṇa and followed it till he pierced the deer with an arrow. Mārīca made a terrible sound by imitating the voice of Rāma, then Sītā sent Lakṣmaṇa forcibly to help Rāma.[179] In the absence of Lakṣmaṇa Rāvaṇa, disguised in the form of a sage, took away Sītā.[180] Hearing Sīta's cries Jaṭāyu challenged Rāvaṇa, but Rāvaṇa injured Jaṭāyū.[181] When Rāma and Lakṣmaṇa came back to the hermitage they did not find Sītā. Rāma began to lament, and started his search for Sītā. Jaṭāyu on their way related the story of Sītā and succumbed to his in injury.[182]

In the Kiṣkindhākāṇḍa of the *Campūrāmāyaṇa* the author describes that Rāma and Lakṣmaṇa reached lake Pampā on the course of their travel.[183] Rāma's emotion had outburst at the site of the natural beauty of the lake which produced a heartrending effect of Rāma.[184] Rāma made friends with Sugrīva and Hanūmān who were in the need of a genuine help in their dire distress. Bāli, the elder brother of Sugrīva was an arch enemy of his who constantly tormented the younger brother. Rāma made an ingenious plan to kill Bāli. Sugrīva would fight with Bāli when Rāma would fell him with his arrow. According to this plan the fight began.[185] In the fight Bāli was killed by Rāma. He gave the kingship to Sugrīva and made Aṅgada the crownprince.[186] After the rainy season Sugrīva sent monkeys for searching Sītā, but they could not find her.[187] At last they saw a vulture Sampāti who told them about Laṇkā and advised them to go to Laṇkā, the capital of Rāvaṇa.[188] Then they proceeded to the mountain Mahendra where they saw the ocean.[189]

In the Sundarakāṇḍa the poet describes the scene of Hanumān flying over the ocean and entering Laṇkā. He saw Sītā in the Aśoka garden.[190] Hanumān appeared before Sītā and disclosed his identity by giving the token ring of Rāma to her.[191] Hanumān destroyed the beautiful Aśoka garden of Rāvaṇa.[192] Hearning the news of the destruction of Aśoka garden, Rāvaṇa sent eighteen thousand fighters who were defeated by Hanumān.[193] Then Indrajit used his divine weapon to capture Hanumān. He took him to court of

Rāvaṇa.[194] Rāvaṇa pronounced death penalty on the offending monkey which was opposed by Vibhīṣaṇa.[195] Then Rāvaṇa ordered his servents to put fire on the tail of the monkey. Accordingly Hanūmān's tail was set ablaze, which gave a chance to Hanūmān to burn Laṇkā.[196] Hanūmān returned to Rāma with a token from Sītā.[197]

In the Yuddhakāṇḍa of the *Campūrāmāyaṇa* Rāma and Sugrīva received the report from Hanumān about his visit Laṇkā.[198] It is started there that Rāvaṇa held a meeting of his council which was attended by his brothers and ministers.[199] He expelled Vibhīṣaṇa his brother who opposed war and advised his brother to return Sītā to Rāma and apologise to him.[200] Bibhīṣaṇa quitted Laṇkā and took refuge with Rāma.[201] Rāma and others who had assembled on the seashore decided to build a bridge on the sea to go to Laṇkā.[202] The construction of the bridge was begun under the leadership of Surgrīva. After completing the bridge Rāma and his entire army reached Laṇkā and immediately the war began.[203] In the war Rāma killed Rāvaṇa,[204] and was reunited with Sītā. Then he returned to Ayodhyā by Puṣpaka Vimāna and the coronation ceremony of Rāma was performed to the great delight of all.[205] In fine, the authors of the *Campūrāmāyaṇa* narrate the same story as found in the *Rāmāyaṇa* of Vālmīki excluding the last few Kāṇḍas of the epic.

4. Literary Study

The principal sentiment (Aṇgī Rasa) and the subordinate sentiment (Aṇga Rasa) of the Campūrāmāyaṇa :

Sanskrit poeticians have discussed thoroughly the principal sentiment (Aṇgirasa) and the subordinate sentiment (Aṇgarasa) present in a dramatical and poetical composition. But no discussion is found regarding the principal and subordinate sentiments in the Alaṃkāra śāstras so far as a Campūkāvya is concerned, Whatever that might be, it is not difficult for scholars with a critical bent to mind of assess the principal and subordinate sentiments in the *Capūrāmāyaṇa.*

Rāma, the hero of the *Capūrāmāyaṇa* is a Vīra. According to Bharata there are three kinds of Vīrarasa or the Heroic sentiments viz. (i) Dānavira, (ii) Dharmavīra and (iii) Yuddhavīra.[206] The heroic sentiment called Dānavīra is associated with the act of charity like that of demon Bali, Dharmavīra refers to the heroic sentiment which is associated with the righteousness of pious persons like Yuddhiṣṭhira. Yuddhavīra denotes the heroism shown in fighting battles and defeating the enemies.

Hemacandra recognises these three types of heroism.[207] But Ānandavardhana[208], Dhanañjaya, the author of the *Daśarūpaka*[209] and Viśvanātha, the author of the *Sāhityadarpaṇa* recognise Dayāvīra or heroism in showing compassion as another type of Vīrarasa.[210] The act of self sacrifice accomplished by persons like Jimūtavāhana in Śrīharṣa's *Nāgānanda* is a case of Dayāvīra. Jīmūtavāhana elevates himself to the position of a Dayāvīra or compassionate hero by the act of self sacrifice made for saving the Nāgas. Hence, the principal sentiment of the *Nāgānanda* is Dayāvīrarasa.

We see that in the *Campūrāmāyaṇa* Rāma is a Yuddhavīra. He fights so many battles against ferocious and powerful demons. He kills Tāḍakā. Khara, Duṣana and finally kills Rāvaṇa, the Lord of Laṇkā He also easily vanquished Paraśurāma in a duel of strength. The authors of the *Campūrāmāyaṇa* like Vālmīki make a serious attempt to glorify Rāma as a great warrior who beats his enemies with his extraordinary might.

Viśvanātha says in his *Sāhityadarpaṇa* that either the erotic sentiment (Śṛṇgārarasa) or the heroic sentiment (Vīrarasa) should be delineated as the principal sentiment of a drama. According to him, other sentiments should occupy only a subordinate position to the erotic or the heroic sentiment delineated as the principal sentiment in it.[211]

The eminent Sanskrit writers like Kālidāsa, Bhavabhūti, Māgha, Bhāravi and Bhaṭṭanārāyaṇa follow the norm mentioned by the author of the *Sāhityadarpaṇa*.

The author of the *Campūrāmāyaṇa* delineates virarasa as the principal sentiment of his *Campūrāmāyaṇa*. Bhoja also delineates all other sentiments in his *Campūrāmāyaṇa* in an appropriate manner. These sentiments naturally occupy a subordinate position to Vīrarasa in the work.

5. The Commentaries Written on the Campūrāmāyaṇa

There is a number of Commentaries on the *Campūrāmāyaṇa* some of which are written by modern authors, M. Krishnamāchāriar in his *History of Classical Sanskrit* literature' give a list of the commentaries written by different commentators[212]. The list includes the names of the following writers :

a) Nārāyaṇa
b) Rāmacandra
c) Kāmeśvara
d) Mānaveda
e) Ghanaśyāma

a) Nārāyaṇa

Nārāyaṇa was the son of Nāgeśvara and disciple of Gopālendrasarasvatī. He was the tenth in decent from Mallinātha of Kolacala family and must therefore had lived about the end of the 15th century. He says in prefatory verses that Mallinātha was honoured by king Vīrarudra of Warrangal and his grandson Peḍḍabhaṭṭa (Commentator of *Naiṣadhacarita*) was bathed in gold by king Sarvagṅa. At the invitation of king Prauḥadevarāya of vijaynagar (1414–1416 A. D.). Mallinātha wrote Vaīśyavaṃśasudhārṇava.[213] Nārāyaṇa's commentary on *Campūrāmāyaṇa* is known as 'Padayojanā'.

b) Rāmacandra

Rāmacandra was the son of Koṇḍapaṇḍita of Śāṇḍilyagotra. He has also commented on *Kṛṣṇa-kamṇāmṛta.*[214] He was also called Mohanabilvamaṇgala.

c) *Kāmeśvara*

Kāmeśvara was the son of Gaṇgādhara of Kodamarti family. He was the disciple of Viśvasvara. He flourished in the 15th century A. D.[215]

d) *Mānaveda*

Mānaveda also known as Eralpattirāja. He lived in calicut in the 7th century A. D. He was an admirer of Nārāyaṇa. Besides a commentary on *Campūrāmāyaṇa* he wrote his *Kṛṣṇagīti or Kṛṣṇanāṭaka*. Rudradāsa describes the marriage of Mānavedarāja with Candralekhā in his Saṭṭaka *Mānavedacarita*.[216]

e) *Ghanaśyāma*

Ghanaśyāma, was originally known as Aryaka. He was the son of Kamalā and Kāśī Mahādeva of Bhārgava family. In his twelfth year he made up the Yuddhakāṇḍa for Bhoja's *Campūrāmāyaṇa*.[217] He wrote sixty-four (64) works in Sanskrit, twenty (20) in Prākṛt and twenty-five (25) in other dialects. On rhetoric he wrote the *Rasārṇava*. Besides his commentary on *Campūrāmāyaṇa*, he wrote commentaries on *Śākuntalā*, *Uttararāmacarita*, *Prabodhacandrodaya Mahāvīracarita*, *Nīlakaṇṭhavijayacampū*, *Bhāratacampū*, *Kādambarī*, *Vāsavadattā and Daśakumāracarita*. His son Candraśekhara wrote a commentary on *Dāmaruka*, which is a puculiar dramatic composition.[218] There are some commentaries written by anonymous authors also which are preserved in certain manuscript libraries in South India.[219] There are some modern commentaries written by the following commentators :

a) Rāmacandra Budhendra
b) V. Śaṇkara Śāstrī and T. R. Ratnam Āyyar
c) Garalapurisa Śāstrī and T. R. Ratnam Āyyar
d) Rāmacandra Miśra
e) Rām Nāth Tripathī Śāstrī

6. Translation

The *Campūrāmāyaṇa* has been translated into different languages of the world. These languages include English. Hindi, Telegu and Bengali. We furnish a list of these translation with details below :

English	-	by Vidyāratna pt. S. Raṇgachar and Vidyālaṃkāra, R. Śrīnivās Sarchar. Sanskrit literature society, Bāṇgālore 4, First ed. 1950.
Hindi	-	by Paṇḍit Rām Nāth Tripāthī Śāstrī, Chaukhambā Amarbhāratī Prakāśan, Vārāṇasī-221001. First ed. 1979.
Telegu	-	by Andhrapradesh Sāhitya Academy, 1915
Bengali	-	by Dr. Anil Chandra Basu, Sanskrit Book Depot Pvt. Ltd., 28/1 Vidhān Sarani, Calcutta.

Different editions of the Campūrāmāyaṇa

There are several editions of the *Campūrāmāyaṇa* The following are some of the important editions of the book.

1. Campūrāmāyaṇa	Ed. by :	Jivanānandha Bhattāchārya Calcutta 1st edition –1878 2nd edition – 1889
2. Campūrāmāyaṇa	Ed. by :	V. Śaṇkara Śāstrī and T. V. Ratnam Āyyar. Madras Oriental Press.
3. Campūrāmāyaṇa	Ed. by :	Rāmacandra Miśra Chaukhambā Vidyā Bhavan 1st edition – 1956 2nd edition – 1971
4. Campūrāmāyaṇa	Ed. by :	T. V. Tattācārya, Madras Vivekānanda Press 1884
5. Campūrāmāyaṇa	Ed. by :	Rāmacandra Budhendra

V. Rāmasvāmi Śāstralu and Sons, 1st edition 1941

6. Campūrāmāyaṇa Ed. by : Vāsudeva Lakṣmaṇśāstrī Paṇśikar, Chaukhambā Sanskrit Saṇsthān, Nirnay Sāgar Press, Bombay 1st edition 1917, reprinted 1982
7. Campūrāmāyaṇa Ed. by : S. Raṇgachar Sanskrit Sāhitya Sadan, Bāṇgālore -4, 1st edition -1950
8. Campūrāmāyaṇa Ed. by : Pandit Rāmnāth Tripāthi Chaukhambā Amarbhāratī Prakāśan, Vārāṇasī -221001 1st edition -1979

7. The Scope and utility of the present study

The *Campūrāmāyaṇa* is a famous Campūkāvya. It is an excellent literary composition. The *Campūrāmāyaṇa* occupies a very important position among the Campū works written in Sanskrit and other languages. It is an immensly important work from the literary and academic point of view. We deeply feel the necessity of a truly exhaustive critical study of *Campūrāmāyaṇa* which will help the readers to appreciate the campūkāvya properly.

References

1. *'miśrāṇi nāṭakādīni teṣāmanyatra vistaraḥ /*
   gadyapadyamayī kāciccampūrityapi Vidyate//
   KDI-31
2. CR. Bālakāṇḍa, Verse 3
3. *'vālmīkigītaraghupuṁgavakīrtileśai*
   stirptiṁ karomi kathamapyadhunā budhānām/
   gaṇgājalairbhuvi Bhagīrathayatnalabdhaiḥ
   kiṁ tarpaṇaṁ na vidadhāti naraḥ pitṛṃām//
   Ibid, Verse 4
4. Ibid, Verse 41.
5. Aufrechet, Cat. Cata. Part I. pp. 418–419.
6. Śāli, Intro. pp. 18-21.
   CIH., p. 334

Cat Cata. Part I, p. 418
Purāṇic Ency. p. 138

7. *'atheśvareṇa krathakaiśikānāṁ svayaṃvarārthaṁ svasurindumatyāḥ/ āptaḥ kumārānayanotsukena Bhojena dūto raghave visṛṣtaḥ*
Raghu. V, Verse 39.

8. SKB. Intro. p. 3.

9. 'Yadā Mālavakamaṇḍale ŚrīBhojarāja rājyaṃ cakāra' Pr. Cin., p. 25.

10. 'Muñja was also known Vākpatirāja II. Utpalarāja, Pṛthivīballabha, Śrīvallabha, was a poet and patron of poets. He was the son of Siyakas. He rule at Dhārā in Mārwar in 974–995 A. D. He was defeated and executed by the Cālukya king Tāilapa'
HCSL Krishnamacariyar. M, p. 401.

11. *Pañcaśatpañcavarṣāṇi saptamāsaṁdinatrayam/*
Bhojarājena bhoktavyaḥ sagauḍaḥ dakṣiṇāpathaḥ//
Bhoja Pra. Verse 6

12. *'Bhojaḥ kṣamābṛtsa khalu na khalaistasyasāmyaṁ narendrai statpratyakṣaṁ kimiti bhavatā nāgataṁhāhatāsmi/*
Yasya Dvāroḍḍamaraśikharakoḍapārāvatānāṁ nādavyājāditi sakaruṇā vyājahāreva dhārā'//
VDC. Ch. 18, Verse 96

13. *'sa ca Bhojanarendraśca dānotkarṣena viśrutau/*
sūrī tasminkṣaṇe tulyaṁ dvāvāstaṃ kavibāndhavau//

14. 'Bhojanṛpaterstyāgalīlāyitam' KP. p. 285

15. HIL, Vol. III, part I, P. 54

16. SKP, p. 136.

17. 'vaṁśeasmin vairisiṁhaḥ kṣitipatirbhavad bhuribūtiprabhāvaḥ.../tasmādvai... śrīsiyakoabhūnnṛpaḥ / tasmād... muñja rājo nṛpaḥ / ... tasyāsīdatha pārthivaḥ pṛthuyaśāḥ śrīsindhu rājo nṛpaḥ / ... tatsūnurbhuvanaikabhūṣaṇambhūdbhūpāla cūḍāmoṇiśchāyadāmbaracumbitāṅghrikamalaḥ śrī Bhojadevo nṛpaḥ...
sadā samakarasyāsya lakṣmīkulagṛhasya ca/
sindhurāja iti vyaktaṁ nāma dugdhodadheriva//
anena vihitānyatra yat sāhasaśatānyataḥ/
navīnasāhasāṅkoayaṁ vīragoṣthiṣu gīyate//
SKB. Intro. pp. 7-8

18. Śṛpra. ed. Rāghavan, V., p. 5.

19. *'dīpapratāpānalasaṁnidhānādbibrat... ...*

.... pṛthivīpatikīrtidhārāṁ dhārāmudārāṁ kavalīcakāra/ bhāgyakṣyānmālavabharturāṣīdekāṁ na dhārāṁ parihartumīśaḥ niḥśeṣnirvāsitarājahaṁsaḥ khaṅgena bālāmbudamecakena......../ Bhojakṣābhṛdbhujapañjareapi yaḥ kīrtiṁhamsīm ..../ Bhojaḥ kṣāmapālavimuktadhārānipātamātreṇa raṇeṣuyasya ..../ dhruvaṁ raṇe yasya jayāmṛtena kṣībaḥ kṣamābharturbhūtkṛpānaḥ ekā gṛhitā yadanena dhārā dhārasahaśraṁ yaśoavakīrṇam//
SKB Intro. p. 11

20. *'cedīśvarendrarathatoggalabhīmamukhyān kaṇāṭalāṭapatigurjararātturuṣkān/ yadbhṛtyamātravijitānavalokya maulā doṣnāṁ balāni kalayanti na yodhṛlokan// Ibid*, p. 10
21. Ibid, p. 11
22. SDT, pp. 179–180, 229–231.
23. 'iti śri vidarbharājaviracite Campūrāmāyaṇe sundarakāṇḍaḥ samāptaḥ. CR. p. 437
24. Bhojapara. pp. 98–101.
25. *'Śrīmatā Bhojadevena Dhārāyaṁ Sarasvatīkaṇṭhābharaṇa nāmnī pāthaśālā sthāpitāsīt/'* SKB Intro. p. 13.
26. *'Mālavādhipatir Bhojaḥ prahitaiḥ svaṃasaṁcayaiḥ/ akārayadyena Kuṇḍayojanaṁ kapaṭeśvare//*
Ibid. p. 12
RJT, VII, Verse 190.
27. 'śrīmato Bhojadevasya svahastākṣaeāṁkitam tāmrapatratrayāmadyāvadhyadhigatam.'
SKB. Intro. p. 14
28. Ibid. p. 9
29. Śr. Pra. ed. Raghavan, V. p. 5
Pra. Carita–p. 200, Verses 75–78.
30. Skt. Poetics, pp. 138–139
31. Uṇādi Sūtra of Bhoja. Govt. Ori, Mss. Lib. Madras, Intro. p. 1.
32. Ibid, Intro., p. 1
33. 'Capernuṁ ca iti Bhojaḥ. 'capśāntvane madhuraṁ vadati campūḥ prabandhabhedah'
Ibid, Sūtra 1–90, p. 19
34. 'Murmura' tuṣādiḥ', Ibid, Sūtra, 1–40.

35. The journal of Sanskrit Academy, Osmania University, Vol. VII, 1985, pp. 4–7.
36. The Uṇādisūtra in various recension, Madras University, Sanskrit series No. 7, Part 6, Intro. p. 1.
37. *'mahārājādhirāja śrīBhojaviracitaṃ Sarasvatīkaṇṭhābharaṇam/ Śri Daṇḍanātha Nārāyaṇa viracita hṛdayahārinī sahitam//* Ibid, p. 1
38. *'vaidarbhī sātha pāñcālī gaurīyāvantikā tathā/ lāṭiyā māgadhī ceti ṣoḍā rītirnigadyate//* SKB. 2–26
39. *'bhūribhārabharākrāntā bādhati skandha aṣate/ tathā na bādhate skandho yathā bādhatibādhate// atra bādhaterātmanepadītvād 'bādhate' iti syāt, na punar 'bādhati' iti',* Ibid. 1. p.4
40. *'śṛṇgāravīrakaruṇādbhūtaraudrahāsya bibhatsavatsabhayānakaśāntanāmaḥ/ āmnāsiṣurdaśa rasān sudhiyo, vayṁ tu śṛṇgārameva rasanād rasaṁāmanāmaḥ//* Śṛ. Pra. p. 487
41. *'sa śṛṇgāraḥ, soabhimānaḥ, sa resaḥ'* Ibid, p. 491.
42. *'dharmaśṛṇgāraḥ, arthaśṛṇgāraḥ, kāmaśṛṇgāraḥ, mokṣaśṛṇgāraḥ iti...*
...tatra pravartamānasya tarāmyānatimāno dharma śṛṇgāraḥ' Ibid, p. 508.
43. *'arthanāmo ātmanaḥ sukhasādhanānām........ prāyataḥ pravṛttau tadavāpti abhimānaḥartha śṛṇgāraḥ* Ibid
44. *'tatra sāmānyaviśeṣakāmārthinaḥ dhīralatitādeḥ nāyakasya tadanukulāyāṁ pravṛttau tadupāyena atikramena atadanubhavābhimānaḥ kāmaśṛṇgāraḥ'* Ibid
45. *'tatvajñānāniḥśreyasādhigamo mokṣaḥ......... puruṣasya ca śāstroktairupāyaiḥ tatvajñadibhiḥ niḥśreyasamīhmānasya gārhasthyoapi tadadhigamo yojñatābhimāno mokṣaśṛṇgāraḥ'* Ibid.
46. *Rājamārtaṇḍa (Āyurvedic granthamālā)* Jādavjī Tricūmjī Ācārya, 2nd ed. 1924.
47. *Samastapathonidhivīcisaṁcaya pravartitāndolanakeli kīrtinā/ Prakāśito Bhojanṛpena dehināṁ hitāya nānāvidhayogasaṁgra haḥ//* Rāja (M), Verse 418.

P. 1. śirorogādhikāra
P. 6. Netra ,,
P. 9. Nāsā ,,
P. 12. Mukha ,,
p. 13. Stona
p. 14. Udara etc.

48. Ibid, pp. 60–65.
49. Cat. Cata. Part I, pp. 418–419
50. The literary remians of Dr. Bhāudāji, ed. by Ghosa, Ramachandra p. 246, 1888, Calcutta Ganakataraṅginī, ed. by Sudhākara Dvivedī, Vārāṇasī p. 964, Bhojarāja', Vārānasi, 1892.
51. Rājamārtaṇḍa (A) ed. Śrīkṛṣṇadāsa, Sudhākara, 1953.
52. *Purvācāryamatejñāḥ yadyat śrastharh laghusphotaṁejñam*
tad budhidaṁ śubhakaraṁ rahasyamtyujñate vaktum/
vaidayaḥ purunvitā mantrā daivajñaśca catūrṇaka
prātaḥ kāleṣu draṣṭravyā nityam svarśrayaḥ iccatā//
Rāja (A), p. 1 Verse 1.
53. *'āyatāṁ caturasraṁ ca vṛttaṁ bhadrasaṁ tathā cakraṁ viṣamabāhusyāt/*
trikoṇa śakatākṛtiḥ daṇḍaḥ raṇasthānaṁ murajaśca vṛhannuthan//
Ibid, Verse 80.
54. *jeṣṭhāṁ saṁbatsaro caiva jeṣṭhamāsasya purṇimā/*
jeṣṭhātena yadāyuktā mahājeṣṭhiprakīrtītā//
aindraśālistraciva prajāpatya ravistathā/
purṇimā jeṣṭhamāsasya mahājesthibhattadā//
jeṣṭhamāse site pakṣe ṣaṣthīvāraṇa saṁyuktā/
vyajanika karāṣtsyāt archanti vipine strīyah// Ibid, p. 128
55. *vṛṣarāśi sthite sūrye śuklapkṣe caturddaśī*
Proktā rudrārcanāvaiba mā ca samyak caturddaśī/
jyeṣthe site caturddaśyāṁ sāvitrivratamuttamm
avaidavyāya kurvanti strīyaḥ śradhāsamanvitam//
Ibid, p. 128
56. SDS. pp. 334–338
57. 'māheśvarastu manyante kāryakāraṇa vidhiduḥkhāntāḥ pañca padārthāḥ paśupatineśvareṇa paśupāśaviṁokṣanāyopadiṣṭāḥ paśupatirīsvarī nimitta kāranamiti varṇayanti' BSŚ, p. 488
58. *'śaivāgameṣu mukhyaṁ patipaśupāśa iti kramāt tritayam/*
tatra patiḥ śiva uktaḥ paśavo hyaṅvoarthapañcakaṁ pāśaḥ// Tattva, Verse–5

59. *'patipaśupāśabhedāt trayaḥ padārthāapi prayoktṛdehasāpekṣaṁ tadardhamkhileadhvani/ kṛtvādhikāraṁ sthityante śivaṁ viśati seścaram/ vinādhikaraṇānyat pradhānvikṛteradhaḥ/ kṛtvādhikāramiśeṣṭamupaiti svādhvasaṁhṛtau//*

Ibid, p. 37

'pāśānte śivatāśruteḥ', SDS, p. 334.

60. *'cittasyanirmalasatvapariṇāmarupasya yā vṛttayoaṅgāṅgi bhāvapariṇāmarupāstāsāṁ nirodho bahirmukhapariṇati ...... yogasya sambhavaḥ/'*

tadvārthamātranirbhāsaṁ svarupaśunyamiva samādhiḥ'

Rāja (Yoga), p. 327, 348

61. *'sattvapuruṣayoḥ śudhisāmaye kaivalyam'*

sattapuruṣāvuktalakṣaṇau tayoḥ śudhisāmye kaivalyaṁ sattvasya sarvakartṛtvābhimānanivṛtyā svakāraneanupraveśaḥ śudhiḥ, puruṣasya śudhirupa caritabhogābhāva iti dvayoḥ samānāyāṁ śudhau puruṣasya kaivalyamutpadyate mokṣo bhavatītyarthaḥ'

Ibid., pp. 357-358.

62. *'tapḥ svādhyāyeśvarapraṇidhāni kriyāyogaḥ'*

tapaḥ śāstrāntaropadiṣṭaṁ kṛcchracāndrāyaṇādi, svādhyā yaḥ praṇavapurvānāṁ mantrānāṁjapaḥ īśvarapraṇi dhānaṁ sarvakriyānāṁ tasminparamagurau phalanira pekṣatayā saṁpaṇam, atāni kriyāyoga ityucyate',

Ibid., p. 338

63. *prātarutthāya vidhinā kuryāddantadhāvanam/*
vāgyaṭaḥ puṇyakāṣṭhena atha Ūrdhaṁ krameṇatu//
dantadhāvanavidhānato nṛnāṁ
mānasaṁ surabhigandhi nirmalam/
jāyate vigata sarvakilibaṣam
svāntamapyavīrataṁ bhavecchuci//

Cāru. Verses 4. 22.

64. *puṇyanirmalatoyena ūṣṇatoyena vā yataḥ*
nalāpakarṣaṇārthaāya snānaṁ kuryātprayatnataḥ..

Ibid., Verse 83

65. *Bhūṣaṇaibhuṣayedaṅgaṁ yathāvibhasārataḥ*
śucisaubhāgyavṛdhyarthaṁ āyurlakṣmabhivṛdhaye/
yena kenāpi ratnena kāñcanena vinirmitam
bhūṣaṇaṁ dhārayennityaṁ sarvadeṣavivarjitam//

Ibid., Verses 147–148.

66. *'atisnigdhaṁ karotyannaṁ viśeṣācchelṣmavardhanam/*
hṛdi gauravamālasyaṁ prasekamarucitathā
Ibid., Verse 342
Ibid., Verses 343–344
67. Ibid., pp. 74–93
68. Ibid., pp. 69–74
69. *'tadurdhvamadhiruḍā syātpañcaśadvātsarāvadhi/*
vṛdhāttparato jñeya suratotsavavarjitā// Ibid., pp. 112
70. Ibid., pp. 98–105.
71. *Khadiramiśritatāmbulam—*
Mukharogakṛmiharaṁ khadirena vimiśritam/
dantānāṁ susthiratvañca vaktradurgandhanāśanam//
vātaśleṣamaharaṁ bhedi raktapīttavibardhanam//
Ibid., pp. 88
72. parṇamūle bhavedvyādhiḥ parṇāgre pāpasambhavaḥ
cūrṇaparṇaṁ haratyāuḥ śirā bhdhivināśinī/
tasmādagraṁ ca mulaṁ ca sirā caiva vivarjayet
cūrṇaparṇaṁ varjayitvā tāmbulaṁ khādayedbudhaḥ//
Ibid., pp. 89
73. BHP, p. 40 Verses 180–185
74. TM, pp. 1–25, Verses 1–78
75. MNS, Vol. I, pp. 83–85
76. Cāru. p. 69
77. Ibid
78. Ibid, p. 70
79. Ibid
80. Ibid, pp. 70–74
81. *'paityaghnañca vraṇaghnañca vaṭapatretu bhojanam/*
garahārī ca tatproktaṁ padmapatre tu bhojanam//
Ibid, 71
82. CKT, pp. 56–62.
83. Yukti, pp. 1–17
84. Ibid, pp. 47–49
85. *nadī śmaśāna śailānāṁ vanasya nikaṭe tathā/*
na vāstukarma kurvvīt na dvandvan nagarāntayoḥ//
sthirarāśi gatebhāno candre ca sthiramodaye/
śudhe kāle dine caiva nagaraṁ kārayetnṛpaḥ//
Ibid, p. 26, 22
86. Ibid, p. 50-61
87. *'revatyaśvidhaniṣṭhāṣu hastādiṣvapi pañcasu/*
guruśukrabudhasyāni vastrālaṁkāradhāranam//
śirastraṁ mukutaṁ hāraḥ kuṇḍalaṁ cāṇgodantathā/

kaṇkaṇaṁ vālakañcaiva mekhalāṣṭāviti kramāt//
muktā vaiduryya nīlañca yathā maraktaṁ kramāt/
ādityādi daśājānāṁ sarva sampamattidāyakāḥ//
Ibid, Verses 39, 41, 43

88. Ibid, pp. 139–176
'astrastu dvividhaṁ proktaṁ nirmmāyaṁ māyikaṁ tathā/
khadgādikantu nirmāyaṁ māyikaṁ dahanādikaṁ//
Ibid, p. 140.

89. *gajaśvādi catuṣpādaṁ dolādi dvipadambhavet/*
naukādyaṁ vipādaṁ jñeyaṁ rathādyaṁ bahūpādakam//
Ibid, p. 7
gajaḥ prasthanadolāyaṁ raṇadolāsuca keśarī/
mṛgo bhramaṇadolāyāṁ kriḍādolāṣu ṣaṭpadaḥ//
Ibid, p. 217

90. *dīrghaṁ vā caturasraṁ vā kārayennṛpaḥ/*
tadvayaṁ vahulambāpi kadācidapikarayet//
dīrghaḥ pādaika prasaraḥ caturasraḥ samocitaḥ/
tribhiḥ pādaih saṁm tryasraṁ vartulaṁvalayākṛtiḥ//
dīrghaṁ syāddīrghakālāya sukhasampatti hetave/
caturasraṁ caturvarga phalāya pṛthivīpateḥ// Ibid, p. 22

91. Śukra, p. 542

92. Kāma. Verses, 23, 33, 44, 45.

93. *'tatra maitrapadasthāne niveśayavanṛpateḥ/*
prasādāḥ prāṇmukhaḥ kāryo yathavat pṛthivīñjayaḥ//
Śālāparikramopeta karmāntairapi cānvitam/
tatraprācyāṁ bhaved gehamādityapadasaṁśritam//
Samarā, p. 64, Verses 16, 18

94. *'athātaḥ sampravkṣyāmi prasādāña śikharānvitān/*
rucakādīṁścatuḥṣaṣthiṁ nāma lakṣaṇataḥ kramāt//
pūrvaṁ yāni vimānāni pañcokānyabhavaṁstataḥ/
tadākārabhṛtaḥ sarve prasādāḥ pañcaviṁśatiḥ//
śikharairvividhākārairekenāṇḍena bhūṣitāḥ/
keciddaṇḍatrayopetāḥ kecit pañcaṇdakānvitāḥ//
īṣadbhedena te jñeyāprasādāḥ sarvakāmadāḥ/
Ibid, Ch. 56 Verses 1–4.

95. *pratimānāatha brūmo lakṣaṇaṁ dravyameva ca/*
suvarṇarupyatā mrāśma dārulekhyāni śaktitaḥ//
citraṁ ceti vinirdiṣtaṁ dravyamarcāsusaptadhā/
suvarṇaṁ puṣṭikṛd vidyād rajataṁ kīrtivardhanam//
netrāśravaṇayormadhyaṁ bhavedaṅgulapañcakam/
karṇau cākṣisamau jñeyāvutsedhād dviguṇāyatau//
Ibid, pp. 596-597.

96. *brahmānlārciḥpratimaḥ kartavyaḥ sumahādyutiḥ/*
sthulāṇgaḥ śvetapuṣpaśca śvetaveṣṭanaveṣṭitaḥ/
kṛṣṇājinottarīyaśca śvetavāsāścaturmukhaḥ//
daṇḍaḥ kamaṇḍaluścāsya kartavyo vāmahastayoḥ/
akṣasūtradharastadā mauñjayā mekhalayāvṛtaḥ//
kāryā vardhayamānastu jagad dakṣinapāṇinā/
avaṁ kṛte tu loke kṣemṁ bhavati sarvataḥ//
Ibid, p. 602–2–5.

97. *kārttikeyasya saṁsthānamidānīma bhīdhīyate/*
taruṇārkanibho raktavāsāḥ pāvakasaṁprabhaḥ/
nagare dvādaśabhujaḥ kheṭake ṣaḍbhujo bhavet/
grāme bhūjadvayopetaḥ kartavyaḥ śubhamicchatā//
nagareṣu sadā kāryaḥ skandaḥ parajayiṣibhiḥ/
kheṭake tu vidhātavyaḥ ṣaṇmukho jvalanaprabhaḥ//
tathā tīkṣṇāyudhopetaḥ ṣradāgāmabhiralaṁkṛtaḥ/
grāmeapi dvibhujaḥ kāryaḥ kāntidyutisamanvitaḥ//
Ibid, p. 604

98. *śṛṇgārahāsyakaruṇā raudrapreyobhayānakāḥ/*
vīra ca bībhatsaścādhutastathā//
śāntaścikādaśetyuktā rasāścitraviśāradaiḥ/
sabhrūkampa tathā premaguṇānvitaḥ/
yatreṣṭalalitā ceṣṭā sa śṛṅgāro rasaḥ smṛtaḥ//
Ibid, p. 632, Verses 2-4.

99. *Patāke tu yadā vakrānāmikā tvaṇgulirbhavet/*
tripatākaḥ sa vijñeyaḥ karma cāsyābhīdhīyate//
Ibid, p. 639.

100. *Tripatāke yadā haste bhaved pṛṣthāvalokinī/*
tarjanī madhyamāyāśca tadāsau kartarimukhaḥ//
Ibid, p. 641.

101. *arālakasya yadā vakrānāmikā traṇgulirbhavet/*
Śukatuṇḍaḥ sa vijñeyaḥ karma cāsyābhidhīyate//
Ibid, p. 644.

102. *'deva proktramatra viṣaye bhagavatā śālihotrena yat–*
kapināṁ medasā doṣo vahnidāhasamubhavaḥ/
aśvānāṁ nāśamabhyeti tamaḥ sūryodaye yathā//'
Pañca. Aparīkṣitakāraka, Verse 75.

103. Yukti, pp. 181–197
Śāli, Aśvayukti, 13, 22 etc.

104. *Bhojastu dvādaśasu kāleṣu kāśāditāḍanamāha/*
tīkṣṇaṁ madhyaṁ punar dvābhyaṁ jaghanyaṁ niṣṭhuris
tribhiḥ// AV. p. 79, 7, 17.

atra Bhojoapi evaṁ aha
grīvāyāṁ bhītaṁ āhaanyāt trastaṁ caivacavājinām/
vibhrāntacittaṁ adhare tyaktśikṣaṁ ca tāḍayet//

Ibid, p. 79-80. 7, 18.

105. *'sito raktastathā pītaḥ sāraṇgaḥ piṇga eva ca/*
nīla kṛṣṇoatha sarveṣāṁ śvetaḥ śreṣṭhatamaḥ smṛtaḥ//

Śāli, Appendix I, p. 20.1.

sotoraktastathā pītaḥ sāraṇgaḥ piṇga eva ca/
nīlaḥ kṛṣṇoatha sarveṣāṁ śvetaḥ śreṣṭhatamaḥ smṛtaḥ//

Ibid, AC, 3.2

106. *śvetābhaḥ śvetapādaśca tathā syācchvetalocanaḥ/*
cakravākaḥ sa vijñeyo rājārho vājisattamaḥ//

Śāli, p. 20. 3

107. *yasya pādāḥ sitāḥ sarve tathā vaktre ca madhyamaḥ/*
kalyānapañcakaḥ proktaḥ sarvakalyāṇakārakaḥ//

Ibid, p. 21.7.

108. *Yasya pādāḥ sitāḥ sarve pucchaṁ vakṣastathaiva*
murdhā bhālaṁ sitaṁ yasya taṁ vidyādaṣṭa maṇgalam//

Ibid, Verse 6

109. *hṛdi skandhe gale caiva katideśe tathaiva ca/*
nābhau kukṣau ca pārśvānte madhyamāste pratkirtitaḥ//

Ibid, Verse 9.

110. *savaśveto hayo yastu bhacchyāmaikakarndkaḥ/*
sa vājī rājayogyaḥ syācchyāmakaṃakaḥ prakīrtiaḥ//

Ibid, p. 20, Verse 4.

111. *'Candrādityau lalātasthau nṛpāṇāṁ jayavardhanau/*
yasya lalāte bhramaradvayaṁ tau Candrādityau
jayakārinau//

Ibid, p. 4 Verse 25.

112. *nṛpaveśmantapūrvage śubhadivase kārayedāgāram/*
sudṛhaḥca suvistīṛṇa vāstugrantho ditātmanāt//

Ibid, p. 18, Verse 129.

113. *varuṇe tu mahāsārakaśādharakuśālayāḥ/*
tatpuraṁ varuṇaṁ jñeyaṁ tāsyā jāyā jayeritā//

Nāma, p. 2, Verse 23.

varuṇe tu mahāsārakaśādharakuśālayāh/
tatpuraṁ varuṇaṁ jñeyaṁ tasya jāyā jayeritā//

Vaija – p. 305

114. 'Bhojanighntuśca samāptaḥ' Nāma. p. 40

115. *Svargaṁ nākalokāgrayasādhāvāsabudhālayaḥ/*
mandākinīdharo divyaṁ khapuraṁ taṁ napuṁsakam//

Indresyuḥ prāgdiśānathamahendradanujārayaḥ/
sarvāṇganayanāgāricintācintāmoṇivarāsanāḥ//

Ibid, p. 1, Verses 2, 5.

116. *ākāśaṁ śabdaguṇakaṁ nakṣatrapadamattyutam/*
vidyādharāpsaroyakṣarakṣogandharvamandiram//

Ibid, p. 6, Verse 43.

117. *divase dṛśyamāneṣu tārakeṣu ca ketavaḥ/*
nabhasi sthānurupeṇa dṛstaṁ yadhoraīlabham//

Ibid, Verse 46.

118. *rātrirniśīthinī kāli niśākarakuṭumbinī/*
niśā syacchuklapakṣe tu praṇā candrikāvatī//

Ibid, p. 7, Verse 53.

119. *ākāśakusumaṁ tāraṁ korakaṁ kārakantakam/*
nirakaṁ nirmalaṁ saṁgyaṁ nakṣatreṣu nigadyate//
śukre kaviḥ śuciḥ kāvyaḥ pūrvadevapurohitaḥ/
gurau vṛhaspatih sūryaḥ surejyaḥ sūrivāsavau//
Candro niśākaraḥ śauriḥ kalaśābdhibhavo bhavaḥ/

Ibid, p. 8, Verses 45, 48, 49

120. *vasundharā ratnagarbhā dhāruṇi dharaṇidharā/*
dhāriṇi bhutradhātri ca viśvadhātri kṣamā sahā//

Ibid, p. 8 Verse 62

121. *dīrgharomā ca bhalluko vikarāloacchabhallukaḥ/*
mahiṣaḥ sauribhoaśvarirjaranto gadgadasvanaḥ//
hirambaḥ kṛṣṇaśṛṅgaśca tulāyaḥ kāsaro guroḥ/
kṛṣṇsah syātkṛṣṇasāre tu nirañjananirañjakau//

Ibid, p. 17

122. *padmarāge ravimoṇiḥ kuruvindaṁ tu korakam/*
pakkadādimabījābhaṁ māṇikyaṁ śikharaṁ matam//
indrnīle masāraṁ syānmahānilaṁ mahipālam/

Ibid, p. 11. verses 86, 87.

123. *varāṇgā tu catrvarṣā dvivarṣā tu dvihāyanī/*
ekavarṣā tu sā dhanyā bahukṣīrā tu vañculaā//

Ibid, p. 19, Verse 149.

124. *bhudevo brāhmaṇo vipro mukhajo vedasaṁbhavaḥ/*
agrajanmā bādavakaḥ śreṣṭhavarṇaḥ karāgnimān//
paramāpto gururbrahmā ātmalābhakaḥ śivaḥ/
varuthaḥ pravaro jñānī brāhmaṇojyotirātmavān//

Ibid, p. verses 172, 184

125. Cat. Cata. Part I, pp. 418–419 HCSL, p. 640.
126. *racitamanilaputreṇātha vālmīkinābdhau*
nihitamamṛtabudhyā prāṇmahānāṭakayat/

sumatinṛpati Bhojenodhṛtaṁ tatkramena
grathitamvatu viśaṁ miśradāmodarena//
Mahānaṭaka, p. 142, Cat. Cata. Part I, p. 438
SKB. Intro. p. 14, HCSL P. 640

127. CIH, p. 109
128. Śāli, Intro p. 20
129. *'Iha hi śiṣṭaśiromaṇi-nikhilaniravadyāvidyānirmānā pūrvaprajāpati-pracaṇḍabhujoḍaṇḍāparākramamārjita caturaśtibirudaprakāśitasvakṛtagranthasamājaḥ śrīBhojarājaḥ śāstrārambhe etc.'*
Śṛ. Pra. ed. by Rāghavan, V., p. 5.
130. *sāhityādikalāvatā śanagaragrāmāvataṁsāyita*
śrīgaṇgādharadhīrasindhuvidhunāgāṇbikā sūnunā/
CR. Yuddhakāṇḍa, Verse 110.
131. *'prāgBhojaditapañcakāṇḍavihitānande'* Ibid
132. *'Bhojena tena racitāmapi pūrayiṣya*
nnalpīyasāpi vacasā kṛtimatyudarām/
na vriḍitoahamadhunā navaratnahāra
saṇgena kinna hṛdi dhāryata eva tantuḥ//
Ibid, Verse 2.
133. *ŚrīBhoja Lakṣmaṇakavindrakṛte prabandhe*
langnaṁ vacoalamapi me bhavita rasādyam//
DC. of Skt. Mss. of Mysore, Ori. Lib. XVI, 8130
134. *'Lakṣmaṇamahākaviḥ Śri Bhoja Lakṣmaṇa mahākaviṁ Śrīmad Bhojarājapranita campūrāṁāyaṇasya paripūrtaye avaśiṣṭhaṁ yuddhakāṇḍaṁ prāripsuḥ'*
DC. of Skt. Mss of Ori. Lib. Madras XXI 8215
135. *'ṣdṣthaṁ śrīlakṣmaṇīyaṁ viṣamalalitaśabdābhirāmṁ cakāṇḍam'* TC. II, 3372.
136. Ādyar Skt. Mss, Cata. II 22
137. Dc Madras Ori. Mss. Lib. XXII, 8615–16
138. HR. Madras, 1905. III, No. 1681.
139. *'gadyapadyamayī kāciccampūrityapi vidyate'* KD. 1/31
140. *'gadyapadyamayī sāṇkā socchvāsā capuḥ'*
Hemcandra KŚ 8/9, Vāgbhaṭa KŚ 1st Ch.
141. *'gadyānubandharasamiśritapadya sūktirhṛdyā hi*
Vādyakalayā kaliteva gītiḥ/
tasmāddadhātu kavimārgajuṣāṁ sukhāya campūprabandharacanāṁ rasanā madīyā//
CR. Bālakāṇḍa, Verse 3.
142. *'gadyapadyamaya kāvyaṁ Campūrityabhidhīyate,*
SD VI. 336

143. *'netāvinito madhurasatyāgī dakṣaḥ priyamvadaḥ/*
raktalokaḥ śucirvāgmī ruḍavaṁśaḥ Sthiro yuvā//
buddhyutsāhasmṛtiprajñakalāmanasanvitaḥ/
śuro dṛḍśca tejasvī śāstracakṣuścadhārnukaḥ//

DR. 11.1.2

tyāgī kṛtī kulīnaḥ suśrīko rupayauvanotsāhī/
dakṣoanuraktalokastejovaidagdhyaśīlavānnetā//

SD 111. 30.

144. *dhīrodhattā dhīralalitā dhīrodāttāstathaivaca/*
dhīrapraśāntakāściva nāyakāḥ parikīrtitaḥ//

NŚ. Ch. 34. 17
DR. 11.3, SD. 31.

145. *'mahāsattvoatigmbhīraḥ kṣamāvānavikatthanaḥ/*
sthiro nigūḥāhaṁkāro dhīrodātto dṛhavrataḥ//

DR. 11.4,
SD 111.32

146. *ādāya tatsaguṇamāśu vidhāya tatra*
sandhāya bāṇamvadhārya tapodhanatvam/
tajjīvitasya dayamānamanā manīṣī
sambhūtaghorasmarddbirarāma ramḥ//

CR. Bālakāṇḍa, Verse 112.

147. *'avikatthanaḥ kṣamāvānatigambhīro mahāsattvaḥ/*
stheyānnigūḥmāno dhīrodātto dṛhavrataḥ kathitaḥ//

SD. 111.32

148. SD. 111.34
149. *'atha nāyikā tribhedā svānyā sādhāraṇā strīti/*
nāyakasāmānyāguṇairbhavati yathāsaṁbhavairyuktā//

SD 111.56

150. CR. Yuddhakāṇḍa, Verse 69
151. Vāl. Rāmā Ayodhyākāṇḍa, Verse 4, 10.
152. CR. Sundarakāṇḍa , pp. 278-280.
153. *'Yuktā Rāmasya bhavati dharmapatnī yasasvīni'*

Ibid. Yuddhakāṇḍa.

154. *'ahaha nihatālaṅkā vālāanalena hanūmataḥ*
paramavanijāpātivratyānalena bhavānapi/
sukhamahamihāsinā śokānaleapi yadīdṛśe
prabhavati na māṁ hantuṁprārayaḥ sa aṣa citānalaḥ//

Ibid., Verse 94

155. Ibid., Bālakāṇḍa, Verses 30-32
156. Ibid., p. 45
157. Ibid., p. 46
158. Ibid., p. 49

159. *'balena tapasā labdhe baletyatibaleti ca/*
vidyete mayi kākutsthaṁ vidye te vitarāmi te//
Ibid., Verse 37
160. *'astrāṇi jṛmbhakādīni....................śāsanāt//*
Ibid., Verse 44.
161. Ibid., pp. 50-54
162. Ibid., p. 100
163. Ibid., p. 102
164. Ibid., pp. 107–112.
165. Ibid., Ayodhyākāṇḍa, p. 129
166. Ibid., p. 195
167. Ibid., p. 198
168. Ibid., p. 200
169. Ibid., pp. 218–219
170. *'tvayā mayā ca kartavyaḥ satyavācaḥ piturvidhiḥ/*
iti pratyādiśadrāmo bhāratīmapi bharatīm/.
Ibid., Verse 81
171. Ibid., p. 222
172. Ibid., p. 223
173. Ibid., Araṇyakāṇḍa, pp. 229–233
174. Ibid., pp. 234–242
175. Ibid., pp. 255–257
176. Ibid., p. 258
177. Ibid., pp. 266–267
178. Ibid., p. 268
179. Ibid., pp. 269–273
180. Ibid., p. 274
181. Ibid., pp. 275–276
182. Ibid., p. 285
183. Ibid., Kiṣkindhākāṇḍa p. 291
184. Ibid., pp. 291–295
185. Ibid., pp. 296–312
186. Ibid., pp. 313–322
187. Ibid., p. 327
188. Ibid., p. 342
189. Ibid., Sundarakāṇḍa 353
190. Ibid., pp. 353–370
191. Ibid., pp. 389–390
192. Ibid., p. 400
193. Ibid., p. 402
194. Ibid., p. 404
195. Ibid., p. 417

196. Ibid., pp. 418–421
197. Ibid., p. 434
198. Ibid., Yuddhakāṇḍa, p.439
199. Ibid., pp. 449–450
200. Ibid., p. 455
201. Ibid., p. 456
202. Ibid., p. 466
203. Ibid., p. 492
204. Ibid., p. 543
205. Ibid., p. 565
206. NŚ. VI, p. 79
207. SD. III, p. 259
208. DV, p. 973
209. DR IV, p. 72
210. SD. III. p. 234
211. *eka eva bhavedaṇgī śṛṅgārovīra eva vā/*
 aṅgamanye rasāḥ sarve kāryo nirvahaneadbhūtaḥ//
 SD. VI. 10
212. HCSL. p. 505
213. DC. XXI. 8212
214. DC. XXI. 8216.
215. TC II, 3372, III. 3789
216. TC III. 4020
217. HCSL p. 248
218. HR. III. 2170
219. TC. Vol. I-V
 List of Skt. Mss. in Private lib, of Southern India by Gustav Oppert. Ph. D., Madras Vol. II, p. 671, 1885.

Chapter II

CAMPŪ KĀVYA : ITS CHARACTERISTICS : ORIGIN AND DEVELOPMENT

1. Definitions of Campūkāvya

It has been discussed above that Campū is a mixed variety of Sanskrit Kāvya in which prose and poetry are blended by the author without any discrimination. The art of mixing prose and verse in a literary work is quite old. Campū has been defined by many authors since the age of Daṇḍin.

(a) Daṇḍin gives the definition of 'Campū' in his *Kāvyādarśa*, viz 'Gadyapadyamayī kāciccampū rityapi vidyate'.[1] The definition means that there is a type of sanskrit poetry where prose and poems are mixed for the same purpose. The expression 'kācit' used in the definition is a significant word. In suggests that though Campū existed in the literary world in Daṇḍin's time, it did not enjoy a covetable position among literary compositions.

(b) The next definition of Campūkāvya is found in a much latter period in the writings of Hemacandra and Vāgbhaṭa. These scholars present an extended meaning of the term 'Campū' which is given in following definition, viz. 'gadyapadyamayī sāṅkā socchvāsā campūḥ.[2] According to them a Campū must be divided into 'aṅkas' and 'ucchvāsa's. In this context it may be mentioned that the *Nalacampū* of Trivikramabhaṭṭa is divided into 'ucchvāsas,[3] while some later Campūs have been divided into 'Aṅkas' or 'Acts'.

(c) Bhoja, the king scholar of Dhārā is the first scholar to give the etymological meaning of 'Campū'. According to him, the word 'Campū' is derived from the verbal root 'cap' by adding 'Uṇādi' suffix 'U'.[4] According to him, a Campū is a literary composition which creates delight in the minds of readers. He says that prose blended with melodious musical poetical compositions create delight in the minds of the readers like a song associated with musical symphony.[5]

(d) Viśvanātha, the author of '*Sāhityadarpaṇa*' follows Daṇḍin's definition of Campūkāvya. He defines the term as follows :

'*Gadyapadyamayaṁ kāvyaṁ Campūrityabhidhīyate*'[6]

(e) Veṅkaṭādhvarin, the author of the *Vīśvaguṇādarśa-campū* says that the mixture of prose and verse in Campū is like a combination of grapes and honey which deeply appeals to the readers, Campū is a literary work in which musical poetry is mixed with elegant prose in order to produce a special aesthetic effect on the minds of its readers.[7]

(f) Another definition of 'Campū' given by an unknown scholar is as follows :

'*gadyapadyamayī sāṅkā socchvāsā kavigumphitā/*
uktipratyuktiviṣkambhaśūṇyā campūrudāhṛtā//[8]

According to this definition, the chapters in a Campū should be named 'Aṅka' and 'Ucchvāsa', but unlike a Sanskrit drama it should be totally free from the dramatic technic called Viṣkambhaka, and also dialogues. It is significant that some Campū Kāvyas have been written in the style of a drama. The *Śrīnivāsacampū* of Veṅkaṭādhvari is a typical example of a dramatical campū. Let us quote a passage from this Campū text in order to substantiate our view :

'Devi-kastvam?
Śrīnivasa – Cakrī.
Devī – (Sāścaryam) narendrālayabhuvi?
tataśca ityuditavati harau rājahastopalakṣi.[9]

(g) Dr. Chavīnāth Tripāthī gives his own definition of Campū in his work. '*Campū kāvya kā ālocanātmak evaṃ aitihāsik adhayan*' in the following way :

'gadyapadyamayaṁ śravyaṁ sambandhaṁ bahuvarṇitam/
sālaṁkṛtaṁ rasaiḥ siktaṁ campūkāvyamudāhṛtam//[10]

2. The origin and development of Campū Kāvya :

(a) The origin of the literary composition called 'Campū' can be traced back to the Vedic period. This style of using prose and verse together in a literary composition appears in the *Taittirīyasaṁhitā* itself, where prose passages appear side by side with poetical passages, though we do not find any narrative in this writing. Thus, we can quote the following passage from the *Taittirīyasaṁhitā* in order to illustrate our point :

yajñasya ghoṣadāsī pratyuṣṭaṁ rakṣaḥ pratyuṣṭā
arātayaḥ preyamagādhiṣaṇa barhiraccha manunā
kṛtā svādhyā vitaṣṭā ta āvahanti kavayaḥ
purastāddevebhyo jusṭhamiha bahirāsade devānāṃ
pariṣūtmasi varṣavṛdhamasi devabarhimātvaanvaṃmā
tiryakparvate rādhyāsamācchettā te māriṣaṁ
devabarhiḥ śatavalśaṃ viroha sahasravalśāḥ/
vivayaṃ ruhema pṛthivyāḥ saṃpṛcaḥ pāhi susaṃbhṛtā
tvā saṃ bharamyādityai rāsnāasīndrāṇyai saṃhananaṃ
pūṣā te granthiṁ granthātu sate māsthaādindrasya
tvā bāhubhyāmudyacche bṛhaspatermūrdhnā
harāmyurvantārikṣamanvihi devaṃgammāsi.'[11]

(b) This Campū style is continued in the Brāhmaṇas and in the Upaniṣads also. In this connection, we can refer to the 'Śunaḥśepa legend' of the *Aitareyabrāhmaṇa* and also in Aindra-mahābhiṣeka chapter of this Brāhmaṇa where we notice this mixed style of composition in a glaring manner. Let us quote below some relevant passages from the *Aitareya Brāhmaṇa* in support of our contention.

(a) *'atha ha śunaḥśepa ikṣāṁcakreamānusamiva vamā*
viśasiṣyanti hantāahaṁ devatā upadhāvāmīti
sa prajāpatimeva prathamṁ devatānāmupasasāra kesya

nūnaṁ katamasyāmṛtānāmityetayarcā/
taṁ prajāpatiruvācāgnirvai devānāṁ
nediṣthastamevopadhācāveti
soagnimupasasārāgnarvayaṁ
prathamasyāmṛtānāmityetayarcā/'[12]

(b) '*atena ha vā aindreṇa mahābhiṣekeṇodamaya ātreyoa-ṇgambhiṣiṣeva tasmādvaṇgaḥ samantaṃ sarvataḥ*
pṛthivīṁ jayanpariyāyāśvena ca medhyeneje/
sā hovācālopaṇgo daśa nāgasahasrāṇi
daśa dāsīsahasrāṇi dadāmi te brāhmaṇopa
māasminyajñe hvayasveti
tadapyete ślokā abhigītāḥ
yābhirgobhirudamayaṁ preyamedhā ayājayan/
dve dve sahasre badhvānāmātreyo
madhyatoadadāta'/[13]

(c) Coming to the Upaniṣadic literature, we find that the same method receives due importance in the Upaniṣads. It is clear from the following texts of the *Kathopaniṣad* and the *Muṇḍako-paniṣad* :

(a) '*uśan ha vai vājaśravasaḥ sarvavedasaṁ dadau/*
tasya ha nāciketā nāma putra āsa/tam ha kumāraṁ
santaṁ dakṣiṇāsu nīyamānāsu śradhāaviveśa
soayamanyat
pītodakā jagdhatṛṇā dugdhadohāḥ nirindriyāḥ/
ānandā nāma te lokāstān sagacchati tā dadat//
sa hovāca pitraṁ tat kasmaimāṁ dāsyati iti/ dvitīyaṁ
tṛtīyaṁ taṁ hovāca mṛtyeva tvā dadāmiti/'[14]

(b) '*om Brahmā devānāṁ prathamaḥ sambhūva viśvasya*
kartā bhuvanasya goptā/
sa brahmavidyāṁ sarvavidyāpratiṣthāmatharvāsya-
jeṣṭha putrāya prāha//
atharvaṇe yaṁ pravadet brahmātharvā tāṁ
puruvācāṃgire brahmavidyām//
sa Bhāradvāyāya satyavahāya prāha Bhāradvājo
aṇgirase parāvarām//
śaunako ha vai mahāśāloaṁgirasaṁ
vidhivadupasannaḥ prapacca/
kasminnu bhagavo vijñāte savamidaṁ vijñataṁ
bhavatite//

dve vidye veditavye itihasma yadbrahmavido
vidantiparācivāparāca/
tatrāparā Ṛgvedo yajurvedaḥ sāmavedoatharvavedaḥ
śikṣākalpo vyākaraṇaṁ niruktaṁ chādojyotiṣamiti
athaparā yayā tadakṣaramadhigmyate//[15]

(d) Dr. Chavināth Tripāthi observes that the origin of the Campūkāvya can be traced back to the *Jātakamālā* and the *Allahabad Stone Pillar Inscription.*[16] We shall discuss the point clearly in a later context.

It will perhaps be improper on our part if we fail to refer to the *Mahābhārata* and the Purāṇas where the similar style removes the boredom of reading endless poetical composition.

(e) The *Mahābhārata* is introduced with a long prose sentence viz.

'Lamaharṣaṇaputra ugraśravāḥ sautiḥ paurāṇiko naimiṣāraṇye śaunakasya kulapaterdvādaśavārṣika satre./'[17]

The initial prose passage is followed by the following verses viz.

sukhāsinānbhyagacchadbrahmarṣīnsaṁśitavratān/
vinayāvanato bhūtvā kadācitsūtanandanaḥ//
tamāśrammanuprāptaṁ naimiṣāraṇavāsinām/
citrāḥ śrotuṁ kathāstatra parivavrutapasvinaḥ//
abhivādya munīṁstāmstu sarvāneva kṛtānjaliḥ/
apṛcchatsa tapovṛdhiṁ sadbhiścivābhipūjitaḥ//[18]

This technic reappears in the Vanaparvan of the Epic. Let us cite one illustration of the technic employed in the Vanaparvan viz.

'avaṁ dyutajtaḥ pārthā kopitāśca durātmabhiḥ/
dhārtaraṣṭriḥ sahāmātyairnikṛtyā dvijasattama//
śrāvitāḥ paruṣā vācaḥ sṛjadbhivairamuttanam/
kiṁkurvata kauravyā mama purvapitāmahaḥ//
kathaṁ caiśvaryavibhraṣṭāḥ sahasā duḥkhameyuṣaḥ/
vane vijahnire pārthāḥ śakrapratimatejasaḥ// (Poetry)
ke vai tānnvavartanta prāptānvyasanamuttamm

kimācāraḥ kimāhāraḥ kva ca vāso mahātmanām/[19]

(Prose)

(f) In the *Viṣṇupurāṇa* we notice a similar method being adopted in the following portion of the text :

Pururjanmejayasatasyāpi pravinvān pracinvataḥ Pravīra pravīrānmanasyośc̄ābhayadasatasyāpi sudyussudyorbahu gatastayāpi saṁyatissaṁyātepahaṁyātistato raudrāśvaḥ/ ṛteṣukakṣeṣusthandileṣukṛtesujaledharmeṣudhṛteṣustha-

lesannateṣuvaneṣunāmāno raudrāśvasya daśa putra

babhubuḥ/ṛteṣorantinātināraḥputro abhūt/ sumatipramatirathaṁ dhruvaṁ cāpyantitāraḥ putrānvāpa/........ mātrā bhastrā pituḥ putro yenajātaḥ sa ava saḥ/ bharasva putraṁ duṣyanta māvamasthāśaśā kuntalām//[20]

(g) *The Allahabad Stone Pillar Inscription* of Hariṣeṇa written as an eulogy of emperor Samudragupta clearly bears the evidence of the Campū composition. One striking feature of this inscription is that in it prose and poetry are used side by side to praise the achievements and the greatness of the Emperor. In this connection, we can point out to the long prose passage viz.

'tasya vividhasamaraśatāvataṃa dakṣasya svabhujabala parākramaikabandhoḥ parākramāṁkasya paraśuśaraśaṁku śaktiprāsāsitomarabhindipālanāracavaitastikādyanekapraharaṇavirudakulavraṇaśatāṁkaśobhāsamudayopacitakantataravaṣmaṇaḥ kośalakamahendramāhākāntārakavyāghrarājakorālamaṇtarāpaiṣṭapurakamahendragirikoṭṭrakasvāmidatte khaṇḍapallakadamanakāṁceyakaviṣrṇugopāvamuktakanīlarāja veṁgayakahastivarmapālakkakograsenadevarāṣtrakakuberakausthalapurakadhanaṃjaya prabhṛtisarvadakṣiṇāpatharājgrahaṇ amokṣānugrahajanitāpratāponmiśramahābhāgyasya............... . ... sucaritaśatālaṁkṛtānekaguṇagaṇotsiktibhiścaraṇa talapramṛṣṭānyanakapatikīrteḥsādhvasādhū-

dayapralayahetupurusasyacintyasya, kṛpaṇadīnānāthāturajanodghara ṇasamantradīkṣābhyupagatamanasaḥ samidhasyavigrahavato lokānugrahasya dhanadava-ruṇendrāntakasamasya... .... mahārājadhirājaśri-Samudraguptasya .... stambhaḥ yasya'

which is preceded by an excellent poem viz 'āryo hītyupaguhyabhāvapiśunairutkīrṇitai romabhiḥ

sabhyeṣūcchvasiteṣu tulyakulajamlānānanodvīkṣītaḥ/
snehavyālulitena vāṣpaguruṇā tatvekṣiṇā cakṣuṣā
yaḥ pitrābhihito nirīkṣya nikhilaṁ pahyevamu
rvīmiti//

which is followed by another poem viz.

pradānabhujavikramapraśamaśātravākyodayai ruparyupari
saṁcayoccaritanaikamārgaṁ yaśaḥ/
punāti bhuvantrayaṁ paśupaterjaṭāntarguhā
nirodhaparimokṣaśīghramiva pāṇḍu gāṇaṁ payaḥ//[21]

(h) The *Jātakamālā* written on the life of Lord Buddha also bears the stamp of a mixed poem of the Campū style. This can be easily corroborated with the help of the following passage :

'bodhisatvabhūtaḥ kilāyaṁ bhagavānparimitakālābhyāsātsātmībhūtopacitapuṇyakarmā kadācicchibīnāṁ rājā babhuva/
sa vālyātprabhṛtyeva vṛdhopāsanaratirvinayānurkta prakṛtiḥ prakṛtimeghāvitvādanekavidyāhigamavipulatara matirutsāhamaṇtraprasādaśaktidaivasampannaḥ svā iva prajāḥ pālayati sma/
tasmistrivargānuguṇā guṇodhāḥ saṁharṣayogādiva sanniviṣṭāḥ//
samastarupā vivarbhūna cāsurvirodhaṣaksobhavipannaśobhāḥ/
biḍamanevāvinayodhatānāṁ
dumedhasāmapadivātikaṣṭā/
alpātmanāṃ yā madireva Lakṣmīrbabhuva sātatra yathārthanāmā//[22]

(i) The *Pañcatantra* of Viṣṇu Śarmā which was written before the third century A. D. may also be considered as an inspiring force for the authors of Campū literature to write out narratives in a mixed style of prose and verse. The *Tantrākhyāyikā* is supposed to be the original version of the original (ādi) *Pañcatantra*. This book has been restored to us by Hertel. The *Pañcatantra* is a glaring example of a mixture of a prose and verse. This work may be another source of the origin of the Campū technique. Let us quote below a few portions from the *Pañcatantra* to be substantiate our view.

vardhamāno mahānsnehaḥ siṁhagovṛṣayorvane/
piśunenātilubdhena jambukena vināśitaḥ//
tadyathānuśruyate—
asti dākṣiṇātye janapade mahilaropyaṁ nāma nagaram/
tatra ca dharmopārjitavṛrtirvardhamānako nāma
śreṣṭhiputro babhūva/ tasya kadāciccittamutpannam/
prabhūteapi vittearthavṛdhiḥ karṇīyeti/
uktaṃ caʃ-
alabdhamarthaṁ lipset labdhaṁ rakṣedavekṣayā/
rakṣitaṁ vardhayeccainaṁ vṛdhaṁ pātreṣu nikṣipet//[23]

So long we have discussed the probable origin of the Campū class of Sanskrit poetry which became very popular after the ninth century A. D. The model of Campū kāvya was cast by Trivikramabhaṭṭa in his *Nalacampū*. The work became so popular within a short time that several hundred campū Kāvyas were written by different authors within a few centuries.

Campū developed into an extensive and highly rich literary composition like a mighty banyan tree spreading out its foliages in all directions. New thoughts, new ideas, new techniques and experience were incorporated in this class of literature. A simple statement i.e. 'gadyapadyamayī kāciccampūrityapi vidyate/'[24] is unable to give its readers a comprehensive idea or the depth and diversity of Campū Kāvyas written by innumerable authors by grafting their experience and imagination in its body.

The theme of some Campū kāvyas is borrowed from the

Rāmāyaṇa, some Campū literature on the stories of the *Mahābhārata*, and some Campūs owe their origin to *Pūrāṇas*.

There are also secular and religious Campū Kāvyas. Moreover, new techniques have been employed in naming the chapters of Campū literature in order to make this class of composition an attractive one. The subject matter of Campū has changed through the ages.

The *Nalacampū*[25] of Trivikramabhaṭṭa is a secular Campū though its theme is borrowed from the Vanaparvan of *Mahābhārata*.

We have discussed above that both religious and secular Campūkāvyas were written which have contributed to development of the Campū class of the ornate poetry. Apart from the secular and sectarian trends which help in the evolution of the Campū literature, there are also some other special features of the different Campū kāvyas which also play a significant role in its evolution. One striking feature which we must note here is the technic followed in naming chapters of a Campūkāvya.

Let us discuss the point clearly below with the help of concrete examples :

(a) The 'Ucchvāsa' division of Campūkāvya

Hemacandra and Vāgbhaṭa remark that the divisions of Campūkāvya should be named as 'Ucchvāsas' and 'Aṅkas'.[26] It may be remembered here that the 'Aṅka' division is found in a regular drama. The name 'Ucchvāsa' is given to the different parts of an *'Ākhyāyikā'*, like the *Harṣacarita* of Bāṇabhaṭṭa.[27] The *Nalacampū* of Trivikramabhaṭṭa is divided into seven Ucchvāsas. The *Nṛsiṁhacampū*[28] of Daivajña Sūrya and the *Gaṅgāvataraṇacampū* of *Saṁkaradīkṣita* also belong to this particular class. The *Nṛsiṁhacampū* is divided into five Ucchvāsas and the *Gaṅgāvataraṇacampū* is divided into seven Ucchvāsas.[29]

(b) Campūkāvya divided into ullāsa

The name 'Ullāsa' or 'flash' is found in the rhetorical text '*Kāvyaprakāśa*' of *Mammaṭa.*[30] This romantic name has been borrowed by a number of authors in naming their Campū works. Thus *Yatirājavijayacampū*[31] of Ahobalasūri contains seventeen Ullāsas but its last Ullāsa is incomplete. The *Kākutsthavijayacampū* of Vallisahāya Kavi possesses eight Ullāsas.[32] The *Nāthamunivijayacampū*[33] of Rāmānuja Dāsa four, the *Ānandakaṇḍacampū*[34] of Mitra Miśra eight and the *Gaṅgādharacampū* contains four Ullāsas.

(c) Some Campūkāvyas have been divided into 'Kāṇḍas'

While studying the history of Campūkāvyas we find some Campū texts like the *Campūrāmāyaṇa* of Bhoja where the different sections have been named 'kāṇḍas'. The word 'kāṇḍa' means a 'Canto'. The *Rāmāyaṇa* of Vālmīki, as we all know, is divided into seven kāṇḍas. Bhoja has named the Cantos of his work as Kāṇḍas by imitating his great predecessor.[35]

(d) The 'Taraṇga' division is found in the Campū texts

Different authors of Campūkāvyas have tried to give new names to the sections of their Campū texts. A Campūkāvya is an artistic product. The writers of this particular class of literature have frequently attempted to choose romantic names for the different parts of their works. Thus, some authors have chosen the term 'taraṇga', in naming the different chapters of their work. 'Taraṇga', in Sanskrit literature literary means 'wave'. The name is applied in the divisions of the '*Kathāsaritsāgara*' of Somadevasūri.[36] Some writers of Campū like Ciranjīva Bhaṭṭācārya, the author of the *Vidvanmodataraṅginīcampū* have divided their works into 'taraṇgas' or waves.[37] The *Gaurīmāyūramāhatmyacampū* of Appaya Dīkṣita is also divided into five 'taraṅgas'.[38]

(e) The 'Āśvāsa' division of Campūkāvyas

'Āśvāsa' is a name which has been innovated by certain

authors of 'kathā' literature. According to Daṇḍin, in a kathā the division of the work are named 'āśvāsas'.[39] This name in a later period has been utilised by certain authors of Campūkāvyas. Thus, Somadevasūri has arranged the different parts of his *Yaśastilakacampū* into 'āśvāsas'.[40] The *Nīlakaṇṭhavijayacampū*[41] of Nīlakaṇṭha Dīkṣita, the *Ānandakāṇḍacampū*[42] of Samarapuṁgava Dīkṣita,[42] and the *Tripuravijayacampū*[43] of Atirātrayājina belong to this class.

(f) The 'Stavaka' division of Campū texts

'Stavaka' is another word which we find in the division of many Campūkāvyas. The word 'stavaka' means a 'bunch of flowers'. The *Bhāgavatacampū*[44] of Abhinavakālidāsa is divided into six stavakas and the *Bhāratacampū*[45] of Ananta Bhaṭṭa into twelve. The *Ānandavṛndāvanacampū*[46] of Kavikarṇapūra, the *Dharmavijayacampū*[47] of Nallā Dīkṣita or 'Bhuminā̄da', the *Mārutivijayacampū*[48] of Raghunātha Kavi and the *Ānandakaṇḍacampū*[49] Śrīnivāsakavi possess the 'stavaka' division.

(g) The 'Manoratha' types of Campū

The word 'Manoratha' means 'desire'. Kālidāsa uses the word significantly in poem in his '*Abhijñānaśākuntalaṃ*[50] The author of the *Bhāgīrathīcampū*[51] utilises this sweet sounding word in the naming of the different sections of his Campūkāvya.

(h) The 'Vilāsa' division of Campū texts

Some authors of the Campū texts use the term 'vilāsa' also like the words 'manoratha', 'taraṅga' etc. used by other authors. The *Varadābhyudayacampū*[52] of the Veṇkaṭadhvari and the *Raghūnāthavijayacampū*[53] of Kṛṣṇakavi contain five vilāsas.

(i) The 'Sarga' division found in some Campūkāvyas

'Sarga' is a regular title used for the different sections of a Mahākāvya. The term has been used by the authors of several Campūkāvyas in naming different parts of their works in order to impart an epic aroma to their Campū composition. The *Śālivāhanakathācampū*[54] of Śivadattasūri and the *Bharateśvarābhyudayacampū*[55] of Āśādhara contain the 'Sarga' division. The author of these works naturally followed the technic of the authors of Mahākāvyas.

(j) The 'Lambaka' division of Campūkāvya

Many authors have used the name 'Lambaka' instead of other names like 'manoratha' in their works. In this context we can refer to the *Jīvandharacampū*[56] of Haricandra as a case where the word 'Lambaka' has been used by the author for different chapters of the work. It may be mentioned here that Somadevasūri in his *Kathāsaritsāgara*[57] has used the names 'Taraṇga' and 'Lambaka' to mean a broad division and a sub-section of his work respectively.

(k) The 'Kallola' division is found in some Campūs

The word 'Kallola' literary means the roaring of the ocean. The word has been used in the *Ācāryadigvijayacampū* of Vallisahāyakavi, who divides his work into different sections by this name. But in the first section of the book, the author uses the word 'Kolāhala' instead of 'Kallola'.[58] Kolāhala is another significant word arbitrarily selected by the author. The word literary means noise.

(l) The 'Bindu' division of Campūkāvya

Some authors of Campū have used the term 'bindu' (dot) in their Campū texts. Thus Kṛṣṇakavi's *Mandāramarandacampū*[59] contain eleven bindus.

(m) The 'Varṇya' division is used in a few campū works

Many authors of Campū literature have used the name 'varṇya' instead of other names like 'bindu' in their works, In this context we can refer to the *Viśvaguṇādarśacampū*[60] of Veṇkaṭadhvari and the *Tattvaguṇādarśacampū*[61] of Annayācārya which belong to this category.

(n) Campū containing the 'pariccheda' division

The name 'pariccheda' is found in the rhetorical work of Viśvanātha kavirāja viz. *Sāhityadarpaṇa*[62].. The *Rāmacandracampū*[63] of Viśvanātha Siṁha is divided into eight paricchedas.

3. The classification of Campūkāvya

We have discussed above some technical aspects of Campū literature which distinguish some Campūkāvyas from others, but apart from this there are also some important points which can be readily considered in the classification of Campūkāvyas. Some Campūkāvyas are purely religious and some are secular. The theme of the Campūs also varies according to the source from which it has been derived. Several Campūs are written on the theme of the *Rāmāyaṇa* and several Campūs are written on the Purāṇas. There are also many other distinctions which we shall discuss in detail below. A critical survey of the whole range of Campū literature shows that there are many Campūs of biographical character. Some other Campūs, again, are of a journey type. There are some historical and monographical Campūs also. Indian philosophies play a dominating role in a few Campū texts of a later period.

(a) The Campūkāvyas written on Epic themes are generally religious Campūs. The *Campūrāmāyaṇa* of Bhoja is a religious Campū based on the Rāma story of Vālmīki's *Rāmāyaṇa* in which the exploits of Rāma are described. Among the religious campū texts some are dedicated to Viṣṇu and some to Śiva. The Vaiṣṇava Campūs are sometimes related to the description of the greatness and exploits of Viṣṇu or his incarnations viz. Rāma and Kṛṣṇa.

(b) Some Campūkāvyas are written on minor Epic characters also. Among these, the *Hanūmadvijayacampū* or *Mārutivijayacampū* of Raghūnātha in which the author deals with the life of Hanūmān in seven 'stavakas' belongs to this type.[64] The theme of this Campūkāvya is based on the Sundarakāṇḍa of the *Rāmāyaṇa* of Vālmīki. The *Gopālacampū*[65] of Jīva Goswāmī and the *Ānandavṛndāvana-*

campū[66] of *Kavikarṇapūra* are based on the Kṛṣṇa legend narrated with a devotional and religious motive. In the second Campūkāvya, Rādhā plays an important part. The *Ānandavṛndāvanacampū* is to a great extent an artificial composition. The early childhood and youth of Lord Kṛṣṇa is described lavishly in a rhetorical style in twelve stavakas in the work. In the *Ānandavṛdāvanacampū* there is a beautiful description of the dance of cowherd ladies with kṛṣna.[67] The principal sentiment of this Campū is Śṛṅgāra, and it is written in the Vaidarbhī style. In the beginning of *Gopālacampū* the poet praises the holy river Gaṅgā[68] and at the end shows the similarity of 'Nīravihāra' and 'Campūvihāra'.[69]

(c) We have stated above that Campūkāvyas were written on the Rāma or the Kṛṣna theme. In a few Campūkāvyas, again, some other incarnation of Viṣṇu is the central character whose exploits are narrated in an excellent manner with a purely religious motive by the author.

Thus, the *Nṛsiṁha Campū* of Keśavabhaṭṭa, son of Nārāyaṇa written in six stavakas is based on the story of the manlion incarnation of Lord Viṣṇu.[70] The *Pārijātaharaṇa-campū*[71] if Śeṣakṛṣṇa, who flourished in the second half of the sixteenth century is concerned with the well known Pūrāṇa legend of Kṛṣṇa carrying away the Pārijāta tree by force from the abode of Indra.[72] The principal sentiment of this Campū is 'Śṛṅgāra' (Erotic sentiment). The book is written in the Gauḍī style.

(d) Apart from Vaiṣṇava Campūkāvyas some other Campūs were also written in India in which Śiva, another Hindu god dominates the theme.

The *Nīlakaṇṭhavijayacampū* is such a campū written by Nīlakaṇṭha Dīkṣita in 1637 A. D. It describes the exploits of Śiva in five āśvāsas.[73] The *Tripuravijayacampū* of Atirātrāyājina, the *Śivacaritacampū* and the *Gaṅgāvataraṇa-campū* are all Śaiva Campūkāvyas. The themes of these Campūkāvyas are based on the story of Śiva narrated in the *Śivapurāṇa* and the *Nāradapurāṇa*.[74]

(e) The Yaśastilakacampū[75] containing eight āśvāsas is a work of Somadeva, a pupil of Nemideva who deals at length some important tenets of the Jaina religion apart from other religious matters. The book is an encyclopedia of Indian religions and philosophy. The story of the *Yaśastilakacampū* is, on the whole, interesting. The object of the author appears to be the propagation of the basic views of Jainism in a kāvya form. Māridatta, the king who is the hero of this campū and who wanted to sacrifice a pair of living beings to the family Goddess Candamāridevatā, is taught the futulity of sacrificing them by a sage Sudatta. The king is ultimately converted to the Jaina faith.[76]

There is another Jaina Campū known as *Jīvandhara Campū* of an uncertain date. It was composed by a Digambara monk Jaina Haricandra. The theme of the Campū is based upon the *Uttarapurāṇa* of Guṇabhadra.[77]

(f) We have discussed above the basic features of some religious Campūkāvyas. Apart from them, many authors have written campūs on secular themes also. The *Nalacampū*[78] of Trivikramabhaṭṭa is such a secular Campū work. The *Nalacampū* written in seven Ucchvāsas, describes the fascinating story of Nala, king of Niṣadha and his love for Damayantī, the princess of Vidarbha. Another very famous secular Campū is the *Varadāmbikāpariṇaya Campū*[79] of queen Tirumālambā.

Besides the two broad divisions of Campūkāvya discussed by us viz. religious and secular Campū, there are also some other important characteristics of many other Campū works which may be duly considered in classifying these Campū works. Let us clarify the point below :

(g) Some Campūkāvyas are purely biographical works Thus, the *Rāmānujacampū*[80] is a biography of Rāmānuja or Rāmānujācārya, a noted Vedāntist philosopher. It consists of ten stavakas, and is written in the Gauḍī style. The *Colacampū*[81] is, again, a monographical Campū written on the life of Virupākṣa. Here the poet gives the detailed description of the Cola dynasty. In this Campū we find also a depcription of Kulutuṅga and his faith in Lord Śiva.

(h) There are some journey types of Campū works also. A typical example of this Campū is the *Yātrāprabandha-campū* of Samarapuṁgava Dīkṣita which is divided into nine āśvāsas, with plenty of interspersed verses. It describes many pilgrimages of Northern and Southern India.[82] Many geographical materials of great importance are available in it. The *Citracampū*[83] of Bāṇeśvara Vidyālaṁkāra was composed in seventh century A. D. It deals with the spiritual journey of the human soul as discussed in Bengal Vaiṣṇavism. Bāṇeśvara describes a pilgrimage which he undertook with Mahārāja Citrasena, king of Vardhamāna.[84]

(i) There are some philosophical Campūs which are based on philosophical themes. The *Tattvaguṇādarśacampū*[85] and the *Vidvanmodataraṅgiṇī*[86] are two examples of this particular class of Campū. The *Tattvaguṇādarśacampū* of Annayācārya describes the comparative merits of Śaivism and Vaiṣṇavism in the form of a conversation between Jaya and Vijaya, a Śaivite and a Vaiṣṇavite saint respectively.[87]

The *Vidvanmodataraṅginīcampū*[88] of Ciranjīva Bhaṭṭācārya written in eight taraṇgas is another philosophical Campū. In this Campū the poet describes various philosophical systems viz. Vaiṣṇava, Śaiva, Śākta, Advaita, Vaiśeṣika, Nyāya, Mīmāṁsā, Sāṁkhya, and Yoga.

(j) The *Viśvaguṇādarśacampū* of Veṇkaṭādhvarin is a dramatical Campū in which two gandharvas Kṛśānu and Viśvavasu give a detailed geographical account of India.[89]

(k) There are some historical Campūs, among which the *Varadambikāpariṇaya* of woman poet Tirumālambā is one, Tirumālambā gives a highly romantic version in the usual style of a historical piece of writtng. The *Varadāmbikā-pariṇayacampū* was written on the illustrious career of King Acyutrāya of Vijaynagar.[90]

(1) Local legend and festivals or praises of deities and

personages were also the inspiring force in the composition of many Campūkāvyas. the *Mārgasahāyacampū* of Navanīta, in which the author praises God Mārgasahāya in six āśvāsas is an example of this type.[91] The *Vyāghrālyeśāṣṭamīmahotsavacampū* of Nārāyaṇabhaṭṭa describes the festivals which are celebrated in the month of Kārtika, These festivals are continued for ten days. The work describes the ten types of festivals performed by the local people.[92]

(m) Apart from the above types of Campū poetry there is a few other Campūs in which the authors present a theme out of his own imagination. The *Udayasundarīkathācampū* of Soḍhala describes in six Ucchvāsas the marriage between Udayasundarī, a Nāga princess and Malayavāhana, king of Pratiṣṭhāna. The model of the writer was the *Harṣacarita* of Bāṇabhaṭṭa. The poet creates beautiful images in the work.[93]

4. The Capurāmāyaṇa and its place among the Campūkāvyas

Now, coming to the *Campūrāmāyaṇa* of Bhoja we find that the present text is a religious work based on the theme the *Rāmāyaṇa* of Vālmīki presented by Bhoja with a religious colour and fervour. Rāma is treated here as an incarnation of Lord Viṣṇu. There is a reference to it in the Bālakāṇḍa of the *Campūrāmāyaṇa* of Bhoja.[94] Thus, the *Campūrāmāyaṇa* is a Vaiṣṇavacampū because Rāma was an incarnation of Lord Viṣṇu. We have already said that the *Campūrāmāyaṇa* has been divided into six Kāṇḍas or Cantos. Bhoja has admitted with reverence his indebtedness to Vālmīki in the following Verse :

'Vālimīkigītaraghupuṁgavakīrtileśai
sṭriptiṁ karomi kathamapyadhunā budhānām/
Gaṅgājalairbhuvi Bhagīrathayatnalabdhaiḥ
kiṁ tarpaṇaṁ na vidadhāti naraḥ pitṛṇām//[95]

The poet has tried to delight the heart of the appreciative learned people by presenting before them the life of Rāma as described by the great sage Vālmīki in a new form. In this Campū the descriptions are highly attractive and are marked by alliterations and excellent similies. In this context we can refer to the following passages of the work :

(a) '*ayaṁ kālaḥ kālapramathanagalābhairabhinavai*
rahaṁyūnāṁ yūnāmapaharati dhairyaṃ
jaladharaiḥ/
smarādhārā dhārāparicitajaḍā vānti sahasā
navasvantaḥ svantaḥ kathamiva viyogaḥ
pariṇmet//[96]

(b) *rāmākarṣaṇabhagnakārmukabhuvā dhvānena*
rodorudhā
dṛptakṣatrayaśaḥ sitacchakule jīmūtanādāyitam/
vīraśrīpratham apraveśasamaye puṇyāhaghoṣāyitaṁ
sītayāḥ kila mānase pariṇaye
māṅgalyaturyāyitam/[97]

It is written in Vaidarbhī style and the principal sentiment of it is Vīra or heroism. Bhoja's *Campūrāmāyaṇa* possesses a special charm. He compares his composition to a melodious song associated with musical concert.[98] This comparison proves true when we closely read the poetical and prose portions of the Campū.[99] The author of the *Campūrāmāyaṇa* displays equal ability in depicting other Rasas also. In the Kīṣkindhākāṇḍa the lamentation of Tārā is a beautiful example of Karuṇarasa. Let us cite one verse from this Kāṇḍa in order to substanciate our view :

'*nāhaṁ suketutanayā na ca saptasālī*
Vālī na ca tribhuvanaprathitaprabhāvaḥ/
tārāsmi vajrahṛdayā viśikhairbhedyā
dhvanī kathaṁ bhavasi rāghava : māmaviddhvā//[100]

In fine, Bhoja proves himself a master in the art of creating a nice and melodious Campū.

References

1. KD. 1/31.
2. KŚ. 8/9 – Hemcandra
   KŚ lstch. – Vāgbhaṭṭa
3. 'iti' Śrītrevikramabhaṭṭaviracitāyāṁ damayantīkathāyāṁ haracaraṇa –sarojāṇkāyāṁ prathamaḥ ucchvāsaḥ samāptaḥ'. NC. p. 82
4. 'capernuṃca iti Bhojaḥ 'cap' 'sāntvane' madhuraṁ vadati campūḥ prabandhabhadaḥ.' Uṇādisūtra 1.90, p. 19

5. *'Gadyānubandharasamiśritapadyasūkti*
hṛdyā hi vādyakalayā kaliteva gītiḥ/
tasmāddadhātu kavimārgajuṣāṁ sukhāya
campūprabandharacanāṁ madiyā//
CR. Bālakāṇḍa, Verse 3.
6. SD. VI, p. 336
7. *'Padyaṁ yadyapi vidyate bahusatāṁ hṛdyaṁ vigadyaṁ na tat gadyaṃ ca pratipadyate na vijahatpadyaṁ budhāsvadyatām/*
ādatte hi tayoḥ prayoga ubhayorāmodabhūmodayam saṃgaḥ kasya hi na svadet manase mādhvīkamṛdvikayoḥ//
VG. Campū 12/4
8. NR. Campū. Into. p. 2.
9. SN. Campū, pp. 115–116
10. CKA, p. 49
11. TS. 1.2, p. 34
12. AB. 33.4, p. 847
13. Ibid, 39.8, pp. 949–950
14. KP. 1/1.2.3.4
15. MUP. 1/1.2.3.4.5
16. CKA. p. 62, 72.
17. Mbh. Ādiparva, Ch. 1, Verse 1.
18. Ibid, Verses 2–4.
19. Ibid, Vanaparva, Ch. 1, Verses 1–4
20. VP, 2, Ch. 19, 1–4, 12.
21. Twenty-five Sanskrit Inscription, pp. 10-13.
22. JM. p. 10 (Śivi Jātakam).
23. Pañca, p. 3.
24. KD. 1/31.
25. Kāśī sans. granthamālā, No. 98, Chaukhambā Sanskrit Sansthān, Vārāṇasī
26. *'Gadyapadyamayī sāṁkā socchvāsā campūḥ'*
K. Ś. Hemcandra
K. Ś. Vāgbhaṭa.
27. *'iti ŚrīBāṇabhaṭṭakṛtau Harṣacariteaṣṭamaḥ ucchvāsaḥ'*
HC. 258
'iti ŚrīTrivikramabhaṭṭaviracitāyāṃ Damayantīkathāyāṃ haracaraṇasarojāṇkāyāṁ saptama ucchvāsaḥ'
NC, p. 456
28. ed. by Dr. Sūryakānta, Kṛṣṇa Brothers, Jalandhar.
29. *'iti Śrīmatsamastaśāstrapāraṇgadīkṣitatuṇḍirājatmaja-sahityapārāvarapāriṇakavitākāntārakaṇthīravasarvasva dānadīkṣāvicakṣaṇaśrīmaddīkṣitabālakṛṣṇa sūnu*

saṅkaraviracite Gaṅgāvataranacampuprabandhe gaṅgācaraṇamge saptama ucchvāsaḥ.'
India Office Cata. 7, 4041/114

30. *'iti kāvyaprakāśedoṣapradarśano nāma saptama ullāsaḥ'*
KPŚ, p. 322

31. *'iti ahobalasūrinā viracite yatirājacaritre Campū prabandhe ṣoraśollāsaḥ/'*
Des. Cata. Madras, 12338

32. *'kākutsthavijayasaṁjñaṃ kāvyaṃballisahāyakaracitam/ paryāptamatulabhāgyāt ullāsenāṣtamena sa sahaiva//*
India Office Cata. 4038/2624

33. Des. Cata. Madras, 12306

34. Sarasvatībhavan texts, No. 36, Vāṇāras, 1931 ed. Gopināth Kavirāj.

35. *'iti Śrīvidarbharājaviracite campūrāmāyaṇa sundarakāṇḍaḥ samāptaḥ'*. CR. p. 437

36. *'Mahākavi Somadevasūri Viracita Kathāsaritsāgara Kathāmukha lambake Pañcama taraṅgaḥ'*.
KTS, p. 224

37. Śrī Veṇkaṭeśvar Press, Bombay, 1985.

38. *'itiviracitamappādīkṣitneśvarasya*
kṣitidharapatikanyāmanyavāmāṁgakasya/
guṇagaṇamaṇimālalaṁkṛtaṁ gadyapadyai
dharata hṛdi budhendrāḥ sādhu
Campūprabandham//
Tanj. Cata. 4158

39. *'ācarya Daṇḍiviracite Daśakumāracarite purvapīthikāyāṁ trtiyocchvāse Somadattacaritam*
Des. Cata., Madras. p. 22.

40. *'...iti Śrī Somadevasūriṇā viracite yaśodharamahārājarcite yaśastilakaparanāmmi mahākāvya kathāvatrāronāma prathamaḥ āśvāsaḥ/'*
YC, p. 149

41. Bālamonaramā Press, Mailapur, Madras, 1941

42. *'iti Śrī Samarapuṁgavakṛtau campūkāvye aṣṭama āsvāsaḥ'*
India Office Cata. 7. 4936/290

43. *'iti'... śrīmadatirātrayājinaḥ kṛtiṣu*
Tripuravijayanāmni Campūkāvye Tripuradānava-
mohanam nām dvitīya āśvāsaḥ'/
Tanj. Cata. No. 4037.

44. *'abhinavapadapurvaḥ kālidāsaḥ pragalbhastrinayanadayi-*
tāyaḥ premaḍimbhastṛtiyaḥ/
viracitayati tayaiva prepritaḥ premapūrvaṁ
hariguṇapari naddhaṁcārucampūprabandham'//
BC. 1.14

45. Vidyābhavan Skt. Granthamālā. 31, Chawkhambhā Vidyābhavan, Vārānasī, 1957.
46. India off. Cata. 4037/462
47. *'ityabhinavabhojarājasahamahīmahendrasundaramukha candrasamdarśanamahimāsandrīkṛtavāgvilāsasya rāmabhadrādhvarivarapriyaśiṣyasya tadiyavaṃśajanmano bhūminādavidvatkaveḥ kṛtau dharmavijaye caturthastavakaḥ/* Tanj. Cata. 4231
48. Ibid, 4106
49. Des. Cata. Madras 12381.
50. *'manorathāya naśaṁse kiṃbāho : spandase mudhā/ purvāvadhīritaṁ śreyo duḥkhaṁ hi parivartate//*

    Abh. 7/13
51. Gopāl Nārāyaṇ Company, Bombay.
52. *'iti Śrīkāñcīnagaranāy akatātacāryabhāgineyasarvapṛṣthāptoryāmadiśrīnivāsāryatanūbhavasya śleṣayamakacakravartīno raghūnātharyayajvanastanayena Śrinivāsakṛpātiśaysuvidita nayena sītāmbāgarbhasaṃbhavena Śrīmadātreyaveṇkaṭārya yajvāna viracitavaradābhyudaye pañcamo vilāsaḥ/'*

    Sans. Series, Mysore, 1908
53. Gopāl Nārāyaṇ Company, Bombay.
54. Des. Cata. Madras
55. Ibid, 12244
56. Sarasvativilās Sirij, Tanjor. ed. Kuppusvāmī, T. S. 1905
57. *'Mahākavi Somadevasūri Viracita Kathāsaritsāgare Kathāmukha lambake Pañcana taraṇgaḥ'*

    KTS. p. 224
58. *'bādhulagotramahaniyaguhāntarodyadballisahāya-kavisiṃha mukhoditeasmin/ ācāryadigvijayasaṃjnamahāprabandhe kolāḥaloaya-mudbhūtprathamaḥ prathiyān//*

    Des. Cata. Madras 12380.
59. *'Śrīmadghatikāśataśatavihitaṣthabhāsasarasa-kavitācamạ nipunasyavāsudevayogīsvarasyāntevāsyanyatamasya guhapuravāśasarmaṇaḥ kṛṣnaśarmanaḥ kaveḥ kṛtau mandāra marande campūprabandhe śeṣabindurekādaśaḥ samāptimagamat/*

    MM. Campū, p. 166

    Nirṇay Sagar Press, Bombay, 1914
60. Nirṇay Sagar Press, Bombay, Yogi B. g, Bakre, M. G. 1923

61. Des. Ċata. Madras, 12295
62. 'ityālaṁkārikacakravartīsāndhivigrahikamahāpātraśrī-Viśvanātha - kavirājakṛte Sāhityadarpaṇe daśamaḥ paricchedaḥ/' SD. p. 64
63. Mitra Cata. No. 1.73.
64. *Cūṃāntarastabakasaptavibhajyamānaṁ*
ṣaṭtriṁśaduttaracatuśśatapadyapūrṅam/
campūṁ paraṃ sakaladeśanivāsidhīrāḥ
paśyantu yāntu ca mudaṁ vidhutābyasūyāḥ//
....
samiravegaṁ kuśakotibudhiṁ sītāsutaṁ
rākṣavaṁśakālam/
nayākaraṁ nanditarāmachadraṁ nityaṁ
hanūmantamahaṁ namāmi//
HV Campū 1-4.1
65. Mitra Cata. No. 72
66. India Off. Cata. 4037/482
67. '*thai thai thai tigaḍatigathai theti paṭhānukṛtyā*
vinyasyantyo bhuvi padataiaṁ dorlatāmantarikṣe/
vamāvarte sakṛdatha sakṛddakṣinavarta ava
nnṛtyantyastaḥ sarasamadhuraṁ maṇḍalastathā virejuḥ//
pādāṇgulyā kṣititalamaladhusphāravakṣojajanuḥ
pārṣṇidvandopaviṣṭā hasitavatī namam ivivistīṃa vakṣāḥ/
aṇguṣṭhau vadhamuṣṭayoḥ kucabhuvi karayornyasya
tālānukṛtyā
laṇkārān kūjayantī gadati tatha tathai thai tathai
theiti theiti//
AVC. p. 200
68. *ambhojanma vamatyanalpakarakāhṛṁgāvalīmekataḥ*
paṁceṣoḥ śaramanyatoardhaśśinaṁ sūte navaṁ
pallavam//
citaṁ cumbati cakravākamithunaṁ proddāmatāraganaṁ
jyotsna kāpi vidhau gata vitanutāṁ gaṇgātaraṃgān
vidheḥ//
GC. p, 2.
69. *madayati mano madiyaṁ tanujaghanabhāratīrasavilāsaḥ/*
kimu sutanu nīravihāro nahi nahi Campūvihāroayaṁ//
Ibid, p. 215
70. *kanakarucidukūlaḥ kuṇḍallollāsigaṇḍaḥ*
śamitabhuvanabhāraḥ koapi līlāvatāraḥ/
tribhuvanasukhakārī śailadhāri mukundaḥ
parikalitarathāṅgo maṁgalaṁ nastanotu//
NṚ Campū. 1/1
71. Kāvyamālā, No. 14
Nirṇay Sāgar Press, Bombay, 1926

72. *Jānāmi te ṣati śakraṁ jānāmi tridaśeśvaram/*
pārijātaṁ tathāapianaṁ mānuṣī hārayāmi te//
tatassamastadevānaṁ sainyaiḥ parivṛtoharim/
prayayau pārijātārthamindro yoddhṛṁ dvijottamam//
VP. 5. 51, 53

73. *nirmmathyamānadudadherabhudvisaṁ maholavanaṁ hālahalāhvamagrataḥ/*
saṁbhṛāntamīnonmakārikacchapāt timidvipagrahatimingi tākulāt//
tataḥ karatalīkṛtya vYāpi halāhalaṁ viṣam/
abhakṣayanmahādevaḥ kṛpayā bhūtabhāvanaḥ//
tasyāpi darśayāmāsa svaviryaṁ jalakalmaṣaḥ/
yaccakāra gale nīlaṁ tacca sādhorvibhuṣaṇam//
Bhā. 8, 6-7

74. *'Bhagīrathasya tapasāt tuṣṭo brahmādadau mune/*
Gaṇgābhāgirathāya yātha cintayāmāsa dhārane//
tataśca śivamārādhya taddvārā svarnanadibhūvam/
ānīyoḥ tajjalai spṛṣṭvā putānninye divaṁ pitṛṇ//
NP. 1, p. 164

75. Kāvyamālā 70, Nirṇay Sāgar Press, Bombay, 1916.
76. *'acalāpatirapi sa māridattaḥ pratihāraniveditāgamana vṛttasya munikumārakayugalasya vilokonā............... .... viśvadyutidarśanānānnabha eva mumoca .... jinaitihyāvagmānmahābhāga iva karuṇarasamavāpa karaṇeṣu praṇidhānaviseṣānmumukṣuriva tamastira ścakārantarātmadiśi/'*
YC, pp. 154–155

77. *'yākathā bhūtadhātrīśaṁ śreṇikaṁ prati vaṃitā/*
sudharmagaṇanāthena tāṁ vaktuṁ prayatāmahe//
madīyavānīramani racitārthā cirādhūt/
vavre jīvandharaṁ devaṁ yā bhāvaunijanāyakam//
Jīvan. Campū, 1–10, 11

78. Kāśī Sans. Granthamālā 98, Chowkhambhā sanskrit Saṁsthān, Vārāṇasi, 1976.
79. Des. Cata. Tanjor
80. Madras Govt. Ori. Manus, Series No. 6, Madras 1942.
81. *'tato yasya śivo guruśca nitarāṁ dāsaḥ śivasyaivayo/*
mātāyasya tu gomatī sa hi virupākṣābhighoyaṁ kaviḥ/
Śrīmatkauśikagotrajaḥ śivavilākhyaṁ śiva prītaye
campūkāvyamidaṁ karoti diśatātsphūrtiṁ paraṁ sāradā//
Tanjor. Sarasvatī mahal series No. 55

82. YP. Campū 5th, 8th āśvāsa
kāvyāmala, 90, Nirṇy Sāgar Press, Bombay. 1936
83. India Office Cata. 4044/939

84. *'dhyātvā Śrī Rāmacandraṁ saha janakasūtā lakṣaṇābhyāṁ prayatnā dājñāmājnaya rājnamapi mukuṭamanerścitrasenāhva-yasya/ sāke kālāṁgatakauṣadhipatiganite kartikeye daśaṁśe purṇā śricitracampū vyatanutadivase śrilavāne śvarākhyaḥ//*

C. Campū 293

85. Des. Cata. Madras, 12295

86. Śrīvenkaṭeśvara Press, Bombay. 1928

87. *'tatvārthanirdhāraṇabuduabudhī matvā svamtyā nikhilaṁ ca śāstram/ modānmithaścakraturapramādaṁ vādaṁ mudā sambhavavaiṣnavau dvau// śāmbhavastamasābudheḥ stambhanādatathātvadṛk/ vaiṣṇavasatvabhavad bhūsṇuhuḥ satvatastatva vittamaḥ//*

'tataḥ kadācana mudā samupajāte prabhāte viracitasnānaḥ kṛtasandhyāy andanādy anuṣṭhānaḥ puraskṛ taśı utismṛtipurāṇetihasadipramāṇānusandhānaḥ paramapuruṣaṁ bhagavantamaravindanayanmavandat svasamayaniyataniyamaniṣnātaḥ śrivaiṣṇavaḥ/

Tatta. Campū, 5, 6

88. *'Śive tu bhaktiḥ pracurā yadi syād bhajecchivatvena harim tathāpi// harau to bhaktiḥ pracurāyadi syād bhajedharitvena śivaṁ tathāapi//*

Vid. Campū. 8/133

89. viśvavasu – *'idaṁbadarikāśramasthalamihaiṣa nārāyaṇa stapasyati namasyatāṁ thiratam tamaḥ śoṣayan/ vikasidhiṣanonmiṣadvisayavarjanāḥ sajjanā janārdanamahardivaṁ bhujagamancamarcantyamī//*

Viś. Campū. 33

90. *'ityekavārākarṇanamātradṛdhāvadhāritanvyakāvyanāṭa-kālaṁkāra purāṇagamarahasyasārasyānubandhasamin-dhānasvābhā-vikapratibhānubhāvayā.... vividhavidyā-pragalbha rājādhirājacyutarāyasārva-bhauma-premasarvasva......viśvāsabhuvā...... tirumālambayā nirmitaṁ Baradāmbikāpariṇayannāma Campūkāvyam ācandratārakaṁ abhivardhatām/'*

Bara. Campū. p. 158

91. *'avaṁ prabhāvaparipāṭikayā prapaṁce prāṁcanviraṁ-cipuramārgasahāyadevaḥ/*

atyadbhutāni caritānyavanau vitaman nityaṁ
taraṅgayati maṅgalamaṁgabhājām//
Mārga. Campū. p. 233.

92. *'prātaḥ prabhūtapaṭamūlamahotsavāni*
madhyāhnabadhadharaṇīvibudhāśanāni/
rātrāvapi prathitadīpamahotsavāni
yātānyaho daśadināni manoharāni//
vyā. Campū. p. 181

93. *'kamalinī bhuvanāntarite ravo vyapagatālikalapasiroruhā/*
paridadhe vidhaveva sudhākaradyutivitānamiṣeṇa
sitāṁaśkam//
cāndraṁ mahahomaṇḍalabhājansthaṁ dugdhaṁ yathā
yāmavatīmahīsyāḥ/
viyoginām dṛgdahanogatāpairullāsitam
vyomatale luloṭha//
Sanskrit Sāhitya Ki Ruprekhā, p. 406

94. *'Nārāyaṇāya nalināyatalocanāya*
nāmāvaśeṣita mahābalivaibhavāya/
nanācarācara vidhāyakajanmadeśa
nābhīpuṭāya puruṣāya namaḥ parasmaiḥ//
CR. Bālakāṇḍa, Verse 16

95. Ibid., Verse 4.
96. Ibid., Kiṣkindhākāṇḍa, Verse 26
97. Ibid., Bālakāṇḍa, Verse 104.
98. *'gadyānubandharasamiśrita padyasūkti*
hṛdyā hi vādya kalayā kaliteva gītiḥ/
tasmāddahātu kavimārgajuṣāṁ sukhāya
campūprabandharacanāṁ rasanā madīyā//
Ibid, Verse 3.

99. *'tatra kaṁcana krauñcamithunādekaṁ pañcaśaravidhamapi vyādhenānuvidhaṁ nidyāyato badhānukampasya bhagavato vālmīkervadanāravindācchandomayī kācidevaṁ nīḥsasāra śarasvatī/'*
Ibid., p. 6

100. Ibid kiṣkindhākāṇḍa, Verse 18

Chapter III

THE RĀMĀYAṆA OF VĀLMĪKI AND THE CAMPŪRĀMĀYAṆA : A CRITICAL AND COMPARATIVE STUDY

It has been already stated that the *Campūrāmāyaṇa* of Bhoja is based on the *Rāmāyaṇa* story given by Vālmīki in his immortal Epic *Rāmāyaṇa*. The Epic is divided into following Kāṇḍas viz. (1) Bālakāṇḍa, (2) Ayodhyākaṇḍa, (3) Araṇyakāṇḍa, (4) Kiṣkindhākāṇḍa, (5) Sundarakāṇḍa, and (6) Yuddhakāṇḍa. Bhoja and Lakṣmaṇasūri also faithfully follow the author of the Epic in this regard. But there is a significant distinction between the *Campūrāmāyaṇa* and the Epic of Vālmīki, while the Epic extends upto the Uttarakāṇḍa where the tragic deparature of Sītā from the World is described, the *Campūrāmāyaṇa* of Bhoja ends with the Yuddhakāṇḍa where the victory of the hero Rāmacandra in a fierce battle in Laṇkā and his glorious return to his motherland Ayodhyā are nicely described. Infact, the *Campūrāmāyaṇa* is a more compact and cohesive Kāvya than the *Rāmāyaṇa* of Vālmīki where the presence of the Uttarakāṇḍa affects to a certain extent the compact character of the Epic.

This is all about broad structure of the *Campūrāmāyaṇa* and its difference from the Epic of Vālmīki. There are many other similarities and differences between the two literary composition.

(1) The *Campūrāmāyaṇa* is started with a benedictory verse dedicated to Lord 'Hairamba' or Gaṇeśa who is imagined to be the dispeller of all impediments.[1] Sanskrit poets, particularly the authors of the Mahākāvyas always

cling to the idea that a poetical composition should begin with an auspicious word or words which are conductive to the spreading of the popularity and fame of the composition.[2] Vālmīki, flourished several centuries before the writers of the Mahākāvyas and ornate poems where this particular norm was introduced. He introduces the Epic with the verse :

> *'tapaḥ svādhyayaniratarṁ tapasvi vāgvidāmvaram/*
> *Nāradarṁ paripapraccha vālmikirmunipuṃgavam//*[3]

or not with any devotional poem or eulogy.

(2) The metre of the *Rāmāyaṇa* is 'Anuṣṭup'.[4] Unlike the authors of the Mahākāvyas and other poems Vālmīki does not try to use wide varieties of metres found in Sanskrit prosody in his Epic. In the *Campūrāmāyaṇa* on the other hand, we notice the presence of other metres. The benedictory verse in the *Campūrāmāyaṇa* is composed in 'Vasantatilaka' metre. The 'vasantatilaka' metre consists of six gaṇas, and it contains fourteen syllables.[5] Bhoja lays great emphasis on composing poems in his *Campūrāmāyaṇa*. Thus in the Bālakāṇḍa of the *Campūrāmāyaṇa* we find one hundred and seventeen poems altogather. In the Ayodhyākāṇḍa there are eighty-six poems. The number of poems is much less in the Araṇyakāṇḍa, the kiṣkindhākāṇḍa and the Sundarakāṇḍa. The Araṇyakāṇḍa, contains fourty-three poems, the Kiṣkindhākāṇḍa fourty-eight and the Sundarakāṇḍa seventy-seven. Lakṣmaṇasūri also lays utmost stress on presenting poems. His Yuddhakāṇḍa is the only Canto of the *Campūrāmāyaṇa* . It contains one hundred and ten poems. This is clear from the treatment of the Rāma-theme by the two authors that both of them are aware of the basic character of the *Rāmāyaṇa* of Vālmīki which is entirely written in verses, inspite of the fact that in a Campūkāvya prose must co-exist with poems.

(3) The Story of the Rāmāyaṇa of Vālmiki and the Campūrāmāyaṇa

There is a great deal of difference in the presentation of the story in the *Rāmāyaṇa* of Vālmīki and the *Campūrāmāyaṇa*. The Rāma-story begins in the Epic of

Vālmīki with an introductory dialogue between the divine sage Nārada and the sage-poet Vālmīki, there Nārada tells poet Vālmīki about the birth of an extraordinary persons in this world as the son of king Daśaratha of Ayodhyā after sometime, his exploits, and the role to be played by him as the protector and benefactor of the people.[6] In fact the central theme of the *Rāmāyaṇa* is narrated in advance by sage Nārada as the Bālakāṇḍa of the Epic.

King Bhoja, on the other hand, does not discuss the details of the Conversation between Nārada and Vālmīki. He abruptly referes to the conversation in a single verse viz.,

> '*vacaṁ niśamya bhagavān sa tu nāradasya*
> *prācetacaḥ pravacasāṁ prathamaḥ kavināṁ/*
> *mādhyandināya niyamāya maharṣisevyāṁ*
> puṇyāmavāpa tamasāṁ tamasāṁ nihantrim//[7]

Readers cannot understand easily about the contents of the very significant conversation between the two sages without studying the Bālakāṇḍa of the *Rāmāyaṇa*. Bhoja is aware of the fact that he is writing a Campū of a resonable dimention not touching the magnitude of the Epic of the sage-poet. He presents the contents of the first two sargas of the Bālakāṇḍa of the Epic within the brief span of two poems[8] and a short prose passages. the 'Krauñca' story of the Rāmāyaṇa is very pathetic. Vālmīki describes it in an attractive manner, but Bhojarāja briefly refers to this story.[9]

(4) There is a noticeable distinction between the method followed by Bhojarāja in introducing the *Rāmāyaṇa* story from that of the Epic poet. While Vālmīki unfolds the story describing the birth of Rāmā and his brothers with proper sequence,[10] Bhoja starts the story practically from the end by introducing Lava-Kuśa, the two child-singers through whom the Rāma story is unfolded.[11] Bhoja narrates the story of Ahalyā[12], as we find in the *Rāmāyaṇa*[13] very briefly.

(5) The legend of the river Gaṇgā descending to the earth thanks to the rigorous penance performed by Bhagīratha, is described in the *Rāmāyaṇa*.[14] Bhoja devotes a number of poems in describing this legend.[15]

(6) Rāma's battle with Tāḍakā also finds a due place in the *Campūrāmāyaṇa*[16], but in the Epic of Vālmīki Rāma's battle with Tāḍakā is described with utmost simplicity.[17]

(7) The story of the sage Viśvāmitra[18] is presented by Bhoja in all details in the Bālākāṇḍa. The legend is simultaneously found in the Bālakāṇḍa of the *Rāmāyaṇa*[19] in a more elaborate form.

(8) The legends of Triśaṇku[20] and Śunaḥśepaḥ[21] are presented in both the works.

(9) The Ayodhyākāṇḍa of the *Rāmāyaṇa* and the Ayodhyākaṇḍa of Bhoja's *Campūrāmāyaṇa* is significantly started with the word 'gacchatā'. While Vālmīki read the verse :

gacchatā mātulakulaṁ Bharatena tadānadhaḥ/
Śatrughno nityaśatrughnonītaḥ prītipuraskṛtaḥ//[22]

Bhoja presents the first verse of the Ayodhyākāṇḍa as

gacchatā daśarathena nivṛtiṁ bhūbhujāmsulabhāṁ bhujābatāt/
mātulasya nagare yudhājitaḥ sthāpitaubharata-lakṣmaṇānujau//[23]

He uses the 'Rathodhatā'[24] metre in this verse.

(10) In the Ayodhyākāṇḍa of the *Rāmāyaṇa* Daśaratha's love for his son Rāmacandra and his desire to install him on the throne is described by the poet in a large number of verses. The emotional condition of the king is nicely described by the author of the Epic in the following verses :

ataistu bahubhiryuktaṁ guṇairanupamaiḥ sutam/
dṛṣṭvā daśaratho rājā cakre cintāṁ paraṁtapaḥ//
atha rājñao bahūvaivaiva vṛdhasya cirajīvinaḥ/
prītireṣā kathaṁ rāmo rājā syānmayi jīvati//
aṣā hyasya parā prītirhṛdi saṁparivartate/
kadānāmasutaṁ drakṣyāmyabhiṣiktamahaṁ priyam//
vṛdhikāmo hi lokasya sarvabhūtānukampakaḥ/
mattaḥ priyataro loke parjanya eva vṛṣṭimān//[25]

In the *Campūrāmāyaṇa*, on the other hand. Daśaratha

expresses his desire to hand over the rein of the kingdom to Rāmacandra in a single verse without any emotion viz.

> *'atha Daśarathaḥ putraṁ Rāmṁ svatastrijagatpatiṁ*
> *svaviṣayamahīmātre kartuṁ patiṁ vidadhematim/*
> *bhuvanamaraṇe kalyaṁ kalyāṇabhūdharamādarā*
> *tsvagṛhapaṭalīdhuryastambhaṁ vidhātumanā iva'//*[26]

The people of Ayodhyā were overwhelmed with emotion, as if their love for the prince was greater than for the king.[27] The ministers of Daśaratha told the king :

> *deve sthiteapi tanayaṁ tava Ramābhadraṁ*
> *lokaḥ svayaṁ bhajatu nāma kimatra citraṁ/*
> *candraṁ vinā yadupalambhanahetubhūtaṁ*
> *kṣīrodamāśrayati kiṁ tṛṣitaścakoraḥ//*[28]

(11) Sage Vālmīki describes in the third Canto, of the Ayodhyākāṇḍa the mirthful preparation for Rāma's installation ceremony.[29] But Bhoja intelligently avoids this description in order to keep his Caṃpū kāvya confined within a reasonable size, and describes the joyful situation of the ceremony in a single verse.[30]

(12) The story of wicked Mantharā who gives wicked advices to Kaikeyī to beg of her husband two boons is described in detail in the Epic.[31] But Bhoja abridges the episode in a single prose passage and a single poem.[32]

(13) Bhoja is adopt in delineating Karuṇarasa. When Kaikeyī begs of her husband two boons by which Rāma was to be banished from the kingdom and Bharata to be enthroned, Daśaratha uttered the verse :

> *'vatsaṁkathorahṛdaye nayanābhirāmṁ*
> *rāmṁ vinā na khalu tiṣṭhati jīvitaṁ me/*
> *dhāturbaladupayamasatvayi jātapūruaḥ*
> *kaikeyī māmupaymaṁ nayatīiti manye//*[33]

Which produces a heartrending effect in the readers.

(14) The description of Rāma's movement to the Jungle[34] and Bharat's persuation of Rāma to return Ayodhyā are described as briefly as possible by Bhoja.[35]

(15) The author of the *Rāmāyaṇa* uses the words 'Nārājake janapade' several times while describing the death of Daśaratha.[36] But Bhoja's description is free from such mechanical uses. He describes the situation in a single prose passage and one poem only.[37]

(16) The Araṇyakāṇḍa of the *Rāmāyaṇa* of Vīlmīki is the turning point of the Rāma story. In this kāṇḍa of the Epic Rāvaṇa eludes Rāmā with the help of a golden deer.[38] Rāvaṇa is mesmerised by the exquisite beauty of Sītā.[39] Vālmīki gives a description of Sītā's heroic remarks defying Rāvaṇa.[40] Such decriptions do not find a place in the *Campūrāmāyaṇa* due to the paucity of space. Bhoja, however, desrcibes the pathetic condition of Rāma and Lakṣmaṇa in a adequate manner.[41]

(17) In the Kiṣkindhākāṇḍa of the *Rāmāyaṇa*, the colourful description of the lake Pampā enhances the beauty of the Epic is given by the poet Vālmīki.[42] There is a reference to the thick bed of the blue lotuses of the Pampā lake in the *Uttararāmacarita* of Bhavabhūti.[43] Bhoja also depicts the Pampā lake with an efficient hand.[44]

(18) The story of the quarrel between Vāli and Sugrīva are described in this Kāṇḍa. Vāli's death in the hands of Rāma and Rāma's friendship with Sugrīva are described in both the works.[45] But Bhoja excels in delineating the Karuṇarasa in the kiṣkindhākāṇḍa, where the lamentation of Tārā, wife of Valī is able to move the heart of every reader.[46] The other episodes of the kīṣkindhākāṇḍa like the enthroning of Sugrīva are described by Bhoja in an attractive manner.[47]

(19) In the Sundarakāṇḍa of the *Campūrāmāyaṇa* the poet presents poetical passages profusely. There are large number of prose passages composed by him in this kaṇḍa.[48] There is a much difference between the episods of the Epic and the *Campūrāmāyaṇa*. The heroic exploits of Hanumān are describe in an efficient manner in both the works.[49]

(20) We have already said that Yuddhakāṇḍa of the *Campūrāmāyaṇa* was composed by Lakṣmaṇasūri. His poems are simple and prose passages are casually long and

lucid.[50] It goes without saying that Vālmīki gives an elaborate and vivid picture of the battle between Rāma and Rāvaṇa.[51] Lakṣmaṇasūri also gives an excellent description of the battle.[52] He gives an account of the different types of divine weapons being used by both parties.[53]

References

1. *Lakṣmīṁ tanotu nitarāmitarānapekṣa*
   maṇgridvayaṁ nigamaśākhiśikhā pravālam/
   Hairambammburuhaḍambaracauryanighnaṁ
   vighnādribhedaśatadhāradhurandharaṁ naḥ//
   CR. Bālakāṇḍa, Verse 1.
2. *'adau 'Lakṣmī' śabdaproyogena varṇagaṇādiśudhiḥ/*
   devatāvācakāḥ śabdā ye ca bhadrādivācakāḥ/
   te sarve naiva nindyāḥ syurlipito gaṇato api vā//'
   Ibid, p. 2
3. *Vāl. Rāmā, Canto 1, Verse–1.*
4. *śloke ṣaṣṭhaṁ gururgyaṁ sarvatralaghupañcamam/*
   dvicaturpadayorhrasvaṁ saptamaṁ dīrghamanyaḥ//
   CM. p. 21
5. *'uktvā vasantalilakā tabhajāḥ jagau gaḥ/'* Ibid. p. 72
6. *ko nvasminsāmpratam loke guṇavānakaśca vīryavān/*
   dharmajñayaśca kṛtajñayaśca satyavākyo dṛhavrathḥ//
   cāritreṇa ca ko yuktaḥ sarvabhūteṣu ko hitaḥ
   vidvānkaḥ kaḥ samathaśca kaścikapriyadarśanaḥ//
   ātmavānko jitakrodho dyutimānkoanasūyakaḥ//
   kasya bibyati devāśca jātaroṣasya saṁyuge//
   atadicchāmyahaṁ śrotuṁ paraṁ kautuhalaṁ hi me/
   maharṣe tavaṁ samarthoasi jñāṭuavaṁidhaṁ naram//
   śrutvā caitattrilokajño vālmīkirnāradau vacḥ/
   śrūyatāmiti cāmanya prahṛṣṭo vākyamabravīt//
   Vāl. Rāmā.Bālākāṇḍa, Canto 1, Verses 2-6
7. CR. Bālakāṇḍa, Verse 5
8. *mā nīsāda pratiṣṭhāṁ tvamagamaḥ śvāsvatīḥsamāḥ/*
   yatkrauñcamithunādekamavadhīḥ kāmamohitam//
   Ibid, Verse 6.
9. *tatra kaṁcana krauñca mithunādekaṁ pañcaśara-vidhymapi vyādhenānuvidhaṁ nidhyāyato baddhānukampasya bhagavato vālmīkervadanāravi-ndacchandomayi kācidevaṁ niḥsasāra sarasvatī.'*
   Ibid, p. 6.
10. *Prodyamāne jagannāthaṁ sarvalokanamaskṛtam/*
    kausalyājanayadrāmṁ divyalakṣaṇasaṁyutam//
    viṣṇoradhaṁ mahābhāgaṁ putramamaikṣvākunadanam/

lohitākṣaṁ mahābāhuṁ raktoṣṭhaṁdundubhisvanam//
kausalyā śuśubhe tena putrenāmitatejasā/
yathā vareṇa devānāmditirvajrapāṇinā//
Bharato nāma kaikeyyāṁ jajñe satyaparākramaḥ/
sākṣād viṣṇoścaturbhāgaḥ sarvaiḥ samuditoguṇaiḥ//
athalakṣmaṇaśatrughnau sumitrājanayatsutau/
Vīrau sarvāstrakusalau viṣṇorardhasamarvitau//

Vāl. Rāma. Bālakāṇḍa, Canto. 18, Verses 10–14

'athasmianapatyatayā dūyamānamānase putrārthaṁ kṛatumaśvamedhaṁ vidhātuṁ mantriviḥ sammṁ mantraya māṇe Daśarathe Sumantraḥ prahṛṣṭamanā............../'

CR. Bālakāṇḍa, p. 15

atha Rāmābhidhānena kaveḥ surabhayan giraḥ/
alaṁcakāra kāruṇyādraghūṇāyṇāyaṁ hariḥ/
tamenamanvajāynta trayastretagnitejasaḥ/
agrajasyānukurvantastaistairlokottarirguṇaiḥ//
Bharatasteṣu kaikeyyāstanayo vinayojjvalaḥ/
anyau Lakṣmaṇa Śatrughanu Sumitrāyāṁ kṛtodayau//

Ibid, Verses, 30-32.

11. *upāgatau militaparasparopamau*
bahuśrutau śrutimadhurasvarānvitau/
vicakṣaṇau vividhanarendralakṣaṇau
Kuśīlavau Kuśalavanāmadhāriṇau//

Ibid, Verse, 9.

12. *atrāgamadgautamadharmadārānanārjajuṣṭena pathā mahendraḥ/*
sa ca krudhā nirvṛṣaṇaṁ bṛṣāṇaṁ bhāryāmadṛśyāṁ ca muniścakāra//
vanametatgate rāme śāpānmukutā bhaviṣiyasi/
ityuktvā gautamaḥ patniṁ himadriṁ tapase yayau//
ithaṁ viditavṛttānte devatānāṁ gaṇe tadā/
pitṛṛnāṁ prābhavāllebhe meṣasya vṛṣaṇaṁ bṛṣā//
tadenāmenaso muktāṁ pratigṛhṇātu gautamaḥ/
iti tasyāśramṁ bheje sākaṁ rāmeṇa kauśikaḥ//
duḥke sukhe ca raja ava babhūva hetu/
ṣtādṛgvidhe mahati gutamadharmapatnyāḥ/
yasmād guṇena rajasā vikṛtiṁ gatā sā.
rāmasya pādarajasā prakṛtiṁ prapede//

Ibid, Verses 90-94

13. *Gautamasya naraśreṣtha pūrvamāsinmahatmanaḥ/*
āśramo divyasaṁkāśaḥ surairapi supūjitaḥ//
sa cātra tapa ātiṣṭhadhalyāsahitaḥ purā/
varṣapūgānyanekāmi rājaputra mahāyaśaḥ//
tasyāntaraṁ viditvā ca sahasrakṣaḥ śacīpatiḥ/
munivesadharo bhūtvā Ahalyāmidamabravīt//

suśrūṣi paritusṭoasmi gamisyāmi yathāgatam/
avaṁ saṁgamya tu tadā niścakāmotjāttataḥ//

....

tathā śaptvā ca vaiśakraṁ bhāryāmapi ca śaptavān/
iha varṣasahasrāṇi bahūni nivasiṣyasi//

....

Trayānāmapi lokānāṁ yāvadrāmasya darśanam
sāpasyāntamupāgamya teṣāṁ darśanamāgatā
Rāghavau tu tadātasyāḥ pādau jagṛhaturmudā/
samaranti Gautamavacaḥ prtijagrāha sā hi tau//

....

Gautamoapi mahātejā Ahalyāsahitaḥ sukhī/
rāmaṁ saṁpūjya vidhivattapstepe mahātapāḥ//

Vāl. Rāmā Bālakāṇḍa, Canto 48–15, 16, 17, 22, 29
Canto 49,–16, 17.21

14. *kathaṁ Gaṅgāvataraṇaṁ kathaṁ teṣāṁ jalakriyā/*
tārayeyaṁ kathaṁ caitāninti cintāparoabhavat//
tasya cintayato nityaṁ dharmeṇa viditātmanaḥ/
putro Bhagīratho nāma jajñe paramadhārmikaḥ//

....

mantrīsvādhāya tadrājyaṁ Gaṅgāvataraṇe rataḥ/
tapo dirghaṁ samatiṣṭhadgokauṇe reghunandana//

....

Gaṅgāyāḥ salilakilinne bhasmneṣāṁ mahātmanām/
svaragaṁ gaccheyurtyantaṁ sarve ca prapitāmahāḥ//

Ibid, Canto 42, Verses - 6,7,12,19

15. *tayā taṭinyā jāhnavyā prāpayattridivaṁ pitṛn/*
Bhagīrathaḥ puraṁ prāpa paripūrṇamanorathaḥ//

CR. Bālakāṇḍa, Verse - 88

16. *tatkāle piśitāśanāsapiśunā sandhyeva kacinmune*
radvānaṁ tarasā rurodha rudhirakṣodāruṇā dāruṇā/

svādhīne hanane purīṁ vidadhatī mṛtyoḥ svakṛtyātayah
krīḍatkiṁkarasaṁghasaṁkaṭamahāśṛṅgāṭakāṁ tāṭakā//
hṛtvādreḥ śikharāṇi tāni paritaḥ kṣiptvā hasitvā krudhā
kṛtvā hastavighaṭṭanaṁ tata itaḥ sthitvā naṭitvā muhuḥ/

siktvā kṣāmasṛjā srajāntrakṛtayā baddhvā kacānkhecarān
dagdhvāgneḥ sadṛśā dṛśā niśicarā rundhanti randhraṁ divaḥ//

Ibid., Verse, 41, 48.

17. *Udhunvānā rajo ghoraṁ Tāḍakā rāghavāvumau/*
rajomeghena mahatā muhūrtaṁ sā vyamohayat//
tatomāyāṁ samāsthāya śilāvarṣeṇa rāghavau.
abākiratsumahatā tataścukrodha rāghavaḥ//

....

Uvāca rajanīṁ tatra ṭāḍakāyā vane sukham/
muktaśāpaṁ vanaṁ tacca tasminneva tadāhani//
vāl. Rāmā Bālakāṇḍa, Canto. 26, Verses -15, 16, 35

18. *'Punarapi kuśanābhastu putrīyanpituḥ prāsādadgādha satvāṅgādhisaṁjñanamasmattātapādānudapādayat/'*
tiṣṭhan kṣatrārahavṛttau munirgamadsāvāśramaṁ brahmasūno
rātithyaṁ tatra labdhvā niravadhi surabheḥ prābhavādityavetya/
sā tena prārthitābhūttadanu munivare nābhyepete cakarṣa
krośantīṁ tāṁ tayaiva pracuravalajuṣā kāndiśiko bahūva//
CR. Bālakāṇḍa, p. 65, Verse -95.

19. *Prajāpatisutastvāsītkuśo, nāma mahīpatiḥ/*
kuśasya putro balavānkuśanābhaḥ sudhārmikaḥ//
kuśanābhasutasatvāsīdgādhitrityeva viśrutaḥ/
gādheḥ putro mahātejā Viśvāmitro mahāmuniḥ//
Viśvāmitro mahātejāḥ pālayāmāsa medinīm/
bahuvarṣasahasrāṇī rājā rajyamakārayat//
jitārājarṣilokāste tapasā kuśikātmajaḥ//
anena tapasā tvāṁ hi rājarṣiriti vidmahe/
avamuktvā mahātejā jagāma sahadaivataiḥ//
triviṣṭapaṁ brahmalokānāṁ parameśvaraḥ//
Viśvāmitroapi tacchutvā hṛiyā kiṁcidvāṇmukhaḥ//
Vāl. Rāmā, Bālakāṇḍa, Canto, 51, 18, 19, 20,
Ibid., Canto 57, 5, 6,7.

20. *'atha sāvitraḥ kṣatriyaśtriśaṇku saśarīraḥ svarga sidhimabhyarthayamāno vasiṣthena pratyākhātastasya .... śaraṇamabhajat. .... ayaṁ mahātmā tapasaḥ prabhāvādāropayāmāsa divaṁ triśaṇkuṁ .... apātayatsvargamupāśrayantaṁ saṁjātamanyu śatamanyurenam .... triśaṇkurgagane pratiṣṭhām.'*
CR. Bālakāṇḍa, p. 90-92

Triśaṇkuriti vikhyāte Ikṣvākukulavardhanaḥ/
gaccheyaṁ svaśarīreṇe devatānāṁparāṁgatim//
viśmāmitraṁ mahatmānmucuḥ sānunayaṁ vacaḥ//
ayaṁ rāja mahābhāga guruśāpaparikṣataḥ/
saśarīro divaṁ yātuṁ nāhartyeva tapodhana
gagane cānyanekāni vaiśvānarapathādbahiḥ/
avākiśarāśtriśaṁkuśca tiṣṭhatvamarasaṁnibhaḥ/
Vāl. Rāmā, Bālakāṇḍa,
Canto 57, 11. 12
Canto 60-24, 25, 31, 32

21 *'...ambarīṣayajñapaśuvināśaprāyaścittārthaṁ.........*
ṛcīkasya madhyamaputraḥ śunaḥśepaḥ śaraṇamayācata...

gāthādvayaprītābhyāmindropendrābhyāmmbarīṣaṁ
Śunaḥśepaṁ ca pūrṇamonorathau kārayāmāsa.'

CR. Bālakāṇḍa, pp. 92–93

'ambarīṣa itikhyāto yaṣṭuṁ samupacakrame...
tasya vacanamśrutvā viśvāmitromahātapā
....
śunaḥśepamuvācārtaṁ rakṣānirāmayam/

Vāl. Rāmā Bālakāṇḍa, Canto 61-62
Verses 5, 8, 18.

22. Vāl. Rāmā, Ayodhyākāṇḍa, Verse 1.
23. Cr. Ayodhyākāṇḍa, Verse 1.
24. 'rātparairraralagai rathodhatā'.

CM. p. 41

25. Vāl. Rāmā, Ayodhyākāṇḍa, Canto 1, Verses 35-38.
26. Cr. Ayodhyākāṇḍa, Verse 2.
27. *'tataḥ prāvṛṣenyapayovāhavyūhastanitanādākarṇana samudīrṇaniratiśayāhlādasaṁsarganiragalanirgalat kekālāpinaḥ kalāpina iva janāḥ pramadabha vakalakalaravamukharitaharinmukhā bhūvūḥ/.*

Ibid, p.121

28. Ibid, Verse 6.
29. *rājñayastūparate vākye janaghoṣo mahanbhūt/*
śanaistasminpraśānte ca janāghoṣe janādhipaḥ//
vasiṣṭhaṁ muniśārdūlaṁ rājāvacanamabravīt/
abhiṣekāya rāmasya yatkarma saparicchadam//
tadadya bhagavānsarvamājñapayitumarhati/
tacchrutvā bhūmipālasya vasiṣṭho munisattamaḥ//
ādideśāgrato rājñaḥ sthitanyuktānkṛtāñjalīn/
suvarṁādini ratnāni balīnsarvauṣadhirapi//
śuklamālyāni lājāṁśca pṛthakśa madhusarpiṣi/
ahatāni ca vāsāṁi rathaṁ sarvāyudhānyapi//

Vāl, Rāmā Ayodhyākāṇḍa, Canto 3. 5-9

30. *āpūrayanmaṇgalatūryaghoṣairāśāvaśāvallabhakarṇa-tālān/*
ujjṛmbhitaḥ koapi girāmabhūmirunmastakaḥ paura janapromodaḥ

CR. Ayodhyākāṇḍa, Verse 8.

31. *jnāntīdāsī yato jātā kaikeyyaā tu sahoṣitā/*
prāsādaṁ candrasaṁkāśamāruroha yadṛcchayā//
dīrghamuṣṇaṁ viniḥsvasya mantharāmidamabravīt//
adya Rāmamitaḥ kṣipraṁ vanaṁ prasthāpayāmyaham/
yauvarājyena Bharataṁ kṣipramadyābhisecaye//
idaṁ tvidānīṁ saṁpasya kenopāyena sādhaye/
Bharataḥ prapnuyādrājyaṁ natu rāmaḥ kathamcana//
purā devāsura yudhe saha rajarṣibhiḥ patiḥ/

agacchatvāmupādaya devarājasya sāhyakṛt//
tatrākaronmahāyudhaṁ rājā Daśarathastadā/
asuraiśca mahāvāhuḥ śastriśca sakalikṛtaḥ//
apavāhyatvayādevi saṁgrāmānnaṣtacetanaḥ/
tatrāpi vikṣataḥ śastraiḥ patiste rakṣitasatvaya//
tuṣtena tena dattau te dvau varau śubhadarśane/
sa tvayoktaḥ patirdevi yadiccheyaṁ tadāvaram//
caturdaśa hi varṣāṇi rāme pravrājite vanam/
avaṁ setsyanti putrasya sarvāthāstava kāminī//

'Vāl Rāmā Ayodhyākāṇḍa Canto 7–1,
Ibid, Canto, 9–1, 3, 11, 15-17,21, 32.

32. *yāṁevāhurniśicarakulunmūlane mūlahetuṁ*
yasyāścittaṁ prakṛtikutilaṁ gātramitra bhūva/
ambhojinyāḥśiśira sarasaṁ kāsarivācchammbhaḥ//
kaikeyyāḥ sā hṛdayamadayaṁ mantharā nirmamantha//

CR. Ayodhayākāṇḍa,
Verse-9,

'saiṣā mantharābhidhānapiśācikāveśaparvaśanijāśayā
pūrvaṁ daṇḍake vaijayantapuravāstavyaśambarā
surasaṁgarasaṁgatavedanāpanodenāthamātmane
vitīrṇaṁvarāya Daśarathāya varadvayaṁ nyavedayat/'
tayorekasya saṁrambho Bharatasyābhiṣecanam/
anyasya vanyavṛtyaiva vane Rāmasya vartanam//

Ibid, p. 128, Verse 11.

33. CR. Ayodhyākāṇḍa, Verse 15.

34. *'atha mithilīnāthaḥ salakṣmaṇaḥ sapradakṣiṇaṁ rājānaṁ jananījanaṁ ca praṇamya pratiṣidha pṛtihāracakro niścakrāma./'* Ibid, p. 170.

35. *'tatra sāntaḥpura ava purānnirgatya śilpivarga samīkṛtasaraṇirbarataḥ purataḥ prasṛtanaragajara thaturaga .... niveśitabalabhāro Bharadvājā bhivandanamakarot/'*
'tataḥ pratipadya saṁjñamanujñayayā guroramarasariti viracitasamucitanivāpakṛtyaṁ praṇīpatya rāmṁ pratinivartayituṁ Bharataḥ prāvartat/'
tvayā mayā ca kartavyaḥ satyavācaḥ piturvidhiḥ/
iti pratyādiśadrāmo bhāratimapi bhāratīm//

Ibid., pp. 209, 218, 220

36. *nārājake janapade vidyunmāli mahāsvanaḥ/*
abhivarṣati parjanyo mahīṁ divyena vāriṇa//
nārājake janapade bījamuṣṭiḥ prakīryate/
nārājake pituḥ putro bhāryā bā vartate vase//
arājake dhanaṁ nāsti nāsti bhāryāapi arājake/
idamatyāhitaṁ cānyatkutaḥ satyamarājake//

nārājake janapade kārayanti sabhaṁ narāh/
udyāṇāni ca ramyāṇi hṛṣṭāḥ puṇyagṛhāni ca//
Vāl. Rāmā, Ayodhyākaṇḍa, Canto 67, Verses 9-12

37. *'atha Daśaratha praśaṁsāmāṁsalaiḥ kaikeyinindākaṇḍa litai Rāmaguṇakīrtana guṇitairavarodhavadhūjana paridevanāravairmukhariteṣu diṅgmukheṣu/'*
abhūdarājakamlānasadga ṇaṁ gaganāṅgaṇam//
ālokyeva tadā śāntamaśeṣaṁ ca mahītalam//
CR. Ayodhyākāṇḍa, p. 196

38. *Kusumānyapacinvantī cacāra rucirānanā/*
anarhā vanavāsasya sā taṁ ratnamayaṁmṛgam//
vismayotfullanayanā sasnehaṁ samudaikṣat/
sa ca tāṁ Rāmadayitāṁ paśyanmāyāmayo mṛgaḥ//
mṛgo hyevaṁvidhao ratnavicitro nāsti rāghava/
jagatyāṁ jagatīnātha māyaiṣā hi na saṁśayaḥ//
avaṁ bruvāṇaṁ kākutsthaṁ prativāryya śucismitā/
uvāca sītā saṁhṛṣṭāchadmanā hṛtacetanā/
babhuva Rāghavasyāpi manovismayamāgatam//
iti sītā vacaḥaṁ śrutvā dṛṣtvā ca mṛgamadbhutam/
asyāmāyāttamasmākaṁ yatkṛtyamṛaghunandana/
ahamenaṁ vadhisyāmi grahiṣyāmyathavā mṛgam//
tena marmaṇi nirvidhaṁśareṇānupamenahi/
mṛgarupaṁ tu tyaktvā rākṣasaṁ rupamāsthitaḥ//
māricasya to māyiṣā pūrvoktā lakṣmaṇena tu/
tattathā hyabhavaccādya māricoayaṁ mayā hataḥ//
hā sīte Lakṣmaṇetyevamākruśya tu mahāsvanam/
mamāre rākṣasaḥ soayaṁ śrutvā sītakathaṁ bhavet//
Vāl. Rāmā. Araṇyakāṇḍa. Canto-42 -32, 34
Ibid Canto. 43 - 89, 9, 23, 47
Canto. 44 - 20, 23, 24

39. *Upatasthe ca vaidehīṁ bhikṣurupeṇa Rāvaṇaḥ/*
abhabyo bhavya rupena bhartāramanuśocatīm//
naivaṁrupā mayā nāri dṛṣṭapūrvā mahitale/
rupamagryaṁ ca lokesu saukumārjaṁ vayaśca te//
Vāl. Rāmā. Araṇyakāṇḍa, Canto. 46, Verses 9, 23.

40. *rāghavasya priyāṁ bhāryāṁ yasatvamicchasi rākṣasa//*
kṣudhitasya ca siṁhasya mṛgaśatrostarasvinaḥ/
āśīviṣasya vadanāddṁṣṭrāmādātumicchasi//
mandaraṁ parvataśresthaṁ pāninā hartumicchasi/
kālakūtaṁ viṣaṁ pītvā svastimāngantumicchasi//
akṣi sūcyā prasṛjasi jihvayā lehi ca kṣuram/
rāghavasya priyāṁ bhāryāmadhigantuṁ tvamicchasi//
avasajjya śilāṁkaṇthe samudraṁ tartumicchasi/
sūryācandramasau cobhau pāṇibhyāṁ hartumicchasi//
yo rāmasya priyāṁ bhāryāṁ pradharsayitumicchasi/

agniṁ prajvalilaṁ dṛṣtvā vastrenahartumicchasi//
kalyanavṛttāṁ yo bhāryāṁ rāmasyahartumicchasi/
ayomukhānāṁ sūlānāṁ madhye caritumicchasi//
Vāl. Rāmā. Araṇyakāṇḍa. , Canto 47, Verses 38-44

41. (a) ayaṁ kathaṁ syāditi bāṣpagarbhamālokyamano vanadevatābhiḥ/
vilokayan kevalaparṇaśālāṁ vinaṣṭacetā vilalāpa Rāmaḥ//

(b) *hā kaṣṭamatra na hi sā kimidaṁ pravṛtta*
mālokayāmi caṭulāmiha pādamudrām/
māṁ vīkṣya nūnamgṛhītamṛgaṁ muhūrta
mantarhitā taruṣu rosavatīvasītā//

(c) *ithaṁ vilapya dayitāṁ vipine vicinvan*
rāmo na tatra dhṛtimānna ca Lakṣmaṇoapi/
tādṛgvidhāmapi kathāṁ kathayan svavācā
valmīkajanmamunireva kaṭhoracetāḥ//
CR. Araṇyakāṇḍa. Verses 35, 36, 41

42. *Saumitre śobhate Pampā, vaidūrjyavimalodakā/*
fullapadmatpalavatī śobhitā vividhairdrumaiḥ//
Sumitre paśya Pampāyāḥ kānanaṁ śubhadarśanam/
yatra rājanti śailā vā drumāh saśikharā iva//
nalinairapi saṁcchannā hyatartha śubhadarśaṇā/
sarpavyālanucaritā mṛgadvijasamākulā//
adhikaṁ pravibhātyetnnīlapitaṁ tu śādvalam/
drumānāṁ vividhaiḥ puṣpapaiḥ paristomairivārpitam//
puṣpabhārasamṛdhāni śikharāni samantataḥ/
latābhiḥ puṣpitāgrābhirupagūhani sarvataḥ//
paśya rupaṇi saumitre vanānāṁ puṣpaśālinām/
sṛjatāṁ puṣpavarṣānivarsaṁ toyamucāmiva//
Vāl. Rāmā, Kiṣkindhākāṇḍa, Canto 1, Verses 3, 4, 7, 8, 9, 11

43. *atasminmadakalamallikākṣapakṣa*
vyadhūtasphuradurudaṇḍapuṇḍarikāḥ/
vāṣpāmbhaḥ paripatanodgamamāntarāle
sandraṣṭāḥ kubalayino bhuvo vibhāgāḥ//
URC. 1.31

44. *'tasminṛsyamūkamārgamupadiśya svargaṁ gate matangāśramavāsinyā tapasvinyā śabaryā kṛtaṁ sarparyāṁ parigṛhya Rāmastadanujñayā manojña vividhavihagakūjtaṁ mṛgagaṇaviharaṇaṁ manoharam gahana padamavagāhya byākośa kuśeśayaparicaya kaṣāyairvanadevatālatādolānukūlaiḥ kūlāyatalilāpara vaśāvallabhamadāmbucumbibhiḥ śambarārātiśara dhiśadṛśatataruhasahakaraśikharavisaradāsavāsāra*

śīkaraśekharairvividhalatālāsikālāsyopadeśadeśikāya mānaiḥ kāyamānasamānābhogalatāgṛhakelilubdha lubdhakapurandhrīśithiladhamillamallikāgandhamāmsa lairmallikākṣapakṣavikṣobhakṣodibhūtapāthaḥ pātheyai staṭavanapavaniranukampyamānaḥ Pampāmabhajat.'

CR Araṇyakāṇḍa. pp. 288–289

45. *'tatastadīyaṁvacanamākarṇya karṇayugalasudhāvarṣi devarṣipratimo dāśarathistamupāśliṣya taddarśitena pathāviracitabhuvanasaukhyaṁ sakyaṁ tapanatanayena sākamagnisākṣikamakarot'.*

CR. Kiṣkindhākāṇḍa, pp. 300-301

Sugrīvo nāma dharmātmā kaścidvānarapuṁgavaḥ/
vīro vinikṛto bhrātā jagatbhramati duḥitaḥ//
avaṁgunagaṇairyuktā yasya syuḥ kāryasādhakāḥ/
tasya sidhyanti sarveathā dūtavākyapracoditāḥ//
tattasya vākyaṁ nipuṇaṁ niśamya prahṛṣṭarupaḥ pavanātmajaḥ kapiḥ/
manaḥ samādhāya jayopapattau sakhyaṁ tadā kartumiyeṣa tābhyām//

Vāl. Rāmā. Kiṣkindhākāṇḍa,
Canto. 3, - 20, 35, 39

Sarve te tvaritaṁ gatvā kiṣkindhāṁ vālinaḥ purīm/
vṛkṣairātmanamāvṛtya hyatiṣṭhangahane vane//
taṁ śrutvā ninadaṁ bhrātuḥ krudho vālimahāvalaḥ/
niṣpapāta susaṁrabdho bhāskaroastataṭādiva//
tataḥ sutumulaṁ yuddhaṁ vālisugrīvayorbhūt /
yagane grahayorgoraṁ budhāṇgārakayoriva/
tadastraṁ tasty vīrasya svargamārgaprabhāvanam/
Rāmabaṇāsanakṣip tamāvahatparamāṁ gatim//

Ibid, Canto, 12–14, 16, 17
Canto, 17–18.

'punarapyavāpya kiṣkindhāṁ parjanya iva garjati.. nijavisālavakṣaḥsthalaḥ kṣititale nipapāta

CR. Kiṣkindhākāṇḍa. p. 313

46. (a) *Kāruṇyaṁ niravadhi yattava prasidhaṁ*
śītāṁśoḥ sahajamivārtihāri śaityaṁ/
tatsarvaṁ manukulanātha ! ramykīrte
matpāpātkathaya kathaṁ tvayānirastam//

(b) *avaṁvidhe priyatameapyanapetajīvāṁ*
māṁ rākṣasīti raghupuṁgava.! sādhu buddhva/
bāṇaṁ vimuñcamayi samprati tāḍkāre/'
śreyo bhaveddayitasaṇgamakariṇaste//

(c) *sadhāraṇī kṣitibhujāṁ mṛgayetipūrva*
muktā tvayiva janasaṁsadi satyavādin/

śākhāmṛgīṁ tadiha māraya māṁ śāṁ śareṇa
ko nāma Rāma : mṛgayurdayate mṛgīṇām//

(d) *saṁtrasya pūvammutastava bandhureṣa*
bheje yathādrimakutobhayamṛṣyamūkam/
bhartā mamāyamapi rāmaśarairbhedyaṁ
prāpto madiyahṛdayacchalamadridurgam//

(e) *nāhaṁ suketutanayā na ca saptasālī*
vālī na ca tribhuvanaprathitaprabhāvaḥ
tārāsmi vajrahṛdayā viśikhairbhedyā
dhvanī kathaṁ bhavasi rāghava ! māmaviddhvā//

(f) *ksitipatitanayānāṁ hanta garbheśvarāṇāṁ*
kimuniravadhi maugdhyaṁ śauryavajjanmasidham/
mama hṛdi nirapāye vartamāne kapīndre
Raghuvara.! Yadmuṣmai tiṣṭhase cāpapāṇiḥ//

CR. Kiṣkindhākāṇḍa, Verses 14–19

47. *'tato Jāmbavatpramukhā valīmukhagaṇā Dāśarathinirdesāt sugrīvaṁ kāñsana kalaśodakairbhyaṣiñcan'/*
'abiṣikte tu sugrīve Rāmaśyāmapayomucā
abhiṣektuṁ sthitā meghāstanmahiṁ mahiṣimiva//

Ibid. p. 321

48. *'tadānīmudnvadullaṇghanadṛhtaranihitacaraṇa niṣpīḍanaṁ sohamakṣamaḥ kṣmābhṛdeṣa nihśeṣaniḥsarannirjharaudhatayā nirantaraniṣpatdvāṣpa varṣa iva itastato vitatajīmutavṛndatayā pāriplavaśithiladhamilla iva,... ....pravadhamānordhvaśavāsa iva vacasāmaviṣayaṁ dauḥsthyamabhajat.*

CR. Sundarakāṇḍa,pp. 353-354

49. *'ānākalokaparikīrtitasaccaritra*
matroparudhya raghuvaṁśapateḥ kalatram/
vaitānavedijanitaṁ pavamānabandhuṁ
vastreṇa bandhumavinīta ! kathaṁ yatethāḥ//

Ibid, Verse 48

ksipramānīyayatāṁ sītā dīyatāṁ rāghavasya ca/
yāvanna harayo vīrā vidhamanti balaṁtava//
vānarāṇāṁ prabvāvoayaṁ na kena viditaḥpurā/
devatānāṁ sakāśaṁ ca ye gacchantinimantritāḥ//

Vāl. Rāmā. Sundarakāṇḍa
Canto. 58–143, 144

50. *vāridādapi ca Rāmanāmataḥ pūritā punarapāṇgadhārayā/*
tatkṣaṇaṁ prati cacāla dakṣiṇaṁ vāhinīśamakhilāpi vāhini//
'atha harīndroapi mahendropāntakāntāraśobhini lobhoniyamalayajātānilebelopavanadeśe raghupaternirdeśena niveśayāmāsa balamakhilam/'

CR. Yuddhakāṇḍa, Verse 5, p. 448

51. Vāl Rāma Yuddhakāṇḍa, Canto 44–109.

52. *tato madaparipalvaplavagavīrasāṁrāviṇa*
kṣaṇakṣubhitakoṇapaprakarapāṇikoṇāhataḥ/
ravairdhikabhiravairuparurodha rodontaraṁ
taraṇgitaghanāghanastanitabandhūbhirdundubhiḥ//
āsāradhārāṁ vikirañśarāṇāmāśvāsayanmānasamā-
śarānām/
vīro harinsṁyati meghanādauvivyādha haṁsāniva
meghanīdaḥ//

CR. Yuddhakāṇḍa, Verses, 40, 42.

53. *'tadanu vāruṇena vaiśvānaraṁ vainateyena vātanghayaṁ vāyavyena vāridaṁ prābhākareṇa tāmistraṁ māhendreṇa dānavaṁ māheśvareṇa vaiṣṇavaṁ ca paraspara mevamastramstreṇa bhindānayorniśamāhavāgrahād viditānyahani sapta vyatīyuḥ/'*

Ibid., p. 542

Chapter IV

LITERARY STUDIES IN THE CAMPŪRĀMĀYAṆA

(A) A general remark about the Language and style of Campūrāmāyaṇa

Bhoja displays his talent as a poet and a prose writer in the *Campūrāmāyaṇa*. As we have already discussed a 'Campū' means a piece of literary work in which prose and verses are blended. Though, generally speaking, this is the salient feature of a Campūkāvya, the *Campūrāmāyaṇa* is much more than that,

Bhoja's language of the *Campūrāmāyaṇa* possesses a special charm. Bhoja compares his composition to a melodious song associated with the musical concert. This statement proves true throughout the poetical and prose portions of *Campūrāmāyaṇa.*

The numerous poems composed by Bhoja in the *Campūrāmāyaṇa* produce a melodious note. The musical quality which he introduces in his poems pervades the entire poetical portions of his work. This quality is not lacking even in the description in the fearful demoness Tāḍakā which ordinarily creates terror in the minds of the readers.

Let us, quote the following passage from the *Campūrāmāyaṇa* to substantiates our view.

'tatkāle piśitāśanāsapiśunā sandhyeva kācinmune
radhvānaṁ tarasā rurodha rudhirakṣodāruṇādāruṇā
svādhīne hanane purīṁ vidadhatī mṛtyoḥ svakṛtyātaya

krīḍatkiṁkarasaṁghasaṁkaṭamahāśṛṅgāṭkaṁ
Tāḍakā.//[1]

We furnish below passages from the *Campūrāmāyaṇa* in order to show Bhoja is proficient in the art of imparting melody to his poems.

(a) *Vālmīkigītaraghupuṁgavakīrtileśaistṛptiṁkarkomi-*
kathamapyadhunā budhānām/
Gaṇgājalairbhuvi Bhagīrathayatnalabdhaiḥ kiṁ
tarpaṇaṁ na vidadhāti naraḥ pitṝṇām//[2]

(b) *Vānivilāsamaparatra kṛtopalambhamambhoja-*
bhūrasahamāna ivāvirāsīt
ābhāti yatkṛtiranekavidhaprapañca-vyājendrajālavi-
dhisādhaka-picchikeva//[3]

(c) *tāmāvasad daśarathaḥ suravanditena sa*
krandanena vihitāsanasaṁvibhāgaḥ/
Vṛndārakārivijaye suralokalabdhamandāramālya
madhuvāsitavāsabhūmiḥ//[4]

(d) *nārāyaṇāya nalināyatalocanāyanāmāvaśeṣitama-*
hābalivaibhavāya /
nanācarācaravidhāyakajanmadeśanābhīpuṭāya
puruṣāya namaḥ parasmai //[5]

The poet employs some high sounding phrases in a few of his poems, but there also the musical note is hard as in the simpler poems. Thus we can quote the following verses in order to corroborate our contention.

(a) *hṛtvādreḥ śikharāṇi tāniparitaḥ kṣiptvā hasitvā*
krudhā
kṛtvā hastavighaṭṭanaṃ tata itaḥ sthitvā
naṭitvāmuhuḥ /
siktvā kṣāmasṛjā srajāntakṛtayā baddhvā
kacānkhecarān
dagdhvāgneḥ sadṛśā dṛśā niśicarā rundhanti
randhraṁdivaḥ //

(b) *Yugapatprāptaguṇayoścāpa bhārgavarāmayoḥ /*
ṛjutā bakratāṁ prāpa vakratāpi tathārjavam // [6]

Similarly, a poem containing Vīra Rasa also possesses the same melody. We quote below the passage :

Yadbāhurāhurasanāyitaśastradhārā
dikpālakīrtimayacandramasaṁ grasanti /
yadvairiṇāṁ raṇamukhe śaraṇa-pradāyī
naivāsti kaścidamumantakamantareṇa //[7]

to substantiate our view.

Some other special features of Bhoja's poems

Bhoja is a master in the art of composing simple and lucid poems very often producing the jingling note of Anuprāsas or alliterations. It should be mentioned here that Sanskrit poets had always a great facination for presenting Anuprāsas which embellish the external form of a poem but not its meaning. Thus, Kālidāsa the greatest of Sanskrit poets displays his fondness for alliteration in such poems of the '*Raghuvaṃśa*' as :

(a) *padmāpadmātapatrena bheje samrājyadīkṣitam /*
parikalpitasānridhyā kāle kāle ca bandiṣu //[8]

(b) *upayayau tanutāṁ madhukhanditā himakarodaya*
pāndumukhacchaviḥ /
sadṛśamiṣṭasamagamanirvṛtiṁ vanitayānitayā
rajanīvadhuḥ //[9]
naravaro ravaśoṣitakesarī[9]

Similarly, Śrīharṣa also finds pleasure in creating alliteration. Śrīharṣa composes some fine poems which contain this particular quality. Here we can refer to the poetical passages like

(a) *athāsyarāgasya dadhā pade pade*
vacāṁści haṁsīva vidarbhajādade //[10]

(b) *apāṁ hi tṛptāya na vāridhārā*
svāduḥ sugandhiḥ svadate tuṣārā /[11]

of the ninth canto of the '*Naiṣadhacarita*'.

Bhoja is a master in the art of employing alliteration which can be readily proved by citing the following poems from the *Campūrāmāyaṇa*.

(a) *nārāyaṇāya nalināyatalocanāya*
nāmāvaśeṣitamahābalivaibhavāya /

nanācarācaravidhāyakajanmadeśa
nābhiputāya puruṣāya namaḥ parasmai //[12]

and

(b) *api kuśalammatyāḥ svāgataṁ sāṁpratam vaḥ*
śamitadanujadambhā kiṁ nu dambholikeliḥ /
api dhiṣaṇamaniṣānirmitā nītimārgā
stridaśanagarayogakṣemarkṛtye kṣamante //[13]

One special feature of the second verse is that poet uses the word 'api' in beginning of the first and the third line of the verse. In another verse of the same kāṇḍa :

anāṁ purāṇanagarīṁ nagarītisālāṁ
sālābhirāmabhujanirjitayakṣarājaḥ /
helābhibhūtajagatāṁ rajanīcarāṇāṁ
rājā cirādavati Rāvaṇanāmadheyaḥ //[14]

The poet repeats the word 'nagarī' and 'sālā' which also adds to the sweetness of the composition. The poet frequently presents couplets. It is worthnoting in this context that immediately after the composition of three long poems, viz.

(a) *nyagrodhapatrasamatāṁ kramaśaḥ prayātāmṅgī-*
cakāra punarapyadaraṁ kṛśāṅgayāḥ /
jīvātave daśamukhorgapīḍitānāṁ garbhacchalena
vasatā prathamena puṁsā //[15]

(b) *madhyaṁ tanutvādavibhāvyamānamākāśa-*
māsīdsitāyatākṣyāḥ /
garbhodaye viṣṇupadāpadeśātkārsyaṁ vihāyāpi
vihāya eva //[16]

(c) *uccasthe grahapañcake suragurau sendau*
navamyāṁ tithau
lagne karkaṭake punarvasuyute meṣaṁ gate
pūṣaṇi /
nirdagdhuṁ nikhilāḥ palāśasamidho medhyāda-
yodhyāraṇe -
rāvirbhūtambhūta pūrvamaparaṁ yatkiṇcidekaṁ
mahaḥ //[17]

the poet abruptly presents four couplets. In another verse, again the poet significantly uses the word 'yogena' in the beginning of the first line of the couplet and 'niyogena' at the very beginning of the second line[18]

Again in another couplet viz.

'balena tapasā labdhe baletyatibaleti ca /
Vidyete mayi kakutstha vidye te vitarāmi te //[19]

two similar expressions viz. 'vidyete' and 'vidyete' have been used. The first verbal form is used in dual number while the second expression, though it is identical in appearance with the first, should be read as 'vidye' and 'te' (those two lores). It reminds us of a passage in the *Śrīmad Ānanda-vṛndāvana-Campū* of Kavikarṇpūra which reads as follows :

'iyaṁ ca kumudvatī mudvatī bhavatyurdhamiti mahat kautukaṁ kau tu kaṁ na rañjayati, iayati.....'[20]

In this passage the first *'Kautukaṃ'* is a single word while the succeeding expression should be read as 'kau', 'tu' and 'kaṃ'.

In another portion of the Bālakāṇḍa of the *Campūrāmāyaṇa* Bhoja repeats the word 'Tāḍakā' four times in four succeeding verses viz. 'mahāśṛṇgāṭakāṃ Tāḍakā,[21] 'karṇamavisattāḍakāguṇaḥ',[22] 'baddhaśradhasya Tāḍakā',[23] and 'Tāḍakāmāthine dadau',[24] Such a repetition, however, does not effect the beauty of the poems.

Again in a poem viz.

'iti vividharasābhiḥ kauśikavyāhṛtābhiḥ
śrutipathamadhurābhiḥ pāvanībhiḥ kathābhiḥ /
galitagahanakṛcchraṁ gacchatordāśarathyoḥ
samakucadiva sadyastādṛśaṁ margadaidhyam //[25]

of the Bālakāṇḍa the suffix 'bhiś' is used five times in succession, which not only does not destroy but enhances the sweetness of the poem. The entire poem containing the instrumental suffix 'bhiś' creates the jingling beauty of 'Anuprāsa'.

One significant feature of the poetical portion of the *Campūrāmāyaṇa* is that the poet presents nice images in many of them. In this connection we can refer to the following poems of the *Campūrāmāyaṇa*, viz.

(a) *Hṛtvādreḥ śikharāṇi tāniparitaḥ kṣiptvā hasitvā krudhā*
kṛtvā hastavighaṭṭanaṁ tata itaḥ sthitvā naṭitvā muhuḥ /
siktvā kṣāmasṛjā srajāntrakṛtayā baddhvā kacānkhecarān
dagdhvāgneḥ sadṛśā dṛśāniśicarā rundhanti randhraiṁ divaḥ //[26]

(b) *'yabvāhurāhurasanāyitaśastradhārā*
dikpālakīrtimayacandramasaṁ grasanti /
yadvairiṇāṁ raṇamukhe śaraṇapradāyī
naivāsti kaśchidamumantakamantareṇa //[27]

In the first poem, there is a vivid description of the angry movement of Tāḍakā. An image is not always identical with a simile or a metaphor, but it is a picture created with the help of words. In the above poem, we find an excellent picture of the exploits of the demoness Tāḍakā.

In the second verse there is a visual image where the mighty arms of Rāvaṇa are described as enveloping the white fame of the gods like the dark demon Rāhu swallowing the white moon.

The poet sometimes deliberately becomes mechanical in composing certain poems. It is clear from three verses of the Bālakāṇḍa, viz.

(a) *'asamañjaṁ sutaṁ lebhe vaidarbhī keśinītayoḥ /*
ṣaṣṭiṁ putrasahasrāṇāṁ sumatiśca yavīyasī //[28]

(b) *'asamañjasacāritramasamanjamapohya saḥ /*
ārabdhahayamedhaḥ sannamuñcat turaṅgamm //[29]

(c) *asamañjasutaṁ pautramaṁśumantamathābravīt /*
saptiṁ hṛtvā samādhattāṁ saptatantuṁ bhavāniti //[30]

He uses the word 'asamañjasa' which gives three different meanings in the three poems. In the first poem, 'asamañjasuta' refers to the son of Vaidarbhī. In the second verse the word 'asamañjasa' means improper and irresponsible. In the third poem 'asamañja' is a part of the compound word 'asamañjasuta'.

The prose passages of the *Campūrāmāyaṇa* are short compared to the prose portions of other Campū texts. The passages are sweet. Let us, quote a few prose passages of the Bālakāṇḍa in support of our contention :

(a) *'purā khalu surāsurāṇāṁ sudhānimittaṁ mithovirodhe pravṛtte māyāṁ viśvamohinīṁ viśvarupaḥ pradarśya daiteyanidhanaṁ śatadhārapāṇinā kārayāmāsa.'*[31]

(b) *'asyāṁ khalu nagaryāmārabdhayajñasya janakasya bhāgadheyātsītā-nāmadheyabhājanama-jījanatkanyāratnaṁ ratnagarbhā bhagavatī'.*[32]

Regarding the prose passages of Lakṣmaṇasūri it can be easily commented that though his prose is sometimes lengthy, it is sweet and full of alliterations. In this regard we can refer to the passages, viz.

'atha tayoraviśrāntavimuktadivyāstrayorākhaṇḍalavṛtr-nibhayorālūneṣumārgaṇeśvabhaṅguraparasparavivaramā-rgaṅeṣu, vicchinneṣudhanurguṇeṣvavyāhatsahajasāha-saguṇādhīneṣu dhurīṇeṣu yāneṣu nirapāya samarā-bhiyāneṣu, nirbhinne sāṁyugīne ca rathe nirbekalya-vijayamanorathamajāyata yaśodhanamāyodhanam.[33]

One special characteristic of Bhoja's *Campūrāmāyaṇa* is that he presents some rare 'nāmdhātus' of verbal forms derived from substantives. One typical examples of such a use is found in the following verse :

rāmākarṣaṇabhagnakārmukabhuva dvānena rodorudhā
dṛptakṣatrayasaḥ sitacchadakule jīmūtanādayitam /
vīraśrīprathamapravesasamaye puṇyāhaghoṣāyitaṁ
sītāyāḥ kila mānase pariṇaye māṅglyatūryāyitam //[34]

where three new words viz. 'māṅgalyatūryāyitam', 'jīmūtanādāyitam' and 'puṇyāhaghoṣāyitam' have decorated the poem by their glaring presents.

(B) Characterisation

The authors of the *Campūrāmāyaṇa* are indbted to a certain extend to Vālmīki in delineating the characters of the *Campūrāmāyaṇa*. However, both Bhoja and Lakṣmaṇasūri deserve a unstinted praise for their ability to portrays the different characters in spite of their allegience to Vālmīki.

Let us, now critically discuss some of the characters of the *Campūrāmāyaṇa*.

(a) Rāma

Rāma is the hero of the *Campūrāmāyaṇa*. The poet adequately describes the heroic, and magnanimous deeds of Rāma like Vālmīki. Rāma is initially an Epic characters which is a unique creation of Vālmīki. He killed the mighty demon Rāvaṇa[34] and the monkey king Vāli[36] who was recognised as a matchless hero in the universe. Rāma is a Dhīrodātta type of hero. He is born in a noble Kṣatriya family.[37]

In the *Campūrāmāyaṇa* Rāma sometimes occupies the position of a super-human person and sometimes he behaves like a normal mortal being. He kills the demoness Tāḍakā[38] and demons Khara and Dūṣaṇa and finally he destroys fourteen thousand demons in an encounter.[39] Rāma's super-human quality is exposed when Ahalyā is reduced to a lady from fossil by the touch of Rāma's feet.[40] But in spite of possessing all these super-human qualities Rāma is simultaneously depicted as a normal human being who is not free from human feelings and emotions. Though, Rāma is worshipped as an Avatāra of Lord Viṣṇu he has a great difference from Vāmana and Narasiṁha. Thus, when he was separated from his beloved wife Sītā he lamented for her like other mortal beings.[41] There is a great difference between Rāma, and Kṛṣṇa of the *Mahābhārata* and the *Bhāgavat purāṇa*.[42] While Kṛṣṇa sometimes appears in his actual form as in the Bhīṣmaparva of the *Mahābhārata* where he assumes the form of Supreme Brahmaṇ,[43] we notice no such extraordinary personality of Rāma. In the *Rāmāyaṇa*, Rāma is saved from his critical situations by Hanūmān.[44]

One very important feature the character of Rāma is that he always behaved like an ideal son and an ideal king.

In the *Campūrāmāyaṇa* Rāma appears as a popular prince. When king Daśaratha proposed to the courtiers that Rāma should be installed as Yuvarāja, they were so delighted that they readily accepted the proposal of Daśaratha who was the rulling king, his courtiers were so partial towards his son, that by forgetting their sense of courtesy, they jubilantly expressed their view in the following manner :

deve stheteapi tanayaṁ tava Rāmabhadraṁ
lokaḥ svayaṁ bhajatu nāma kimatra citram /
candraṁ vinā yadupalambhanaheturbhūtaṁ
kṣīrodamāśrayati kim tṛsitaścakora //[45]

But Daśaratha's dream did not materialise due to the interference Kaikeyī. Rāma was compelled to leave for the forest for fourteen years.[46] But as in the *Rāmāyaṇa* of Vālmīki so in the *Campūrāmāyaṇa*. Rāma is depicted as remaining unpurturbed over the situation.[47] He left for the forest without any hesitation or grudge. In the Ayodhyākāṇḍa of the *Campūrāmāyaṇa* the author describes that when Kaikeyī ordered Rāma to go to exile, Rāma accepted the evil design of Kaikeyī as a flower garlands.[48] Such a character is rare in this world.

In ancient days the kings in India had many wives. Daśaratha himself is an example of this. But Rāma is the singular representative of monogamy. His life was occupied by Sītā and no other woman.

In the *Campūrāmāyaṇa* Rāma is an ideal hero who dedicated himself to the cause of the sages. Thus, he saved the religious order by destroying the wicked demons who constantly disturbed the peaceful recluse of Viśvāmitra.[49]

Rāma stood always for Dharmayuddha and adopted only righteous methods in battle. Though he was a prince coming from a high royal family he did not feel the sense of vanity. He was a liberal person who expressed the genuine sense of love for the Caṇḍāla king Guhaka and the monkey chief Hanūmān whom he embraced without any hesitation.[50] Such sincere love and friendship are rare in this world. Rāma had always a high reverence for womanhood. He possessed a deep regard for Kaikeyī though she was bent upon causing immense harm to his interest.[51] Though Rāma was an amiable and loving personality who generally remained calm and cool even in difficult situation, he was a real Kṣatriya prince, who became occasionally angry. As we notice in the Yuddhakāṇḍa of Lakṣmaṇasūri, he was angry with the recalcitrant attitude of the ocean who refused to offer him a passage to Laṇkā.[52] After all, a human being is bundle of varying emotions. He is not a latent block of stone.[53]

Daśaratha

Daśaratha was the king of Ayodhyā. In the *Campūrāmāyaṇa* the author Bhoja describes him as a great king who defeated mighty demons. In the following verse of the *Campūrāmāyaṇa*, king Daśaratha is depicted as the lover of Gods.

tāmāvasaddaśarathaḥ suravanditena
Sakrandanena vihitāsanasamvibhāgāḥ /
vṛndārakārivijaye suralokalabdha
mandāramālyamadhuvāsitavāsabhumiḥ //[54]

He had no son but at the advice of minister Sumantra he performed Aśvamedha sacrifice and Putrakāmeṣṭi sacrifice.[55] As a result performing sacrifices, four sons were born to him. They were Rāma, Lakṣmaṇa, Bharata and Śatrughana. Though as a father he loved all his four sons the author of the *Campūrāmāyaṇa* shows that he had a greater wickness for his eldest son Rāma. This can be easily realised from an episode of the *Campūrāmāyaṇa*. When Viśvāmitra requested Daśaratha to send his son Rāma with him to kill demons, Daśaratha felt worried and sad.[56] But at the advice of priest Vasiṣṭha Daśaratha ultimately sent Rāma with Viśvamitra.[57] Daśaratha is depicted as an ideal person who does not violate his commitment under any circumstances. Daśaratha was, however, not free from human wicknesses. He had a greater love for his young queen Kaikeyī. He promised to her to grant two boons. Kaikeyī demanded suddenly that Rāma be banished and Bharata should be installed as Yuvarāja. The demand of Kaikeyī caused a serious conflict in the minds of Daśaratha which is nicely described by the poet.[58] Daśaratha died from the shock he received at the ruthless prayer of Kaikeyī.

Lakṣmaṇa

The character of Lakṣmaṇa is portrayed by the authors of the *Campūrāmāyaṇa* with equal ability. Lakṣmaṇa's attachment to Rāma is a limitless and passionate attachment.[59] Equally sincere is his devotion to Sītā.[60] When Rāma refused to allow him to accompany him to the forest, Lakṣmaṇa fell at Rāma's feet and pleaded with him to consider his pious wish.[61] Lakṣmaṇa is always outspoken and firm. Bhoja describes that he rebuked even his father for the decision to send Rāma to the forest.[62] Rāma always turned to Lakṣmaṇa for any counsel when he needed such a counsel. Rāma was moved by Lakṣmaṇa's devotion to him. Lakṣmaṇa is depicted as a devoted younger brother of Rāma in the *Rāmāyaṇa*[63] of Vālmīki and also the *Campūrāmāyaṇa*. Bhoja says in the Araṇyakāṇḍa that when Lakṣmaṇa remained by his side Rāma felt that his own father was alive and protecting him.[64] Lakṣmaṇa's thoughts were very high. He always behaved modestly with Rāma in spite of being a great hero. He killed Rākṣasas without much difficulty. Sometimes he behaved rashly. Thus, he chopped off the nose of Śūrpaṇakhā when she behaved in an indecent manner with Sītā.[65]

Bharata

Bharata was the son of Kaikeyī. In the *Campūrāmāyaṇa* his love for his brothers and for duty as well as his devotion towards Rāma has been appropriately depicted.[66] He loved Rāma so deeply that he was not the least tempted by the throne of Ayodhyā. Like Lakṣmaṇa Bharata was also outspoken. He rebuked Kaikeyī for sending Rāma to the forest.[67] After the cremation ceremony of his father he went along with his ministers to bring Rāma back to Ayodhyā.[68] Lakṣmaṇa suspected Bharata's motive of coming to meet Rāma.[69] He admonished him and said that Bharata was inspired by an evil design.[70] When Bharata saw Rāma he was overwhelmed with emotion. He fainted at Rāma's feet by uttering the word 'Ārya', Bhoja describes the scene of Bharata's love and allegiance to Rāma with the help of the following passage :

'....... *pādayornipatya..........vikarttanakulasya...... tādṛsamāsayaṁ prakāśayantī Bharatopajña vijñapanā*'.[71]

The entire scene is another excellent specimen of Bhoja's great poetic genious. In fine, Bharata was a devotee of Rāma. He was dutiful and modest.

Śatrughna

The character of Śatrughna in the *Campūrāmāyaṇa* does not reach the height of Rāma and Bharata. But Śatrughna is another excellent character in Bhoja's work. He is a Kṣatriya prince with a lesser capacity of controling his passions. When he saw Mantharā he felt a sudden fit of anger and tried to kill her for her wickedness.[72] Śatrughna followed Bharata when the latter went to Bharadvāja's āśrama to bring Rāma back.[73]

Sages in the Campūrāmāyaṇa

The sages Vasiṣṭha, Viśvāmitra and Bharadvāja play their role in the *Campūrāmāyaṇa* most adequately.

Vasiṣṭha

Vasiṣṭha appears in the Bālakāṇḍa of the *Campūrāmāyaṇa*. He was a family priest of the Ikṣvāku dynasty. In the Bālakāṇḍa of the *Campūrāmāyaṇa*, when king Daśaratha refuses to send Rāma and Lakṣmaṇa with Viśvāmitra, Vasiṣṭha interferes and advises Daśaratha to send Rāma as demanded by Viśvāmitra.[74] He knew that

Rāma was inconquerable and he alone could vanquish the demons. When Rāma was banished and kaikeyī gave bark dresses to Sītā and Rāma, Vasiṣṭha was swept out of his usual majestic calm.[75] When Rāma came back from exile with Sītā and Lakṣmaṇa he was very happy and made him crown prince.[76]

Viśvāmitra

Viśvāmitra was a celebrated sage. He was originally a Kṣatriya, and the king of Kānyakubja.[77]

Viśvāmitra is a more pictureque figure in the *Campūrāmāyaṇa.* When Daśaratha refused to send Rāma with him Viśvāmitra was full of ire. But Vasiṣṭha advised Daśaratha to send Rāma as demanded by Viśvāmitra.[78] After that, when Rāma and Lakṣmaṇa went into his hermitage with him, he was their playful companion. He told them many stories of past. They crossed the river Sarayū and passed through many āśramas.[79] On their way, Viśvāmitra imparted to Rāma and Lakṣmaṇa two mantras named Balā and Atibalā.[80] He also taught them the use of certain rare weapons to Rāma like the divine weapon called Jṛmbhakāśtra.[81] Rāma killed demoness Tāḍakā. After killing her Rāma also killed two other demons viz. Subāhu and Mārīca.[82] After that, Viśvāmitra, left with the princess to the court king Janaka to attend the svayambara of Sītā.[83]

The character of Viśvāmitra is nicely depicted in the *Rāmāyaṇa*[84] and in the *Mahābhārata.*[85] He appears more as a great sage possessing extraordinary divine powers. Though he was occasionally angry, he was a pleasant comparison of Rāma and Lakṣmaṇa. Viśvāmitra's past history is adequately narrated in the *Campūrāmāyaṇa.*[86]

Bharadvāja

The description of Bharadvāja is one of the highlights of the *Campūrāmāyaṇa.* His wonderful power of penance is glowingly described in Ayodhyākāṇḍa. Acting on his advice, Rāma wẹnt to the Citrakūṭa hill. When Bharata went to fetch Rāma, Bharadvāja gave him a grand reception.[87] He told Bharata that Rāma's exile would prove a service of great blessing to the universe. When Rāma returned along with Sītā and Lakṣmaṇa and his innumerable new allies and followers, the sage requested him to stay in his hermitage for a day and pertake of the unparalled and lavish hospitality offered by him.[88]

The characters of sages Atri,[89] Śarabhaṇga,[90] Sthūlaśirāḥ,[91] Mātaṇga,[92] and Sutīkṣṇa[93] are briefly drawn in the *Campūrāmāyaṇa.*

Śarabhaṇga was another meritorious sage. Rāma was a Priyatithi or a dear and adorable guest for him, for which he possponed his journey to Brahmaloka when Rāma appeared on his Āśrama.[94]

Agastya

The great sage Agastya is described in an illuminating manner in the *Campūrāmāyaṇa.* Agastya is portrayed as a mighty and eminent sage and a protector of virtues. Agastya rendered a very valuable service to Rāma by presenting to him some priceless gifts like a bow of Viṣṇu, a divine missile of Brahmā and two inexhausible quivers and a golden arrow which were necessary for Rāma to destroy his enemies.[95]

Śatānanda

Śatānanda was the purohita (priest) of Janaka.[96] He was the son of Gautama and Ahalyā. He possessed a very charming trait. He was overjoyed at the sight of his mother Ahalyā being restored to her previous status from a stone by the grace of Rāma. It is he who told Rāma the marvellous history of Viśvāmitra's life.[97]

Guha

Our assessment of the male characters in the *Campūrāmāyaṇa* will remain incomplete if we fail to mention the character of Guha, another most illustrious character in the *Rāmāyaṇa*[98] of Vālmīki and in the *Campūrāmāyaṇa*. Though he was born in a Niṣada family, he proves himself as a mejestic character in the *Campūrāmāyaṇa*. He is described a great friend of Rāma. He gave shelter to his new friend whom he loved with great ardour.[99]

Female characters in the Campūrāmāyaṇa

Sītā

The character of Sītā as depicted in the *Campūrāmāyaṇa* is almost the same as found in the *Rāmāyaṇa*. Sītā was the adopted daughter of Janaka. The birth of Sītā is described in the *Campūrāmāyaṇa* in a following way :

> *....... janakasya bhāgadheyātsītā*
> *nāmadheyabhājanamajī*
> *janatkanyāratnaṁ ratnagarbhābhagavatī.*[100]

Sītā known as Dharaṇitanayā, Jānakī, Maithilī.[101]

Sītā occupies a conspicuous place in Indian literature by her great devotion to her husband, her indomitable spirit, her self-sacrifices and other noble qualities.

In the Ayodhyākāṇḍa of the *Campūrāmāyaṇa*, the author describes that when Sītā heard about the banishment of Rāma, she was shocked like a peacock hearing the sounds of a hunter's bow. The poet describes it in the following passage—

> *kalyāṇavādasukhitāṁ sahastva kāntāṁ*
> *kāntāracārakathayā kaluṣīcakāra /*
> *ambhodānadamuditāṁ vipine mayūrīṁ*
> *saṃtrāsayanniva dhanurdhvaninā pulindaḥ //*[102]

The poet says that when Sītā wore 'valkala' garments her tears removed the hardness of 'valkala.[103] Sītā is a very beautiful and accomplished lady. Śūrpaṇakhā, sister of Rāvaṇa, also describes the beauty of Sītā.[104] In the Araṇyakāṇḍa Sītā's lamantation at the separation from Rāma and her miserable plight is nicely described by the Bhoja as—

'hā nātha ! kva cirāyasīti bahuśo vyākruśya bāṣpāvilaṁ cakṣurdikṣu vimuncatīṁ Daśarathasyādyāmvekṣya snuṣām //[105]

In the Sundarakāṇḍa of the *Campūrāmāyaṇa* we find her moral greatness at its sublimest hight. She lived a famished, ill-fated, grief-stricken life in Aśokavana of Rāvaṇa.[106] Her lotus eyes and moonface are described by Rāma in the following passages—

'taruṇi dharaṇīsute.........vidhumukhi .... kañjalocane ... ...'[107]

Hanūmān says that Laṇkā was burnt by Sītā's glory.[108] In the *Campūrāmāyaṇa* the authors refer to various sweet charming traits of her character such as her softness and sweetness and splendour of speech, her patience, her courtesy and such other important qualities. But when Rāma declined to take her with him to the forest, she showed her great mental strength and obstinacy, and even rebuked Rāma.[109]

When Rāma took an oath to destroy the cruel sinful Rākṣasas, she gently demonstrated and argued with him for trying to harm persons who never harmed him. These episodes stand out very prominently in her life. Like Rāma she exihibits the virtue of the protection of the helpless and weak. She would not allow Hanūmān to punish the demonesses who had persecuted her. Hanūmān is moved by her noble forgiveness and said that she was fit to be called the 'pativratā' wife of Rāma.[110] When she faced the fire ordeal, she maintained her love and tenderness for Rāma and entered the fire without hesitation. All the gods declared her purity, and Rāma himself send that he imposed the fire test only to convince the word about her purity.[111]

Other female characters of the Campūrāmāyaṇa

We hear only the names of the consorts of Rāma's brother viz. Urmilā, Māṇḍavī and Śrutakīrti in the *Campūrāmāyaṇa.*[112] They do not play any part in the story of the *Campūrāmāyaṇa.* But the author has clearly portrayed the queens of Daśaratha, viz. Kausalyā, Kaikeyī and Sumitrā in his work.

Kausalyā

In the Bālakāṇḍa of the *Campūrāmāyaṇa*, Bhoja describes Kausalyā as a dignified lady. She had a reverential love for Daśaratha and passionate and boundless love for Rāma.[113] Kausalyā was a very pious woman. She prays to God Nārāyaṇa to bless her son in exile.[114] She was not angry with Daśaratha for his unkind action but she went with Bharata in his fruitless mission to fetch Rāma. As a mother, she was extremely delighted when Rāma returned to Ayodhyā after exile.[115]

Kaikeyī

The author of the *Campūrāmāyaṇa* gives as a full length portrait of Kaikeyī. She loves Daśaratha as a true pativrata woman. But at the same time she exhibits the weakness of her character. She was guided by the advice of Mantharā and asked the king to give her the promised boons which suddenly changed the entire situation. When Kaikeyī heard from her maid Mantharā about the proposed coronation of Rāma as Yuvarāja, her first reaction was one of joy. But she was swayed by description of the coming distress to herself and specially to her son Bharata. Mantharā's word carried her immediately to the other direction.[116] She became furious with Daśaratha. She insisted on the king to grant her the two boons promised to her on an earlier occasion. She demanded that Rāma be banished for fourteen years to the forest and that Bharata be crowned Yuvarāja.[117] She was so blind with greed for the throne of Ayodhyā that she unhesitatingly gave bark drasses to Rāma, Lakṣmaṇa and even Sītā as a token of sending them to the forest.[118] But Bharata's high-minded attitude which defeated all her plans gave her the rudest shock in life.[119] All her attempts to capture the coveted throne for Bharata proved fulfil at the reprisal of her son to occupy the throne. Kaikeyī excellently exhibits her motherly weakness for her son even at the cost of virtue and righteousness.

Sumitrā

Bhoja refers to Sumitrā, mother of Lakṣmaṇa.[120] But he does not present the character directly in his work.

Mantharā

Bhoja blends his power of poetic subtility and humour in delineating the character of Mantharā. As soon as Mantharā heard about the coronation of Rāma as Yuvarāja her anger knew no bounds.[121] Her crookedness of character is appropriately described by Vālmīki[122] and Bhoja.[123] In fact Mantharā plays the pivotal role in turning the history of Ayodhyā into a different direction.

The other female characters in the *Campūrāmāyaṇa* are but few and deserve only a slight mention.

Śabarī

The character of Śabarī very clearly and delicately drawn by the author. Śabarī belonged to the caste of Śabaras (hunters) and performed panances for meeting Rāma and obtaining his grace.[124]

Gautama's wife Ahalyā[125] and Atri's wife Anasūyā[126] are also briefly sketched in the *Campūrāmāyaṇa.*

Svayamprabhā in her wonderful cave is one of the marvellous creations of poet's imagination. The monkeys who moved to the south in search of Sītā met her in her underground golden cave. She possessed a great spiritual power by means of which she led them out of her cave.[127]

Other male characters in the Campūrāmāyaṇa

Hanūmān

The character of Hanūmān is one of the most lovable and admirable characters ever painted by the poets Bhoja and Lakṣmaṇasūri. His physical, heroic and devotional characteristics are depicted in the *Campūrāmāyaṇa.* He was the son of wind God Vāyu.[128] He was strong and powerful like a mountain. This supreme quality is rare in other characters. Sugrīva and Jambuvān could understand his strength, valour, wisdom and skill.[129] Even the ocean could surpass him in courage with his physical power.[130] He could assume horrible forms and manifest his powers according to the valour of his opponent. Hanūmān is said to be an 'Uttamadūta' or an excellent messenger. In the *Campūrāmāyaṇa*[131] and the *Bhaṭṭikāvya,*[132] he is depicted as endowed with extraordinary qualities. Hanūmān was a devoted and faithful servant of Rāma. He was greatly enraged when he saw Rāvaṇa talking with Sītā in Aśokavana.[133] As a devotee of Rāma, he will remain over supreme in the world. In fact, he saved Rāma from catastrophe in many difficult situations. He was equally devoted to Sītā. In his speech, Hanūmān appears as true, forceful and logical. He was a sly monkey who saved himself from the sharp eyes of the Rākṣasas while entering Laṇkā. He passed on unnoticed by all the Rākṣasas.[134] He did not fight Rākṣasas without proper calculation fearing that Sītā's life might be endangered by thoughless encounters with them.[135] He was expert in accomplishing his own objects. He spoke to Rāvaṇa very modestly and declared himself to be a messenger rather than an aggressor.[136] He was a peace-loving dūta and advised Rāvaṇa to give back Sītā and enjoy his prosperity.[137]

So, three characteristics of Hanūmāna viz. as powerful monkey, a messenger and devotee of Rāma are depicted in the *Campūrāmāyaṇa.*

Sugrīva

Sugrīva was a noble and powerful Monkey king who is described as ruler dwelling in the Ṛṣyamūka mountain.[138] He captured the throne of Kiṣkindhā by killing his arch enemy Vāli with the help of Rāma. Though he was installed on the throne by destroying Vāli he was not a traitor, because he suffered terribly in the hands of Vāli for a long period.[139] In the *Campūrāmāyaṇa* he is depicted as a real friend of Rāma. He advises his Vānara army to search Sītā who was kidnapped by Rāvaṇa. Of course for sometime he indulged in sexual pleasures and neglected his duty and the vow of assisting Rāma to salvage Sītā.[140] But this is quite natural for a person who was separated from his wife for a long time and was banished in the mountain. No person in the world is perfect. None is free from passions and normal weakness. Therefore, a temporary digression of Sugrīva from his commitment cannot be blamed.

He is described as a peace-loving and friendly king. He was a conscious and wise politician who declared Aṇgada as his successor.[141] Sugrīva was obeyed by the other Vānaras.[142] His tacit political moves are certainly praiseworthy.

Vāli

Vāli is one of the greatest heroes depicted in the Epic of Vālmīki. Vāli's nature is even more imperious than that of Sugrīva. He was even more attached to pleasures than his brother. Vāli was a mighty king and hero who could easily subdue Rāvaṇa, a great hero of world-wide fame. He was initially a good fellow. But his misunderstanding with Sugrīva led to a quarrel with his brother. When he was shot at and fatally wounded by Rāma, he rebuked Rāma, but he soon realised his mistake.[143]

Jambuvān

The character of Jambuvān is not clearly depicted in *Campūrāmāyaṇa* as in the Epic of Vālmīki. Jambuvān was wise and experienced in worldly life. On two critical occasions he saved his friends. When monkeys were unable to cross the ocean, it is he who advised Hanūmān to perform this apparently impossible task.[144] When Lakṣmaṇa swooned in the battle in Laṇkā it is he who suggested that Haṇūmān should bring the Sanjivanī herb to save the life of Lakṣmaṇa. Such wise person with the presence of mind are always necessary for kings to conduct royal affairs smoothly.[145]

Tārā

Of the female characters of the monkey group Tārā alone is fully delineated by the poet Bhoja. Tārā was the wife of Vāli. In the *Campūrāmāyaṇa,* the lamentation of Tārā after the sad death of her husband Vāli gives rise to the tragic sentiment. Vāli had the highest regard for her wisdom. She knew the powers of goodness of Rāma and was evidently consciousness of his divinity. She emerges in few passages as an impressive character, as the loving and devoted wife of Vāli. The poet Bhoja exhausts all his power of poetic ingenuity and insight while expressing the pathos of Tārā and also her deep love and devotion to her husband. Tārā was not vindictive of her enemies. She had a great respect for Rāma in spite of the fact that he was her husband's enemy.

Bhoja describes the lamenting scene of Tārā in the most effective manner which appeals deeply to the readers. This can be clearly realised from the following verses :

(a) *nāhaṁ suketutanayā na ca saptasālī*
Vāli na ca tribhuvanaprathitaprabhāvaḥ /
tārāsmi vajrahṛdayā viśikhairbhedyā
dhvanī kathaṁ bhavasi rāghava !
māmaviddhvā //[146]

(b) *kiṣitipatitanayānāṁ hanta garbheśvarānāṁ*
kimuniravadhi maugdhyaṃ śaurjabjjanmasidham /
mama hṛdi nirapāye vartamāne kapīndre
raghuvara ! yadmuṣmai tiṣṭhase cāpapāṇiḥ //[147]

Rākṣasa characters in the Campūrāmāyaṇa

Rāvaṇa

Authors of the *Campūrāmāyaṇa* describes Rāvaṇa in the same manner as Vālmīki. Among the Rākṣasa characters, Rāvaṇa naturally stands out as the supreme figure. Kuvera, Rāvaṇa, Kumbhakarṇa and Vibhīṣaṇa were the sons of sage Viśraśravas. Rāvaṇa got boons from Brahmā and Śiva and defeated Kuvera and took away his Puṣpaka vimāna and aspired to conquer and rule and oppress the entire universe.[148] In the Sundarakāṇḍa of the *Campūrāmāyaṇa*, Hanūmān gives a physical description of Rāvaṇa in the following manner :

(a) *āpāṭalādharapuṭāntavirājamāna*
daṁṣṭrāmahaḥ prasaraśāraśarīrakāntim /
saṁdhyāmbudāntaritamadhyasudhāmayūkha
rekhābhirāmamiva vāsavanīlaśilam //[149]

(b) *saṁgrāmakeliparighaṭṭanabhagnamagna*
digdantidantakṛtamudrabhujāntarālam
chāyātmanā pratitaraṇgavirājamāna
śītāṁśumaṇḍalasanāthamivāmburāśim //[150]

(c) *niḥśreyasapraṇayinīṁ padavīṁ niroddhuṁ*
trailokyapāpaparipākamivāttarupam /
sūrjendupāvakamahāṁsi tapobalena
jitvā yathecchamabhiṣiktamivāndhakāram //[151]

He is depicted as an extraordinary person who practised the most austere penance for ten thousand years in order to propitiate the God Brahmā.[152] He gained a boon from Brahmā on the strength of which he grew very tyrannical, and oppressed all beings. In the *Campūrāmāyaṇa*, he is described a mighty demon king who could order even the Fire God Agni to act his royal cook.[153] One occasion he tried to uplift the mountain.[154] But his fingers were curshed under its pressure. He prayed to Śiva to loudly to save him that the God gave him the name 'Rāvaṇa'.[155] Viṣṇu descended on earth for the destruction of this very demon. Rāvaṇa carried off Rāma's wife Sītā and urged her to become his wife.[156] Rāma assisted by the monkey warriors invaded Laṇkā, annihilated Rāvaṇa's forces and killed the demon. This is the story found about Rāvaṇa in the *Rāmāyaṇa* of Vālmīki.[157] The story is retold in the *Campūrāmāyaṇa*. We see a long achivalrous battle scene in the Yuddhakāṇḍa of the *Campūrāmāyaṇa*.[158] Rāvaṇa is the villain of the *Rāmāyaṇa* of Vālmīki and the *Campūrāmāyaṇa*. He is a fit match for Rāma as his arch opponent. He was a matchless warrior and conqueror in the universe, who was finally subdued by Rāma whose glory was enhanced by the task. Of course, Rāvaṇa was defeated by Vāli and Kārtavīrya also.[159] In the *Rāmāyaṇa*, Vālmīki says that Rāma and

Rāvaṇa have no equals but themselves just as the sky and sea have only themselves to be compared to themselves.[160] Rāvaṇa's character is described by Vālmīki in the most excellent manner. In the *Campūrāmāyaṇa*, and the *Śiśupālabadha* of Māgha also, his exploits are described in an equally appropriate manner.[161]

Vibhīṣaṇa

Although Vibhīṣaṇa was a Rākṣasa, his character is unlike that of a general demon. He was a wise and virguous demon. He again and again urged Rāvaṇa to restrain from mischievous activities.[162] He always tried to uphold righteousness. When Rāvaṇa became hostile to him, he sought shelter at Rāma's feet.[163] He accepted the empire of Laṇkā at Rāma's command and restored the reign of virtue there.[164] His wife Saramā was a friend of Sītā, who addressed Sītā as 'Sakhī Vaidehi'.[165] Vibhīṣaṇa was gentle, peace-loving and sincere in his love for Rāvaṇa. He argued in the interest of safeguarding the kingdom of Rāvaṇa and his life.

The character of Vibhīṣaṇa is depicted by Vālmīki,[166] and Bhaṭṭi the author of the *Bhaṭṭikāvya*[167] as an illustrious character. Some critics may blame Vibhisana for joining hands with Rāma and helping him in destroying the forces of Rāvaṇa, his own brother. But Vibhīṣaṇa never defended immoral, improper and atrocious activities, which merely ruin the healthy social order. This is a main reason for which he took the side of Rāma. The rash and thoughtless behaviour of Rāvaṇa also provoked him to help righteous Rāma in the battle.

Kumbhakarṇa

Kumbhakarṇa, another brother of Rāvaṇa, is a heroic and the sametime a comic character in the *Rāmāyaṇa* of Vālmīki. He earns a reputation as hero of tremendous physical power, a voracious eater, and a conspicuous figure who sleeps for months. Kumbhakarṇa was the real brother of Rāvaṇa who died for him. He was defeated and killed by Rāma after a great battle.[168]

Indrajit

Indrajit or Meghanāda, the son of Rāvaṇa possessed some divine weapons like Brahmāstra. With the help of Brahmāstra Indrajit captured the mighty Hanūmān.[169] He was a great warrior who defeated Indra and resisted the missiles of his enemies effectively.[170] Indrajit knew that the art of cleverly hiding himself by means of magic power. This was instrumental in fighting against his enemies.[171]

Akṣakumāra

In the *Campūrāmāyaṇa* simply describes Akṣakumāra was the son of Rāvaṇa. He came to fight against Hanūmān but was killed by him.[172]

Minor female characters

Among the female characters Tāḍakā, Śūrpaṇakhā and Mandodarī are described by the authors of the *Campūrāmāyaṇa.*

Tāḍakā

Tāḍakā was a fearful demoness. Her chivalrous and fearful activities are nicely described in the Bālakāṇḍa of the *Campūrāmāyaṇa.*[173]

Śūrpaṇakhā

·Śūrpaṇakhā appears in the *Campūrāmāyaṇa* in two distinct forms, viz. in the form of beautiful damsel and in her fearful form of an ugly Rākṣasī. Her amorous feelings are appropriately described by Bhoja in the following verse :

> *vṛṣasyantī vṛṣaskandhaṁ Rāghavaṁ Rāvaṇānujā /*
> *bhūyaḥ śūrpaṇakhā bheje śūrpakārātibādhitā //*[174]

She became jealous of Sītā who stood between her lovers and her desire.[175] She suddenly assumed the form of an angry and fierce demoness and was instantly punished by

Lakṣmaṇa.[176] Śūrpaṇakhā was responsible for the bloody strife between Rāma and Rāvaṇa. She persuaded Rāvaṇa to kidnap beautiful Sītā which ultimately caused debase for Rāvaṇa and his Laṇkā.[177]

Mandodarī

The name of Mandodarī appears in the Yuddhakāṇḍa of the *Campūrāmāyaṇa.* She was a devoted wife of Rāvaṇa. When her husband died in the battle of Laṇkā, she lamented for husband in a heart rending manner. Lakṣmaṇasūri describes the bewailing scene of Mandodarī in a graphic manner in the following verses :

(a) *janakaḥ svayaṁ danujavaṁśanāyako dayito jagattritayajaitraśāsanaḥ /*
tanayaḥ puraṁdarajayīti garvitā vidhinā hamevadhunāviḍambitā //[178]

(b) *ahaha nihatā laṁkā vālānalena hanūmataḥ*
paramavanijāpātivratyānalena bhavānapi /
sukhamahamihasīnā śokānaleapi yadīdṛśe
prabhavati na māṁ hantuṁ prāyaḥ as asa
citānalaḥ //[179]

Bird characters of the Campūrāmāyaṇa

Jaṭāyu

Jaṭāyu the king of vultures was a friend of Daśaratha.[180] He once saved the life of Daśaratha when he swirled through spacc towards the earth at the wrath of Saturn. He was a noble and illustrious character. He sacrificed the life in an attempt to save Sītā from the hands of Rāvaṇa.[181]

Sampāti

Sampāti was the brother of Jaṭāyu. In the Kiṣkindhākāṇḍa of the *Campūrāmāyaṇa* the author describes that when the monkey troops of Sugrīva were searching Sītā, he gave them some valuable information about her abduction by Rāvaṇa. He rendered an important service to the monkeys to locate the whereabout of Sītā and inform their king of the matter.[182]

Thus, Sampāti is another important character in the *Campūrāmāyaṇa* though he appears only for a brief while in the Campūkāvya.

(C) Delineation of Rasas in the Campūrāmāyaṇa

Sanskrit rhetoricians lay great emphasis on the delineation of Rasas or Sentiments in Sanskrit dramas and Mahākāvyas. They have recognised many Rasas.[183] Viśvanātha, author of the *Sāhityadarpaṇa* suggests that only one Rasa should be delineated as the principal Rasa (Aṅgīrasa) in a Mahākāvya and other Rasas should be delineated as subordinate or aṅgarasas to the principal one.[184] However, there is no discussion on the treatment of Rasas in a Campūkāvya for the probable reason that Campū is a much later variety of poetic composition. In spite of this difficulty we shall try to examine the sentiments of the *Campūrāmāyaṇa.* In the *Campūrāmāyaṇa* Bhoja and Lakṣmaṇasūri present different Rasas. Let us now critically examine the point below :

Vīrarasa

Bharata, the author of the *Nātyaśāstra* opines that the basic mood of vīrarása or heroic sentiment is 'Utsāha' or 'Enthusiasm'.[185] According to him vīrarasa can be classified into three types viz. Dānavīra, Yuddhavīra and Dharmavīra.[186] Later poeticians like Viśvanātha says that 'Dayāvīra' is the another type of heroic sentiment.[187] A 'Dayāvīra' is one who shows extravagance in showing charity or compassion.

Now coming to the *Campūrāmāyaṇa* we find that Rāma the hero of the Epic *Rāmāyaṇa* and the *Campūrāmāyaṇa* does not belong to the classes of Dharmavīra and Dānavira. He is a perfect Yuddhavīra. He vanquished his enemies in battles. The principal sentiment or Aṅgīrasa of *Campūrāmāyaṇa* is vira as evidenced by the activities of

Rāma and other characters. If we now critically examine some passages of the *Campūrāmāyaṇa*, we notice that the heroic sentiment is appropriately delineated in them. Rāma fights with Rākṣasas most valiantly and kills them with his missiles. He succeeds in extirpating Rāvaṇa; the most dreaded demon of the three worlds. Rāma decended to the mortal world in order to destory demons who were arch enemies of honest people or the sacrificial cult. Thus, Rāma performs a noble service to peace-loving human beings. The Vīrarasa in the *Campūrāmāyaṇa* is confined primarily in the battle field. But sometimes it is delineated elsewhere also. This is clear for the scene of breaking Haradhanu by Rāma. Rāma displays a extraordinary valour throughout the *Campūrāmāyaṇa*. It is not possible for us to quote all the relevant passages of the *Campūrāmāyaṇa* containing Vīrarasa. We present below a physical speciman of Vīrarasa in order to substantiate over statement that *Campūrāmāyaṇa* is a primarily a Kāvya which contain Vīra is the principal sentiment :

Rāme bāhubalaṁ vivṛṇvati dhanuryajñe guṇāropaṇaṁ
mā bhūtkevalamātmanā tilakite vaśeapi vaikartane /
ākṛṣṭaṁ nitarāṁ tadeva na paraṁ sītāmanoapi drutaṁ
bhaṅgastasya na kevalaṁ kṣitibhujāṁ doḥstambhadam-bhasya ca //[188]

Śṛṅgārarasa

Sanskrit alaṁkārikas lays great stress on the delineation of Śṛṅgārarasa or Erotic sentiment in a Kāvya composition. Viśvanātha, the author of the *Sāhityadarpaṇa* says that the principal sentiment in a Kāvya must be either Śṛṅgāra or Vīra.[189] According to the Sanskrit poeticians Rati (love) is the permanent mood or Sthāyībhāva of Śṛṅgārarasa.[190]

Śṛṅgārarasa is broadly divided into two types viz. Sambhoga Śṛṅgāra and Vipralambha Śṛṅgāra.[191] Vipralambha is further divided into four types by Viśvanātha. They are (i) Purvarāga Vipralambha, (ii) Māna Vipralambha (iii) Pravāsa Vipralambha and (iv) Karuṇa Vipralambha.[192]

In the case of pathetic love-in-separation or 'Karuṇa

Vipralambha' Hemacandra says 'saṇgatayoreva anyatravyāpādekaruṇaḥ'[193] and cites Aja's lamentations over Indumatī's loss as its instance.[194] Physical pleasure of lovers constitutes the essence of 'Sambhoga Śṛṇgāra', while the 'Vipralambha' is characterised by the separation of lovers resulting in their unbearable lovelorn condition.

'Vibhāva' is classified by the poeticians into Ālambana Vibhāva' and 'Uddīpana Vibhāva'. While the hero and heroine are known as Ālambana Vibhāva, the phenomena exciting love are called Uddīpana Vibhāvas.[195]

In the *Campūrāmāyaṇa* some of the Uddīpana Vibhāvas which help in arousing the amorous sentiment are nicely presented by the authors. Thus in the Araṇyakāṇḍa of the *Campūrāmāyaṇa* there is an excellent description of the (false) beauty of the elusive demoness Śūrpaṇakhā. Wc quote the relevant passage in support of our view :

vṛṣasyantī vṛṣaskandhaṁ rāghavaṁ rāvaṇānujā /
bhūyaḥ śūrpaṇakhā bheje śūrpakārātibādhitā //[196]

This description is an appropriate case of Uddīpana Vibhāva or the Amorous sentiment in the *Campūrāmāyaṇa.* The poet vividly describes the Hemanta season in the Araṇyakāṇḍa while drawing a picture of the Pañcavaṭī āśrama. This description is also an appropriate medium for arousing the amorous feeling.[197] Bhoja delineates an amorous scene in the Araṇyakāṇḍa where Śūrpaṇakhā, the sister of Rāvaṇa is overpowered with amorous feelings at the sight of uncommon beauty of Rāma. She remarks with a overwhelming feeling of love for Rāma in the following way :

lāvaṇyambunidheramuṣya dayitāmenamivaranaṁ janaṁ
kasmānnāsṛjadasmadanvayagurorutpattibhūḥ
padmabhūḥ /
āstāṁ tāvadaraṇyavāsarasike ha kaṣṭamasminnimāṁ
kāntiṁ kānanacandrikāsamadaśāṁ kiṁ nirmame
nirmame //[198]

Apart from this we hardly find any erotic scene in the *Campūrāmāyaṇa.* In the *Rāmāyaṇa* of Vālmiki, Rāvaṇa loses his patience at the sight of the exquisite beauty of Sītā.[199] But Bhojarāja avoids any reference to Sītā's uncommon beauty or Rāvaṇa's love for her. The probable reason is that Sītā is adored as a goddess and Bhoja thinks that any description of a love scene centering Sītā is improper. Bhoja presents a few verses in the Araṇyakāṇḍa which are full of Karuṇa Vipralambha Śṛṅgāra generated by Rāma's loss of his beloved wife. We quote these verses below in order to show how effectively the author presents Karuṇa Vipralambha :

(a) *tvadabhilaṣita pūtyā vañcitaḥ pañcavaṭyā*
macaramacaramoahaṁ mohabhājāṁ prajānām /
tadiha saralabudhe ! naisa roṣasya kālaḥ Sumukhi!
mama mukhaṁ kiṁ sodhasītāviyogam //[200]

(b) *yadyasti kautukamapūrvamṛge mṛgākṣi /*
cāndraṁ harami hariṇaṁ mama sannidhehi //
yāvanna muñcasi mayā hṛtamenamenaṁ
tāvaddadhātu tava vaktratulāṁ mṛgāṇkaḥ //[201]

The 'Karuṇa Vipralambha' is also found in the description of the love lorn condition of Sītā in the Araṇyakāṇḍa of the *Campūrāmāyaṇa* after she was separated from Rāma by the wicked demon king Rāvaṇa.[202]

Raudrarasa

According to Bharata's *Nāṭyaśāstra*, the sthāyībhāva or peṛmanent mood of the Raudra rasa is Krodha or anger. This particular sentiment is characterised by the frowning of eyes and other angry movements of the body etc. of the hero. The 'Ālambana Vibhāva' of the Raudra Rasa is the person who has done the wrong to the hero or any other person. His offensive deed, arrogant behaviour, insolence etc. awaken this sentiment and act as the Uddīpana Vibhāva of the sentiment.[203]

Reddened eyes, smattering teeth, heated talk, handling of weapons, offering a duel fight are the characteristics of this sentiment.[204]

In the *Campūrāmāyaṇa* the Raudra Rasa is delivered

through the character of Bharata, when Bharata came to learn about the banishment of Rāma he felt suddenly agitated. He started to rebuke his mother Kaikeyī for her mischievious behaviour.[205]

The author also describes an angry scene where Rāvaṇa being obstracted by Jaṭāyu was infuriated with him. This scene naturally contains Raudra Rasa.[206]

Bhayānaka Rasa

Sanskrit poeticians describes that fear is the permanent mood or sthāyībhāva of Bhayānaka Rasa. The essential characteristics of this particular rasa are described by Bharata and his followers. According to Bharata peculiar sounds and appearances etc. are the causes of Bhayānakarasa.[207] Viśvanātha, the author of the *Sāhityadarpaṇa* corroborates the view expressed by Bharata on essential characteristics of the Bhayānaka Rasa.[208]

In the *Campūrāmāyaṇa* Bhoja presents a terror striking scene in the angry movements of Tāḍakā which is found in the following verse of the work :

hṛtvādreḥ śikharāṇi tāni paritaḥ kṣptvā hasitvā krudhā
kṛtvā hastavibhaṭṭanaṁ tata itaḥ sthitvā
naṭitvā muhuḥ /
siktvā kṣāmasṛjā srajāntrakṛtayā baddhvā
kacānkhecarān
dagdhvāgneḥ sadṛśā dṛśā niśicarā rundhanti
randhraṁ divaḥ //[209]

In this verse poet stresses that the demoness Tāḍakā frequently pulled dunesand rocks of the mountain. She appeared like a mass radiant feme. It is a appropriate scene of Bhayānaka Rasa.

Adbhuta Rasa

According to Bharata the mental state of surprise or Vismaya is the permanent mood or Sthāyībhāva of Adbhūtarasa. Bharata says that wonderful object or an unexpected incident or performance of the impossible like the feasts of jugglers became the Ālambana Vibhāva of the Adbhūtarasa.[210] He says that this sentiment should be expressed by a character with the help of various unusual signs like the expansion of the eyes and looking at an object intently and appearance horripilation of the body, perspiration etc. which are the vyabhicārībhāvas of Adbhūtarasa.[211]

Coming to the *Campūrāmāyaṇa* we find that Rāma creates wonder through his extraordinary exploits. Though all the essential characteristics of Adbhūtarasa as discussed by Bharata are not strictly applicable to the activities of Rāma, it is a fact some of his extraordinary exploits definitely create vismaya in the minds of the readers. Thus, we see in the Bālakāṇḍa that Rāma throws out the demon Mārīca into the middle of the ocean with the help of his missile.

māricanīcamatirāhavamāracayya
kṣiptaḥ kṣanena raghunāyakasāyakena /
madhyepayonidhi bhayena nimagna mūrtirveṣaṁ
pupuṣa jalamānuṣanirviśeṣam //[212]

The wonderman Rāma performs another unusual fit when he breaks the mighty bow of Śiva at ease. The author describes his fit as

navaḥ kaṭhinakarṣaṇatruṭitacāpajanmā kṣaṇā
ddiśāṃ dviradadhīṇkṛtaḥ kṛtaharitpatisvāgataḥ /
jagadbhramaṇakautukoccalitarāmakīrtyaṅganā
prayāṇapaṭhadhvaniṁ prathayati sma
tāradhvaniḥ //[213]

Karuṇarasa

Bharata, the author of the *Nāṭyaśāstra* says that the death of relatives, the affiliation caused by a curse imprisonment, loss of property etc. are the causes of the emergence of Karuṇarasa or the tragic sentiment. He says that a character should express the tragic sentiment by shedding tears, having sigh, loss of memory and such other external signs are Anubhāvas.[214] Sorrow, fatigue, inxiety, infatuation, fear etc. are the vyabhicārībhāvas of Karuṇarasa.[215]

In the *Campūrāmāyaṇa* Bhoja displays great ability in delineating this sentiment particularly in the Kiṣkindhākāṇḍa at least three heart rending poems. Tārā's lamentation for her husband Vāli are nicely described in these poems.

(a) *avaṁvidhe priyatameapyanapetajīvāṁ.*
mām rākṣasīti raghupuṇgava ! sādhu budhvā /
bāṇaṁ vimuñca mayi samprati taṭakāre !
śreyo bhaveddayitasaṇgamakāriṇaste //[216]

(b) *sādhāraṇī kṣitibhujāṁ mṛgayeti pūrva*
muktā tvayaiva janasaṁsadisatyavādin /
śākhāmṛgīṁ tadiha māraya māṁ śāṁ śareṇa
ko nāma rāma ! mṛgayurdayate mṛgīṇām //[217]

(c) *nāhaṁ suketutanayā na ca saptaśālī*
Vāli na ca tribhuvanaprathitaprabhāvaḥ /
tārāsmi vajrahṛdayā viśikhairbhedyā
dhavnī kathaṁ bhavasi rāghava !
māmaviddhvā //[218]

It reminds us of a passage of the *Kumārasambhava* where the poet describes the lamentation of Rati after the death of her beloved Madana (cupid) by the third eye of Lord Śiva is also a clear case of Karuṇarasa.[219]

Bībhatsarasa

Sanskrit poeticians describes that 'jugupsā' or abhorance is the permanent mood or sthāyībhāva of Bībhatsarasa.[220] Bībhatsarasa generally aroused by filthy description, obscence sights and talks, dislike turning of face etc.[221]

The author of *Campūrāmāyaṇa* delineates Bībhatsarasa or the sentiment of abhorance in the few passages. This sentiment is found in the battle-fields were bodies were lying strewn on the earth. The blood, injuries on the body of Rāvaṇa in the battle-field are the objects which generates this sentiment.

daśānanaśarakṣatikṣaradasṛgjarībudbuda
staraṇgitamahendrakaṅkaṭasahasracakṣupathaḥ /

raṇe raghukulodbhavaḥ kṣaṇamamāni vaimānikai
yathā daśasatekṣaṇo balaruṣā kaṣāyekṣaṇaḥ //[222]

(D) Alaṁkāras in the Campūrāmāyaṇa

Sanskrit poets lay great emphasis on alaṁkāras or figure of speech in their poetical composition since the age of Vālmīki. The word 'alaṁkāra' means 'the embellisher of poetry. According to Sanskrit rhetoricians there are two broad groups of Alaṁkāras viz. Śabdālaṁkāras and Arthālaṁkāras or figure of word and figures of sense, while Anuprāsa and Yamaka belong to the first category, Upamā, Rūpaka, Dṛṣṭānta etc. are recognised as figure of sense. According to Sanskrit poets they are more important embellishers than Śabdālaṁkāras which decorate the surface of a poem but does not evoke much aesthetic interest of readers.

Bhojarāja employs a wide variety of alaṁkāras in his *Campūrāmāyaṇa* in order to make his literary work a truely decorative one.

Figures of Words

Bhoja uses Anuprāsa equally in prose and poetry like many other Sanskrit poets.

(a) Anuprāsa or alliteration

Anuprāsa or alliteration is a typc of Śabdālaṁkāra in which same letters are repeated in different ways.[223] This is an old device in Sanskrit poetical literature which generates auditary pleasure to readers. Sanskrit rhetoricians have classified Anuprāsa into different groups like Chekānuprāsa. Vṛttyānuprāsa, and Lāṭānuprāsa. Like many other Sanskrit poets Bhoja also employs this figure of words in his *Campūrāmāyaṇa* in a reasonable manner.

(a) Chekānuprāsa

Chekānuprāsa means that particular variety of Anuprāsa

or alliteration in which consonants belonging to different categories are repeated only once. The author of the *Sāhityadarpaṇa* defines Chekānuprāsa as follows :

'cheko vyañjanasaṇghasya sakṛtsāmyam anekadhā'[224]

He quotes a poem viz.

ādyā vakulagandhānandhīkurvan pade pade bhramarān /
ayameti mandaṁ mandaṁ kāverīvāripāvanaḥ pavanaḥ //[225]

In the above poem conjunct consonants in 'gandhān andhī' non-conjunct consonants 'kāverīvāri' and also consonants 'pāvanaḥ and pavanaḥ' are repeated only once. Bhoja, in the course of narrating the Rāma story presents this Alaṁkāra in the following verse of the Kiṣkindhākāṇḍa :

'ayaṁ kālaḥ kālapramathanagalābairabhinavai
rahaṁyūnāṁ yūnāmapaharati dhairyaṁ jaladharaiḥ /
smarādhārā dhārā paricitajaḍā vānti sahasā
nabhasvantaḥ svantaḥ kathamiva viyogaḥ pariṇamet //[226]

In the above poem there is a repetition of the consonants 'kāla kāla and yunā yunā dhiaryam' etc.

(b) Vṛttyanuprāsa

The author of the *Sāhityadarpaṇa* defines Vṛttyānuprāsa as follows :

'anekasyaikadhā sāmyamsakṛdvāpyanekadhā /
ekasya sakṛdyeṣa vṛttyānuprāsa ucyate //[227]

According to this definition when several consonants are repeated in the same manner or otherwise it is a case of Vṛttyānuprāsa.

Bhoja uses Vṛttyānuprāsa in the verse :
vācaṁ niśamya bhagavān sa tu nāradasya
prācetasaḥ pravacasāṁ prathamaḥ kavīnām /
mādhyandināya niyamāya maharṣisevyāṁ
puṇyamavāpa tamasāṁ tamasāṁ nihantrīm //[228]

in which there is a repetition of the word 'tamasāṁ'. Such a repitition of 'ta', 'ma' and 'sa' gives rise two Vṛttyānuprāsa in literature.

(c) Lāṭānuprāsa

Lāṭānuprāsa is a type of alliteration in which words identical in form but differing in meaning are presented in succession. Viśvanātha defines Lāṭānuprāsa as follows :

'śabdārthayaḥ paunaruktyaṁ bhede
lāṭparyamātrataḥ /[229]

Bhoja presents this Alaṁkāra in the following verse of the Bālakāṇḍa of the *Campūrāmāyaṇa.*

'paryāptabhāgyāya bhavānmuṣmai kuryātsaparyāṁ
kuśikātmajāya /
niryātudhānaṁ vasudhāṁ vidhātuṁ niryātuṁ rāmaḥ
saha Lakṣmaṇena //[230]

In the above poem the expression 'niryātu' found in 'niryātudhānam' and 'niryātum' are identical in appearance. But they give different meanings. In the first word viz. 'niryātudhānam' 'niryātu' is a part of compound word. The second 'niryātu' is also a part of an infinitive expression 'niryātum'. Hence, there is a clear case of Lāṭānuprāsa in the above verse.

(i) Upamā (Simile)

Upamā or simile is a common Arthālaṁkāra of Sanskrit poets in which two things are compared in such a manner as to create the poetic delight in the minds of the readers. We find a typical example of Upamā in the very beginning of the *Campūrāmāyaṇa.* Bhoja compares his *Campūrāmāyaṇa* which is a mixed composition of elegant prose and melodious verses to a musical orchastra.[231] That the poet is found of this very popular Alaṁkāra can be understood from the following poem also viz.

vāṇīvilāsamaparatra kṛtopalambha
mmbhojabhūrasahamāna ivāvirāsīt /

ābhāti yatkṛtiranekavidhaprapañca
vyājndrajālavidhisādhakapicchikeva //[232]

of which he creates innumerable unreal objects. Brahmā, the creator also creates a beautiful universe with all its diversities by means of his divine power. Thus, the poem contains an excellent Upamā (simile).

There are different kinds of Upamā in Alaṁkāra texts. One striking variety of Upamā is Ārthī Upamā in which the common quality of the Upamāna and the Upameya is not expressed with the help of 'iva' etc.[233] But the sense 'iva' and such other words remains implied. The author of the *Sāhityadarpaṇa* presents a typical illustration of Ārthī Upamā by citing the following verse :

'*saurabhammbhoruhavanmukhasya kumbhavivastanau pīnau /*
hṛdayaṁ madayati vadanaṁ tava śaradinduryathā bāle //'[234]

Bhojarāja also gives a verse viz.

'*indranīlācalodañcaccandrikādhavalasmitaḥ /*
vācamūce sudhādhāraṁ madhurāṁ madhusūdanaḥ //[235]

in which we find a similar technic. In the first line of the verse there is an expression viz. (candrikā iva dhavala) remains implied. We find some more verses and passages in the *Campūrāmāyaṇa* where this particular Alaṁkāra receives a due importance. Let us give an idea of this Alaṁkāra by citing some appropriate passages from the *Campūrāmāyaṇa* :

'*tatkṣaṇamaśanihata iva parvataḥ sarvataḥ parītadavadahana iva vanaspatiḥ divaspatipada-bhraṁśavidhura iva Nahuṣaḥ papāta niḥsaṁjñaḥ paṅktirathaḥ /*'[236]

In the above passages Bhojarāja proves his real worth by presenting excellent Upamā, where the poet compares the mental state of king Daśaratha to a steady mountain (aśanihata iva parvataḥ) and compares trees surrounded by jungle fire (davadahana iva vanaspatiḥ) and also to sorrowful Nahuṣa who had fallen from heaven (vidhura iva Nahuṣaḥ). Hence, these descriptions of Daśaratha are a clear examples of Upamā alaṁkāra.

Like Bhojarāja Lakṣmaṇasūri also employs Upamā-alaṁkāra in his Yuddhakāṇḍa. We notice the existence of this particular figure in a number of passages in the Yuddhakāṇḍa of the *Campūrāmāyaṇa*. Let us cite a poem to substanciate our view :

āsāradhārāṁ vikirañśarāṇāmāsvāsayanmāna-
samāśarāṇam /
vīro harīnsaṁyati meghanādo vivyādha haṁsāniva
meghanādaḥ //[237]

In the above poem there is an expression 'meghanādo meghanādaḥ' in which the sense of 'iva' (Meghanādo iva meghanādaḥ) remains implied. Here the first word 'meghanādo' means 'rain' and the second 'meghanādaḥ' means 'son of Rāvaṇa'. Similarly, poet compares 'haṁsan (swan) iva harīn (monkey). So, it is a clear instance of Ārthī upamā in the above verse.

(ii) Rūpaka (Metaphore)

Rūpaka or Metaphore is another popular figure in which the Upamāna and Upameya are identified by the speaker. Viśvanātha, the author of the *Sāhityadarpaṇa* defines Rūpaka as 'Rūpakaṁ rupitāropād viṣaye nirapahnave'.[238]

According to him though there is an identification between two objects in the Rūpaka the Upameya or the object compared does not lose of its identity in the figure (viṣayenirapahnave).

Bhoja employs Rūpaka Alaṁkāra in the following poem of the *Campūrāmāyaṇa* :

yadbāhurāhurasanāyitaśastradhārā
dikpālakīrtimayacandramasaṁ grasanti /
yadvairiṇāṁ raṇamukhe śaraṇpradāyī
naivāsti kaścidamumantakamanareṇa //[239]

In the above poem though the two objects 'bāhu' and 'rāhu' and 'kīrtimayacandrasami' seems to be identical but actually they bears quite different meanings and does not lose their identity. Commentator Rāmacandra Budhendra adequately explains this figure. The commentator says that 'bāhurāhu ityatra kīrtimayacandrasami tyatra rūpakālaṁkāraḥ'.[240]

(iii) Ekāvalī (Neclace)

Ekāvalī is an excellent figure of sense like Upamā. Viśvanātha defines Ekāvalī in the following way :

pūrvaṁ pūrvaṁ prati viśeṣaṇatvena paraṁ param /
sthāpyateapohyate vā cetsyāttaikavali dvidhā //[241]

It means that if each succeeding thing which is affirmed or denied is an attribute of each preceeding thing, there is Ekavali. One striking illustration of Ekavali Alaṁkara which is frequently quoted in the following poem of the *Bhaṭṭikāvya* :

'na tajjalaṁ yanna sucārupaṇkajaṁ na paṇkajaṁ
tadyadlīnaṣaṭpadam /
na ṣaṭpadoasu na juguñja yaḥ kalaṁ na guñjitaṁ
tanna jahāra yanmanaḥ //[242]

Bhoja presents this figure in the following poem of the Bālakāṇḍa of his Campū text.

'uccairgatirjagati sidhayati dharmataśce
tasya pramā ca vacanaiḥ kṛtaketariścet /
teṣāṁ prakāśanadaśā ca mahīsuraiśce
ttānntareṇa nipatet kvanu matpraṇāmaḥ //[243]

In this poem the word 'pramā' etc. act as the attributes of the preceeding word 'dharma' etc. and hence there is a clear case of Ekāvalī Alaṁkāra. Rāmacandra Budhendra explains the figure adequately as :

'atrottarottarasya purvaṁ purvaṁ prati viśeṣaṇāt-
vādekava lyalaṁkāra.'[244]

(iv) Utprekṣā (poetical fancy)

Utprekṣā or poetical fancy is another favourite Alaṁkāra of Sanskrit poets. The very expression poetical fancy conveys the idea that the poet imagines a particular thing as something else in this figure, which evokes the aesthetic pleasure of the readers. The author of the *Sāhityadarpaṇa* adequately defines this figure as :

'bhavetsambhāvanotprekṣā prakṛtasya parātmanā'[245]

Bhoja has successfully employed this Alaṁkāra in his *Campūrāmāyaṇa.* In this connection, we can refer to the verse :

'apahṛtavibudhārtervāmanasyājamūrte
rakhilabhuvanabhikṣoāśramanokahānām /
tatiriyamatinīlā vyāptadigvyomasīmā
svayamapi parimātuṁ lokamabhyaudyateva /[246]

in the Bālakāṇḍa of his work. In the above verse he describes the trees luxuriantly growing in the hermitage of Vāmana (the Dwarf incarnation of Viṣṇu). He says in the verse that the trees have expanded their branches in all direction as if with a desire to measure the vast expanse of the universe.

Now, trees are trees. They have grown and expanded under the law of nature. From a practical point of view it is impossible on the part of the trees to make an extraordinary attempt to expand themselves with an intention to measure the universe. But a poet is a poet. He superimposes a new idea on a natural phenomenon in order to create aesthetic delight in our minds. The entire description is a fit of the poet's extraordinary imagination.

In the similar manner poet Bhoja describes in the following verse of Ayodhyākāṇḍa.

'nṛpasukhavimukhena svena kāntena sākaṁ
duhitari vidhipākātkānanāya vrajantyām /
akuśalamiti matvā nūnamahnāya dhātrī
parijanamukhabāṣpaṁ pāṁsubhiḥ paryahārṣīt //[247]

that the earth rubs of the tears from her eyes with the help of dust realising that her tears may be an ominous sign for Rāma and Sītā in days of their distress. In fact, there was a dust storm at the time of Rāma entering into the forests. This reality has been presented otherwise by the poet with the help of his fancy. The figure occurs in the following prose passage also in the *Campūrāmāyaṇa* :

> *'athakadācidupacīyamānamanobhavavaibhavaḥ 'pākakapiśa' kalamamañjarīpuñjapinjrībhūta ....kādambakadambasyā pyanatithipriyaṁ ... nīhārātaṅkaśaṅkayā hṛdayakamalamiva gopāyantamaśrāntadantavīṇāvyāpāravepamānādhara-puṭatayā śītikāpiśācikānirharaṇāya nipuṇaṁ ...'*[248]

The indeclinable 'iva' used in the passage represents the Utprekṣā Alaṁkāra and it should not be confused with Upamā.

Bhojarāja proves his real worth by presenting excellent visual images in the above passages.

Lakṣmaṇasūri also displays his ability in successfully employing the figure Utprekṣā. Thus, in the following poem viz.

> *'alakṣitamahīdharagrahaṇamasphuṭakṣepaṇaṁ*
> *vicitraghaṭṭnaṁ tato virācito nalenāmunā /*
> *abodhi hariyūthapairadhipayodhi seturmahān*
> *bhuvobhuja ivā bhayaṁnijatanūbhuvo lambhayan //*[249]

Lakṣmaṇasūri's fancies the stone bridge built by Rāma's army in the ocean as an extended hand of the Earth. It instantly reminds us a passage the Allāhābad Stone Pillar Inscription of Samudragupta viz.

> *'Mahārājādhirāja śrīsamudraguptasya sarvapṛthi-vīvijayajanitodaya vyāpta nikhilāvanitālaṁ kīrtimita stridaśapatibhavana gamanāvāpta lalitasukha vicaraṇāmācakṣāṇahavabhuvau bāhuraya-mucchritaḥ stambhaḥ yasya'.*[250]

(v) Dṛṣṭānta (Exemplification)

Dṛṣṭānta or Exemplification is another common Alaṁkāra found in Sanskrit poetry. In this particular kind of Alaṁkāra there is a type (Bimba) and the prototype (Pratibimba) relationship between two objects. They are presented in the poem with the help of two distinct sentences. Viśvanātha defines this figure as :

> *'dṛṣṭāntastu sadharmasya vastunaḥ pratibimbanam*
> *sadharmasyeti prativastūpamāvyavacchedaḥ'.*[251]

Now coming to the *Campūrāmāyaṇa*, we find that Bhoja employs this figure in verse viz.

> *'Vālmīkigītaraghupuṁgavakīrtileśai*
> *stṛptiṁ karomi kathamapyadhunā budhānām /*
> *gaṅgājalairbhubi bhagīrathayatnalabdhaiḥ*
> *kiṁ tarpaṇaṁ na vidadhāti naraḥ pitṛṇām //*[252]

In the above verse the poet expresses his inability to satisfy his readers by reciting the Rāma story because it has been already presented by Vālmīki in a delighting manner. But he has made a humble attempt to sing the Rāma story. In this connection, Bhoja states that though the river Gaṇgā was flown to the Earth by Bhagīratha to liberate his deceased forefathers with the help of its holy water which was a great task of the prince, still common people also perform 'tarpaṇa' with the water of the Gaṇgā though they deserve little credit for that. A critical examination of the poem shows that there is a type and prototype relationship between the activities of Vālmīki and Bhagīratha on the one hand, and the activities of Bhoja and the common people on the other.

(vi) Nidarśanā (Illustration)

In Nidarśanā Alaṁkāra also there is a type and prototype relationship between a pair of objects. The relationship between the two objects may be ordinarily possible or impossible in this world. But still the poet tries to bring them together through his imagination. The author of the *Sāhityadarpaṇa* defines this Alaṁkāras as follows :

'sambhavanvastusambandhoasambhavanvapi kutracit /
yatra bimbānubimbatvaṁ bodhayetsā nidarśanā //[253]

In the *Campūrāmāyaṇa* the author presents this Alaṁkāra in the following verse :

'anujaracitapaṃāgārahṛdyāsu mādya
tparabhṛtagalañcatpañcamairñcitasu /
janakaduhitṛyogājjātasāketasaukhya
ściramaramata rāmaścitrakūṭasthalīṣu //[254]

In this verse the poet states that Rāma who was living in his forest-hut with Sītā in Citrakūṭa, enjoyed the happiness of living in Ayodhyā. Though, royal comforts cannot be enjoyed in a petty hut in the jungle, the poet imagines it as such. Hence, there is a clear case of Nidarśanā Alaṁkāra in the poem. Again in a poem of the Sundarakāṇḍa viz.

'tatra tatpatrasaṁchannagātraḥ putro nabhasvataḥ /
nyagrodhadalasaṁlīnajanardanadaśāṁ dadhau //[255]

Bhoja describes Hanūmān hiding among the green leaves of a Siṁśapā tree (Dalbergia latifalia) as Lord Viṣṇu dwelling among the leaves of a Vaṭavṛkṣa (Ficus Bengalensis). In this description though there is no direct relationship between the activities of Hanūmān and Viṣṇu, the poet tries to bring them together through Nidarśanā. We notice the presence of this Alaṁkāra in the following verse also of the Sundarakāṇḍa :

'ānākalokaparikīrtitasaccaritra
matroparudhya raghuvaṁśapateḥ kalatram /
vaitānavedijanitaṁ pavamānbandhuṁ
vastreṇa bandhumavinīta ! kathaṁ yatethāḥ //[256]

where the poet angrily remarks that Rāvaṇa by making Sītā a captive in Laṇkā has tied a mass of flame in a wrapper. This poem reminds us of a poetical passage of Kālidāsa's *Abhijñanaśākuntalam.* viz.

idaṁ kilavyājamanoharaṁ vapustapaḥkṣamaḥ
sādhayituṁ ya icchati /
dhruvaṁ sa nīlotpala patradhārayā śamī-latāṁ
chettumṛsivyavasyati' //[257]

Incidentally we remember a passage of the *Rāmāyaṇa* of Vālmīki where Sītā angrily remarks before Rāvaṇa as follows :

'Rāghavasya priyāṁ bhāryāṁ yasatvamicchasi rākṣasa /
kṣudhitasya sa siṁhasya mṛgaśatrotrasvinaḥ /
āśīviṣayasya vadanāddaṁstrāmādātumicchasi //
mandaraṁ parvataśresṭhaṁ pāṇinā hartumicchasi /
kālakūṭaṁ viṣaṁ pītvā svastimāngantumicchasi //
akṣi sucyā prasṛjasi jīhvayā lehi ca kṣuraṁ /
rāghavasya priyāṁ bhāryaṁ bhāryāmadhigantum tvamicchasi //
avasajjya śilāṁ kaṇṭhe samudraṁ tartumicchasi /
sūryacandramasau cobhau pāṇibhyāṁ hartumicchasi //
yo rāmasya priyāṁ bhāryāṁ pradharṣayitumicchasi /
agniṁ prajvalitaṁ dṛṣṭvā vastreṇāhartumicchasi' /[258]

(vii) Atiśayokti (Hyperbole)

Atiśayokti or Hyperbole is another important figure in Sanskrit literature. The essential characteristics of this figure is that in it, the Upameya or the object compared is completely concealed. Viśvanātha defines it as :

'sidhatveadhyavasāyasyātiśayortirnigadyate /'

Now in the *Campūrāmāyaṇa* of Bhoja we find that this figure has been employed by the poet in the Bālakāṇḍa of his work. In this connection we can refer to the following verses of the Bālakāṇḍa.

(a) *Prahlādasya vyasanamamitaṁ daityavargasya dambhaṁ*
stambhaṁ vakṣaḥsthalamapi riporyogapadyena bhettum /
baddhaśradhaṁ puruṣavapuṣā miśrite viśvadṛṣṭe
daṁṣṭrārocirviśadabhuvane raṁhasā siṁhaveṣe //[259]

(b) *'astipraśastavibhavairvibudhairlaṅghyā*
laṇketi nāma rajanīcararājadhānī /
māṇikyamandirabhuvāṁ mahasāṁ prarohai
stejastrayāya dinadīpadaśā diśantī //[260]

The commentator Rāmacandra Budhendra had

adequately explained this figure continued by the above poems.[261] While explaining the second verse, the commentator says that

'tejastraye dinadīpadaśāasambandheapi tatsambandhavarṇanādatiśayoktiralaṁkāraḥ'.[262]

Lakṣmaṇasūri also presents this Alaṁkāra adequately in several poems in the Yuddhakāṇḍa. We give below an examples of the employment of this figure by the poet :

(a) *ākarṇya kiṁnaramukhādanadhe svavaṁśe*
kākutsthadāharanopagataṁ kalaṇkam /
hāheti mīlitadṛśaḥ karayoryugaṁ ta
daṣṭau śrutīrapi kathaṁ pidadhātu dhātuḥ //[263]

in which the Upameya or the object compared is completely concealed. The commentator Rāmacandra Budhendra while explaining the verse says

'Brahmāatmanaḥ sarvathā viśudhe vaṁśe tvatkṛtaṁ sūryakulāvataṁsaśrīrāmabhāryāpaharaṇarupaṁ kalaṁkaṁ kinnaragaṇamukhādākarya .... svakarṇān pidhātumichamicchānnapi karadvayenāṣṭau karṇān kathaṁ pidadhātvityarthaḥ.' atra Brahmaṇastvādṛśavyavahārāsambandheapi tatsambandhokteratiśayoktiḥ /'[264]

(viii) Pariṇāma (Communication)

Pariṇāma or communication is a poetic figure which is casually presented by sanskrit writers. We find the following definition of *Sāhityadarpaṇa* as follows :

'viṣayātmatayāropye prakṛtārthopayogini /
pariṇāmo bhavettulyālulyādhikaraṇo dvidhā //[265]

He clearifies the meaning of the definition adequately in the following way :

'āropyamāṇasyāropaviṣayātmatayā parinamātpariṇāmaḥ' /[266]

A critical examination of the defination of Viśvanātha

shows that in Pariṇāma two distinct object are described, while one of them is superimposed upon the other, and this serves a useful purpose in the description.

In Bhoja's work this figure appears in the following poem of Ayodhyākāṇḍa where Bharata taunts his mother Kaikeī for her rash and thoughtless act.

'tātaḥ svavācā vyavahṛtya hṛdyaṁ vatsābhiṣekotsava-maṅgalaṁ me /
praṇāmasaṁjñasya mayārpitasya kiṁ pūrṇapātra-sya na pātramāsīt //[267]

In this poem the salute (praṇāma) made by Bharata is figuratively reduced to a 'pūrṇapātra'[268] of a yajña by Bharata himself in his statement. Now, because the salute is reduced to a poetical 'purṇapātra' by the speaker, it is a clear case of Pariṇāma Alaṁkāra, Bharata's statement instantly reminds us of a poem given by Viśvanātha as an illustration of the figure.

'smitenopāyanaṁ dūrāgatasya kṛtaṁ mama /
stanopapīḍamāśleṣaḥ kṛto dyūte paṇastayā //[269]

(ix) Apahnuti (Concealment)

Apahnuti is a significant term. Literally term means 'concealment'. Apahnuti is another common Alaṁkāra used by Sanskrit poets. When a real thing is concealed in a poem, and it is presented as a different object, the Alaṁkāra arising therefore it is called Aphnuti. Viśvanātha defines it appropriately as :

'gopanīyaṁ kamapyarthaṁ dyotayitvā kathaṁcan /
yadi śleṣenānyathā vānyathayetsāpyahnutiḥ //[270]

The author of the *Campūrāmāyaṇa,* casually employs this Alaṁkāra in a few poems of the Ayodhyākāṇḍa and the Kiṣkindhākāṇḍa. In the Ayodhyākāṇḍa, Bharata admonishes his mother Kaikeyī. While doing so he describes his mother as 'akīrtersavitrī' or the mother of 'infamy'. Thus, prince Bharata conceals the fact that Kaikeyī is his mother and depicts as what she is not. Hence, it is a clear example of Aphnuti Alaṁkāra.[271]

(x) Arthāntaranyāsa (Corroboration)

According to the Sanskrit rhetoricians when a general statement is supported by a particular statement or particular by a general in poetry which gives rise to poetic embellishment, it is a case of Arthāntaranyāsa Alaṁkāra. Viśvanātha defines Arthāntaranyāsa as follows :

'sāmānyaṁ vā viśeṣeṇa viśeṣastena vā yadi /
kāryaṁ ca kāraṇenedaṁ kāryeṇa ca samarthyate //
sādharmyeṇetareṇarthāntaranyāsoastodhā tataḥ //[272]

Kālidāsa is famous for employing this Alaṁkāra in his *Meghadūta.*[273]

Bhoja and Lakṣmaṇasūri also presents this figure in few poems in the *Campūrāmāyaṇa.* In this connection we can refer the following verses of the *Campūrāmāyaṇa* where this figure is used by the poets.

(a) *nūnaṁ janena puruṣe mahati prayukta*
māgaḥ paraṁ tadanurupaphalaṁ prasūte /
kṛtvā raghūdvahagateḥ kṣanamantarāyaṁ
yadbhārgavaḥ paragatervihartiṁ prapede //[274]

(b) *Bhojena ten racitāmapi pūrayiṣya*
nnalpiyasāpi vacasā kṛtimatyudarām /
na vriḍitoahamadhunā navaratnahāra
saṅgena kinna hṛdi dhāryata eva tantuḥ //[275]

(c) *śreyaḥ padātpadamupaiti vidheḥ prasādā*
tprāyastadaya phalitaṁ hi vibhīṣaṇa tu /
rekhātapatrasahitaṁ padamasya gṛhna
nnekātapatrasahitaṁ padameṣa bheje //[276]

In the first verse the miserable plight meet by Paraśurāma in the hands of Rāma by challenging him in a battle. The poet says that when a man commits an offence against a venerable person he meets the punishment of his act. In the above verse a general statement 'nunaṁ janena' etc. is supported by a particular statement viz.

'kṛtvā raghūdvahagateḥ kṣaṇamantarayaṁ' etc.
bhārgavaḥ paragatervihatiṁ prapede'.

Hence, there is a clear case of Arthāntaranyāsa Alaṁkāra in the verse.

In the second poem Lakṣmaṇasūri says that he is completing the incompleting text of Bhoja's *Campū-rāmāyaṇa.* Though his task is a small one, compared to that of Bhoja, he is not ashamed of it. In this connection he states that his act is like a broad thread in his neck along with a necklace (i.e. the major work of Bhoja). In this poem a particular statement viz. 'Bhojena ten racitāmapi... statement is supported by a general statement viz. 'na vrīḍitoahamadhunā navaratnahāra saṁgenenakinna hṛdi dhāryata eva tantuḥ'.

In the third verse Lakṣmaṇasūri refers to ascendancy of Vibhīṣaṇa on the throne of Laṇkā. He Says that it is by the grace of Vidhi (fate) miracules things suddenly happen. In this poem also a general statement i.e. 'śreyaḥpadāt padamupaiti vidheḥ prasādātprāyastadadya phalitaṁ hi vibhīṣaṇo tu' is supported by a particular statement 'rekhātpatrasahitaṁ padamasya gṛhnnekātapatrasahitaṁ podameṣa bheje'.

(xi) Vibhāvanā (Peculiar Causation)

When the poet describes in his poem the emergence of a effect without a cause, the Alaṁkāra involved in the poetical passage concern is called Vibhāvanā. The author of the *Sāhityadarpaṇa* defines this Alaṁkāra appropriately in the following manner.

'vibhāvanā vinā hetuṁ kāryotpattiryaducyate'[277]

Bhoja casually employes this Alaṁkāra in his work. This is clearly noticed in a verse of the Ayodhyākāṇḍa. viz.

nākrātastridivaḥ paraḥ sumanasāṁ kāntā na vandīkṛtā
nākīṇaṁ puruhūtāśasanadharāḥ sāketabāhyāṇ-gaṇaṁ/
nādiṣṭāḥ sacivāśca bhūtalaporitrāṇāya yadyapasau
nākaṁ śokavasśādgāddaśaratho nāsthāṁ vahanvāhane.//[278]

In the above poem there is a reference to death of king Daśaratha. Instead of directly mentioning that Daśaratha died, the poet expresses the idea in a figurative way that the king went to the abode of Gods. In this connection he states that though the abode of Gods was not assailed by him, though divine damsels were not made captive, though the outskirt of the city of Ayodhyā was devoid of divine servants and, though the charge of the kingdom was not laid on the ministers, Daśaratha ascended to heaven. In this poem Daśaratha's movement to heaven is without any case whatsoever. Thus, there is a case of Vibhāvanā Alaṁkāra according to the said definition. The poem, however, bears the stamp of artificiality, which is a characteristic of Sanskrit ornamental poetry.

(xii) Viṣama (Incongruity)

This figure of speech is rarely used by Sanskrit poets. But it occupies a significant position among Alaṁkāras. Sometimes an activity produce an expected and contradictory result not intended by a person. When in poetry this particular feature is noticed the figure arising from the description is called Viṣama.[279]

In the *Campūrāmayaṇa* of Bhoja we notice the presence of such a passage viz.

Vanabhuvi tanumātratrāṇamājñapitaṁ me
sakalabhuvanabhāraḥ sthāpito vatsamūrdhni/
tadih sukaratāyāmāvayostatirtāyāṁ
mayi patati garīyānamba te pakṣapātaḥ//[280]

In the above poem Bharata remarks before Kaikeyī that while Kaikeyī tried to make him a fortunate prince by asking the two boons from her husband she had practically made him unhappy through her action. Thus, in the above poem there is a reference to an unexpected and contradictory result of the action of Kaikeyī. Hence, there is a case of Viṣama Alaṁkāra in this poem.

(xiii) Virodhabhāsa (Contradiction)

Viśvanātha defines the Virodhābhāsa Alaṁkāras as :

'jātiścaturbhijātyādyairguṇo guṇādibhistribhiḥ
kriyā kriyādravyābhyāṁ yad dravyaṁ dravyeṇavā mithaḥ
virudhamiva bhāset virodhoasau daśāṛtiḥ/[281]

According to this definition Virodhābhāsa or Virodha is characterised by assumed contradiction. We notice Virodhābhāsa Alaṁkāra in following verses of the *Campūrāmāyaṇa.*

(a) *māturājñaṁ vahanmūrdhnā mālāmiva mahāyaśāḥ/*
vanāya rāmo vavrāja jagatāmavanāya ca//[282]

(b) *niśicarapatirityavetya roṣādaśaninipātanibhena tāḍanena/*
asurahitamamuṁ prahṛtya daityaṁ surahitameva cakārabāli sūnuḥ//[283]

In the first verse the expression 'vanāya' in Rāmo vanāya' is contradictory to 'avanāya ca'. The superficial meaning of the expression is that Rāma went to the forest ('vanāya') and 'non-forest' (avanāya). But the expression 'avanāya' or rather 'jagatāmavanāya' actually means for the protection of the world. Thus, there is no practical contradiction in the statement.

In the second poem there is an apparent contradiction between 'asurahitam' and 'surahitaṁ'. But the word 'Asurahitaṁ' should be read 'asu rahitaṁ' (lifeless). Hence, there is no contradiction between the expressions.

(xiv) Svabhāvokti (Natural Description)

Svabhāvokti is a excellent figure of sence. In which description and action in a natural way. Viśvanātha describes Svabhāvokti Alaṁkāra in the following manner –

'svabhāvoktirduruhārthasvakriyārupavaṇanam'[284]

Bhoja present this figure in the following passages in the Kiṣkindhākāṇḍa of the *Campūrāmāyaṇa.*

'... tārāpathāṁ ghanaravamukharitaharinmukhābhogāṁ kadambavanapavanā kampaniraḍambarakadam-bakuṭumbāmabu dakadambakavalitāmbarāṁ śilīndhrasaṁbandha-bandhura vasundharāṁ vikacakuṭajanicayakvacitamahāraṇyāṁ prābṛṣeṇyāṁ prakriyāṁ...[285]

In the above passage poet gives a natural description of rainy season mostly by using the Svabhāvokti alaṁkāra, in which the poet avoids all artificiality as presents a scene in a natural way.

We have discussed above some common figures of speech found in the *Campūrāmāyaṇa*. Apart from them, Bhoja and Lakṣmaṇasūri have employed figures like Saṁkara,[286] Saṁsṛṣṭi,[287], Tulyayogitā,[288] Sahokti, [289] Arthāpatti,[290] Kāvyaliṅga[291], Pratīpa,[292] Parisaṁkhyā,[293] and Samucchaya,[294], In fine, the whole of the *Campūrāmāyaṇa* is a neatly worked out and embellished kāvya, where figures of word and sense employed adequate representation.

(E) Imagery in the Campūrāmāyaṇa

Like Kālidāsa and other Sanskrit poets Bhoja and Lakṣmaṇasūri also presents a number of beautiful images in the *Campūrāmāyaṇa*. The creation of new images of a attractive nature proves the real worth of a poet. An image is a picture made out of words. In Sanskrit there is no synonym for image. Sanskrit ālaṁkārikas have tried to convey the idea of images with the help of the figures like Upamā, Rūpaka, Utprekṣā and Dṛṣṭānta. However, a large number of new images have emerged in Sanskrit literature through the ages.

(a) Bhoja presents a number of excellent visual images in his *Campūrāmāyaṇa*. He proves his worth as a creator of beautiful images from the very beginnings. He lays special emphasis in depiction the demoness Tāḍakā in which a graphic and fearful picture of the man-eater demoness in the follwing poem of the Bālakāṇḍa.

'hṛtvādreḥ śikharāṇi tāni paritaḥ kṣiptvāhasitvākrudhā
Kṛtvā hastavighaṭṭanaṁ tata itaḥ sthitvā naṭitvā muhuḥ/
siktvā kṣāmasṛjā srajāntrakṛtayā baddhvā kacānkhecarān
dagdhvāgneḥ sadṛśā dṛśā niśicarā rundhanti randhraṁ divaḥ//[295]

He presents in an attractive manner the violent movements of Tāḍakā which create an awe in our mind.

(b) Sometimes Bhoja draws a placid but delightful picture of nature also. Thus while describing the hermitage of Dwarf God Viṣṇu he says that the trees of the hermitage have spread to all directions as if with a desire to measure the expanse of the Universe.[236]

(c) The poet portrays an attractive picture of Mother Earth in the following verse :

'devyā yasyā vasanamudadhiḥ pīṭhikā hāṭakādri
hāraḥ sindhuḥ sagaratanayasvargamārgaika bandhuḥ/
krīḍāśailaḥ prathamapuruṣakroḍadaṁṣṭrā ca tasyāḥ
sītāmāturjagati mithilāṁ sūtikāgehamāhuḥ//[297]

(d) In a passage of the Ayodhyākāṇḍa the poet presents an image of a Pulinda hunter frightening a female peacock with the twang of the bow. Bhoja says that when Rāma divulged the news of his banishment to Sītā, she was startled, as it were, by the sound of the bow created by a hunter of the Pulinda tribe aiming his arrow at an innocent female peacock.[298] Like other Sanskrit poets Bhoja also frequently uses images in the form of different Alaṁkāras throughout his work. We make an attempt to discuss here only a few striking imagery of the poet.

(e) Bhojarāja gives a panoramic description of Nature. While doing so he creates some attractive images in the Sundarakāṇḍa of his work. In this kānda of the book he draws a picture of mighty Hanūmān who limped to the sky from the Mahendra mountain. The poet narrates that under the pressure of the monkey hero's feet a fountain suddenly oozed from the mountain. Bhoja describes the phenomenon with the help of an image which proves his extraordinary poetic faculty. While Hanūmān started his extraordinary fit of limping to the sky, the deer were fleeting out of terror. Their sharp hoofs raised the red dust. The poet transform this natural phenomenon into an excellent visual image. He says that the moutain was bleeding.[299] It instantly reminds us of the first sentence in Maxim Gorky's short story 'Malva' viz. 'the sea was laughing'.

Bhoja displays his power of lofty imagination throughout the description of the Mahendra mountain. When Hanūmān jumped from the Mahendra mountain pieces of crystals rolled down the mountain and felled Kīcaka bamboos, and wind passing through these bamboos suddenly produced a melodious sound. The poet imagines that the Mahendra mountain was heavily which produced this sound.[300]

(f) Bhoja not only creates attractive visual images but also shows equal efficiency in creating auditary images. This can be clearly understood from the following poem of his work :

'Rāmākarṣaṇabhagnakārmukābhuvā dvānena rodorudhā
dṛptakṣatrayasaḥsitacchadakule jīmūtanādāyitam /
Vīraśrīprathamapraveśasamaye puṇyāhaghoṣāyitaṁ
sītāyāḥ kila mānase pariṇaye māṅgalayaturyāyitam //[301]

The poet significantly uses three high sounding words viz. Jīmūtanādāyitam, puṇyāhaghoṣāyitam and māṅgalyaturyāitam in the passage which produce the auditary effect :

(g) Like Bhoja Lakṣmaṇasūri also displays equal efficiency in presenting imagery. This is clearly noticed in the following prose passage of the Yuddhakāṇḍa :

'Krameṇ ca kupitakapivīradurikṛtanirṭavīra....... astaṁ bhajati bhānumati, ... dūramantaritaharidābhoge saṁdhyārāge samudañcite vikrāntaharinakhākrānta dantāvalavipulakumbhasthalamuktamuktākalāpa iva vijjṛmbhamāṇeviyati tārāgaṇe..... turagapadātiga

japadāhataviśvam bharāntarālajanuṣi rajasīva bhuvanamaskandati tamasi, ...pramadākare kumudākare/ /'.[302]

In this long prose passage, Lakṣmaṇasūri describes the evening stars gradually covering the sky as innumerable dazzling pearls pouring from the tample of a jungle-elephant pierced by a lion.[303]

In fine, both Bhoja and Lakṣmaṇasūri possess the faculty of creating new imagery which is a always desirable in the case of a poet. Ezra Pound remarks in his 'Literary Essays': 'It is better to present one image in a lifetime than to produce voluminous works.[304] His observation is correct.

(F) The treatment of Nature in Bhoja's Campūrāmāyaṇa

Nature has played a prominent role in the poetical works of many poets both Western and Eastern, modern and old. Wordsworth, Shelley, Keats, Byron and in modern times eminent poets like T.S. Eliot have treated Nature in a significant manner in their works. In India Nature has occupied the queen's seat in the *Rāmāyaṇa*[305] of Ādikavi Vālmīki, Kālidāsa and Bhavabhūti. In Kālidāsa's *Abhijñānaśākuntalam*[306] and *Kumārasambhavavam,*[307] Nature plays a pivotal role. Bhavabhūti puts flesh and blood in the body of Nature and converts them into living beings. In the '*Uttararāmacarita*', the author transforms Vanlakṣmī Vāsantī and the rivers Tamasā and Muralā into three goddesses who sympathise with the love-lorn condition of Rāma and Sītā.[308]

Bhoja is no less a poet than many of his great predecessors in the treatment of Nature in his Campūkāvya. He presents a penoramic picture of the river Gaṅgā which is the life-line of the people of India in the following verses of the Bālakāṇḍa of the *Campūrāmāyaṇa.*

(a) *'athavīcīcayacchannadigantagaganāntarā /*
śaśāṅkaśaṅkhasaṁbhinnatārāmauktikadanturā//[309]

(b) *taraṇgakṛṣṭamātaṇḍaturaṇgāyāsitaruṇā /*
phenacchannasvamātaṇgamargaṇavyagravāsavā//[310]

(c) *Gaṇgā saptākṛtirjātā nyapatadharamūrdhani /*
tena stutyā prasannena kṣiptā bindusarasyapi//[311]

In the first verse Bhoja portrays a picture of the river Gaṇgā descending to the Earth with the help of few excellent visual images. The poet is a pastmaster in the art of depicting the Indian forest in a lively manner. However, he is not a naturalist. He gives excellent poetic description of trees,[312] beast[313] and birds[314] of the Indian forest by adding his soaring imagination. Thus, when Bharata enters into the forest of Citrakūṭa with the Caṇḍāla chief Guha, the poet describes that the forest wind fragrant with the sweet smell of ghee offered by hermits in the fire was blowing. The hermitage of Bharadvāja remained strewn with flowers, and poet remarks that sylvan deities had offered worship to their gods by showering these flowers on them. The trees were extending hospitality, as it were to their honourable guest Bharata by means of fruits and flowers.[315]

Like the author of the *Nalacampū*, Bhoja also presents almost unending descriptions of Nature thickened with the names of innumerable trees in order to make the entire forest scene a lively and appropriate one. In fact, his description of the jungle is like the thick and intricate tropical forest of India.[316] It is due to the courtesy of Bhojarāja we learn about the wide varieties of Indian flora which are gradually waning due to the pressure of human population. In the Sundarakāṇḍa, the poet mentions innumerable trees like Nāga, Puṃnāga, Tāla, Hintāla, Tamāla and Sarala.[317] We have already given a list of trees with their relevant Botanical names in our present dissertation. Like Vālmīki[318] and Kālidāsa[319], Bhoja also lays adequate emphasis on the treatment of Indian seasons and particularly of Hemanta (cool) and Varṣā (rainy season). He depicts a nice scene of the Hemanta (the cool season) season with all its diverse phenomena. In the Araṇyakāṇḍa the description of the Hemanta or (cool season) plays the role of Anubhāvas or objective-correlatives of the amorous sentiment of Śūrpaṇakhā.[330] Bhoja says that in this season men and women smear their bodies with sandal-paste, and frequently bathe in tanks and wells. They paint their bodies with saffron and wrap their bodies with soft rugs. Paddy plants with ripe seeds decorate the farms of cultivators in this season which is a common village scene of India.

> *'athakadācidupacīyamānamanobhavavaibhavaḥ pākakapiśa kalamañjarīpuñjapinjarībhūtakedāraprapañcaḥ pañca bāṇaraṇaprayāṇocitavīrapāṇavatpatraputạpātra......... .... candanānulepane............ vātāyanasevane nirutsukatāṁ.........vāpikūpopakaṇṭhe............ śaśodararomamṛdukambalasya ca kālāgarudhūmasya ca kāsmīrāṇgarāgasya ca nirdhūmāṇgāra bharitahasantikāyantrasya ca subhagaṁkaraḥ......... .... nirbhayanilīnanidādhabhāvodivā bhītavrātasyā .... kṣemaṇkarasudhākaraḥ........ .... romakambalakṛtāṇgarakṣamiva .... kṣīṇahimaprakarairadhwagāntaḥkaraṇānisimantayanheman tasamayaḥ samudajṛmbhat'.*[321]

The poet gives a typical description of the rainy season or Varṣā mostly by using the Svabhavokti-Alaṁkāra. Natural description or Svabhāvokti is a type of figure in which the poet avoids all artificiality and presents a scene in a natural way. While depicting the Varṣā or rainy season the poet remarks :

(a) *mahāsamarasūcakaḥ pratidiśaṁ manojanmano*
mayūragalakāhalīkalakalaḥ samujjṛmbhate /
payodamaline dine paruṣaviprayogavyathāṁ
nareṣu vanitāṣu vā dadhati hanta ke kā iti //[322]

(b) *ambhodharodaravinirgatavāridhārā*
sammadamāṁsalasamīrasamīryamānaiḥ /
āmodavīcinicayaiḥ kuṭajaprasunai
rākāśametadavakāśavihīnamāsīt //[323]

(c) *ghanaśyāmalapatrasya vyomanyagodhaśākhinaḥ /*
prarohā iva lakṣyante vāridhārā dharāṁ
gataḥ //[324]

The expressions like 'mayūragalakāhalīkalakalaḥ samujjṛmbhate' and 'ambhodharodaravinirgatavāridhārāsammadamāṁsalasamīrasamīryamāṇaiḥ' possess some excellent images which create immense delight in our minds. Kālidāsa[325] and the author of the *Nalacampū*[326] also try to present this season in an adequately attractive poetic language. Bhoja excels in a passage of the Sundarakāṇḍa when he describes the limping of Hanūmān from the Mahendra mountain.[327] The poet says that when Hanūmān made an effort to limp from this mountain towards Laṅkā a fountain immediately emerged under his pressure. Bhoja imagines that the mountain was weeping under great pressure exerted by Hanūmān. He present a lively picture of deer shooting to an fro out of panic. The red dust raised with their feet, is imagined by the poet as a gush of blood flowing from the body of the mountain.[328] The entire scene is not only delighting but it also represents some other important facts. The author of the *Campūrāmāyaṇa* reduces the insensible mountain into a lively form capable of feeling the pain of the termantation caused by Hanūmān's feet. It also contains a few new imagery. Thus, Bhoja can be easily declared as a successful poet of nature.

(G) Metres in the Campūrāmāyaṇa

Bhoja and Lakṣmaṇasūri show their artistic skills in handling the metres found in Sanskrit prosodical texts. As a whole twenty-five metres have been used in the *Campūrāmāyaṇa*. These metres are Vasantatilaka, Anuṣṭubh, Mālinī, Rucirā, Upendravajrā, Mandākrāntā, Indravajrā, Drutavilambita, Rathodhatā, Śārdulavikrīḍita, Upajāti, Sragdharā, Pṛthvī, Hariṇī, Puṣpitāgrā, Śikhariṇī, Āryājāti, Aupacchandika, Kuṭaka, Mañjubhāṣini, Pramitākṣarā, Narḍaṭakam, Toṭakam. This shows the command of the two poets over the poetic craft employed in arranging their statements into different metrical order. We give below a list of the different metres used by Bhoja and Lakṣmaṇasūri in a systematic manner below :

1. *Vasantatilaka*

Bālakāṇḍa	:	1-5, 7, 12, 16, 18, 27, 38, 50, 52, 94, 112, 115, 116
Ayodhyākāṇḍa	:	4-8, 12, 15, 21, 28, 30, 31, 33, 44, 46, 49, 50, 53, 55, 70
Araṇyakāṇḍa	:	6, 8, 13, 22, 26, 28, 34, 50
Kiṣkindhākāṇḍa	:	8, 13, 15, 17, 33, 35, 36, 40

Sundarakāṇḍa : 7, 12, 18, 20, 26, 30, 34, 36, 43-48, 50-56, 62, 64-66, 70
Yuddhakāṇḍa : 2, 4, 5, 7, 9, 14, 17, 19, 20, 22, 23, 30, 32, 34, 35, 38, 48, 51, 53, 67, 69, 70, 78, 80, 84, 88, 90, 91, 96, 97, 99, 103, 106.

2. *Anuṣṭubh*
Bālakāṇḍa : 6, 22, 30-33, 35-38, 42-44, 51, 54-64, 114

3. *Mālinī*
Bālakāṇḍa : 8, 45-47, 53, 99, 109
Ayodhyākāṇḍa : 3, 10, 13, 20, 25, 38, 45, 52, 64, 66-69, 73-75
Araṇyakāṇḍa : 9. 11, 22, 24, 25, 27, 31, 37, 42-46
Kiṣkindhākāṇḍa : 5, 6, 12, 19, 38, 45, 47
Sundarakāṇḍa : 19, 21, 39, 69
Yuddhakāṇḍa : 13, 16, 29, 31, 89.

4. *Rucirā*
Bālakāṇḍa : 9
Yuddhakāṇḍa : 44, 108.

5. *Upendravajrā*
Bālakāṇḍa : 10, 25
Ayodhyākāṇḍa : 43
Kiṣkindhākāṇḍa : 41
Sundarakāṇḍa : 23
Yuddhakāṇḍa : 12

6. *Mandākrāntā*
Bālakāṇḍa : 13, 15, 23, 100
Ayodhyākāṇḍa : 9
Kiṣkindhākāṇḍa : 4
Yuddhakāṇḍa : 15

7. *Indravajrā*
Bālakāṇḍa : 11, 28, 34, 39, 49, 96
Ayodhyākāṇḍa : 42
Sundarakāṇḍa : 75
Yuddhakāṇḍa : 42

8. *Drūtavilambita*
Bālakāṇḍa : 24

Araṇyakāṇḍa : 3, 16
Kiṣkindhākāṇḍa : 3

9. *Rathodhatā*
Bālakāṇḍa : 26, 113
Ayodhyākāṇḍa : 16, 86
Kiṣkindhākāṇḍa : 11

10. *Śārdūlavikriḍita*
Bālakāṇḍa : 29, 41, 48, 103
Ayodhyākāṇḍa : 14, 23, 29, 48, 54, 57
Araṇyakāṇḍa : 29
Kiṣkindhākāṇḍa : 34, 48
Sundarakāṇḍa : 2, 13, 17, 33, 40, 49, 57, 61, 63, 70
Yuddhakāṇḍa : 1, 3, 10, 26, 33, 36, 37, 46, 55, 58, 59, 68, 77, 83, 85, 87, 109, 110.

11. *Upajāti*
Bālakāṇḍa : 84-90, 97
Ayodhyākāṇḍa : 19, 26
Araṇyakāṇḍa : 23, 34
Kiṣkindhākāṇḍa : 1

12. *Sragdharā*
Bālakāṇḍa : 94
Araṇyakāṇḍa : 15
Kiṣkindhākāṇḍa : 24, 46
Sundarakāṇḍa : 38, 59, 67

13. *Pṛthvī*
Bālakāṇḍa : 105
Ayodhyākāṇḍa : 32
Kiṣkindhākāṇḍa : 27
Sundarakāṇḍa : 15
Yuddhakāṇḍa : 8, 24, 28, 40, 41, 43, 65, 73, 86, 105, 107.

14. *Rathodhatā*
Bālakāṇḍa : 26, 113
Ayodhyākāṇḍa : 1, 16, 86
Sundarakāṇḍa : 51, 53, 54

15. *Harinī*
Ayodhyākāṇḍa : 2

16. *Praharṣiṇi*
Kiṣkindhākāṇḍa : 14

17. *Śālinī*

Ayodhyākāṇḍa	:	23

18. *Puṣpitāgrā*

Araṇyakāṇḍa	:	7
Kiṣkindhākāṇḍa	:	39
Yuddhakāṇḍa	:	25, 66, 96

19. *Śikhariṇī*

Ayodhyākāṇḍa	:	76-79
Kiṣkindhākāṇḍa	:	26
Sundarakāṇḍa	:	37

20. *Āryājāti*

Kiṣkindhākāṇḍa	:	26

21. *Aupacchandika*

Sundarakāṇḍa	:	6

22. *Kuṭaka*

Sundarakāṇḍa	:	32

23. *Mañjubhāṣini*

Yuddhakāṇḍa	:	18, 57, 76

24. *Pramitākṣarā*

Yuddhakāṇḍa	:	50, 63, 64

25. *Nardaṭaka*

Yuddhakāṇḍa	:	11, 27, 39, 49, 56, 60, 62, 82, 100.

References

1. CR. Bālakāṇḍa –verse 41.
2. Ibid., Verse 4.
3. Ibid., Verse 7.
4. Ibid., Verse 12.
5. Ibid., Verse 16.
6. Ibid., Verse, 48, 114.
7. Ibid., Verse 20.
8. Raghu, Canto. 4, Verses 5, 6.
9. Ibid., Canto. 9, Verses 38.
10. Nai. Car. 9/14.
11. Ibid., 3/93.
12. CR. Bālakāṇḍa, Verse 16.
13. Ibid., Verse 17.
14. CR. Bālakāṇḍa, Verse 19.
15. Ibid., Verse 27.
16. Ibid., Verse 28.

17. Ibid., Verse 29.
18. *yogena labhyo yaḥ puṁsāṁ saṁsārāpetacetasām /*
niyogena pituḥ soayaṁ rāmaḥ kauśikamanvagāt //
Ibid., Verse 35.
19. Ibid., Verse 37.
20. AVC, pp. 392-393.
21. CR. Bālakāṇḍa, Verse 41.
22. Ibid., Verse 42.
23. Ibid., Verse 43.
24. Ibid., Verse 44.
25. Ibid., Verse 47.
26. Ibid., Verse 48.
27. Ibid., Verse 20.
28. Ibid., Verse 66.
29. Ibid., Verse 67.
30. Ibid., Verse 71.
31. Ibid., p. 82.
32. Ibid., p. 97.
33. Ibid., Yuddhakāṇḍa, p. 539.
34. Ibid., Bālakāṇḍa, Verse 104.
35. Cr. Yuddhakāṇḍa, Verse 87.
36. '..... *nija viśālavakṣaḥsthalaḥ kṣititale nipapāta'*
Ibid., Kiṣkindhākāṇḍa, p. 313.
37. Ibid., Bālakāṇḍa, p. 32.
38. Ibid., Verse 43.
39. Ibid., Araṇyakāṇḍa, pp. 258-259.
40. *'duḥkhe sukhe ca raja eva babhūva hetu stādṛgvidhe*
mahati Gautamadharmapatnyāḥ /
yasmād guṇena rajasā vikrtiṁ gatā sā rāmasya
pādarajasā prakṛtiṁ prapede //
Ibid., Bālakāṇḍa, Verse 94.
41. Ibid., Araṇyakāṇḍa, pp. 280-283.
42. Bhā. 10th Skanda, Ch. 89, Verses 48-51.
43. *paśayame pārtha rupāṇi śataśoatha sahasraśaḥ /*
nānāvidhāni divyāni nānāvaṇākṛtāni ca //
paśyādityān vasun rudrānaśvinau marutstathā /
bahunyadṛstapūrvāṇi paśyāścāyāṇi bhārata //
Mbh. Bhīṣmaparva, Ch. 35, Verses 5-6.
44. Vāl. Rāmā. Yuddhakāṇḍa, Canto 91.
45. Ibid., Ayodhyākāṇḍa, Verse 6.
46. Ibid., Verse 7.
47. Ibid., Verse 26.
48. *māturājñayāṁ vahanmūrdhnā mālāṃiva mahāyaśāḥ /*
vanāya rāmo vavrāja jagatāmavanāya ca //
Ibid., Verse 27.

49. Ibid., Bālakāṇḍa, Verse 45.
50. Ibid., Ayodhyākāṇḍa, pp. 141-143.
    Ibid., Araṇyakāṇḍa, pp. 255-256.
51. Ibid., Ayodhyākāṇḍa, Verse 24.
52. *vyāparayannatha vilocanakoṇamabdhau*
    kopāruṇaṁ kuṭilitabhrukuṭīviṭaṅkaḥ /
    ādātumaihata dhanuḥ prathamo raghūṇāṁ
    paitāmohaprathamasargasamāpanāya //
    Ibid., Yuddhakāṇḍa, Verse 22.
53. Ibid., Araṇyakāṇḍa, Verse 36.
54. Ibid., Bālakāṇḍa, Verse 12.
55. '...... sumantravacanā .... aśvamedhādhvaraṁ.... putrīyāmiṣṭimvidhivatkarumārabhat'.
    Ibid., p. 16.
56. *'atadākarṇya karṇaparuṣaṁ maharṣibhāṣita matimātraputravātsalyātkausalyājaniḥ saślyāntaḥ karaṇoabhūt'*
    Ibid., p. 45.
57. Ibid., p. 43.
58. Ibid., Ayodhyākāṇḍa, pp. 129-195.
59. Ibid., p. 159.
60. 'mātṛsamparkasaukhyam' Ibid., Araṇyakāṇḍa, Verse 27.
61. Ibid., Ayodhyākāṇḍa, p. 156.
62. Ibid., Verse 29.
63. *na devalokakramanaṁ nāmaratvāmahaṁ vṛṇe /*
    aiśvaryaṁ cāpi lokānāṁ kāmaye na tvayāvinā //
    Vāl. Rāmā. Ayodhyākāṇḍa, 31, Verse 5.
64. *Sītā pateḥ kisalayaiḥ ....*
    puṇyalabhyādsvapna eva vanavartmani Lakṣmaṇo abhūt //
    CR. Ayodhyākāṇḍa, Verse 56.
65. Ibid., Verse 19.
66. Ibid., Ayodhyākāṇḍa, p. 208.
67. *pariṇatiparuṣāṇāṁ pāpamanāṁ sannipātā*
    nna hi bhavasi Caturṇāṁ sa tvamasmākammbā /
    tadiha tanayavatyaḥ saṁlapiṣyanti kāmṁ
    śrutipuṭaracitatersatvāṁ savitrimakirteḥ //
    Ibid., Verse 66.
68. Ibid., pp. 209-210.
69. Ibid., Verse 79.
70. Ibid., pp. 214-217.
71. Ibid., pp. 217-218.
72. Ibid., p. 205, Verse 71.
73. Ibid., pp. 209-210.
74. Ibid., Bālakāṇḍa, pp. 46-47.
75. Ibid., Ayodhyākāṇḍa, Verse 39.

76. Ibid., Yuddhakāṇḍa, p. 564.
77. Ibid., Bālakāṇḍa, p. 65.
78. Ibid., pp. 46-47.
79. Ibid., p. 49.
80. Ibid., Verse 37.
81. Ibid., Verse 44.
82. Ibid., pp. 54-61.
83. Ibid., p. 96.
84. Vāl. Rāmā. Bālakāṇḍa, 19-39, 52, 67.
85. Mbh. Ādiparva, Ch. 175, 176.
86. CR. Bālakāṇḍa, pp. 88-95.
87. Ibid., Ayodhyākāṇḍa, pp. 210-213.
88. Ibid., Yuddhakāṇḍa, pp. 558-559.
89. Ibid., Ayodhyākāṇḍa, p. 223.
90. Ibid., Araṇyakāṇḍa, pp. 234-285.
91. Ibid., p. 286.
92. Ibid., p. 288.
93. Ibid., p. 236.
94. *'daśaśatanayaneapi vīkṣyamāṇe daśaratha putrāśiṣe-*
viṣaiva jātā /
manasijaśarabhaṅgakārivṛttermanasi muneḥ
śarabhaṅganāmabhājaḥ //
Ibid., Araṇyakāṇḍa, p. 234.
95. *'tataḥ parmaharṣeṇa maharṣiṇā....sarasijāsanastraṁ sautrāmaṇaṁ tūṇīryugmaṁ rukmamayakośaṁ khadgaṁ ca pratigrhya....'*
Ibid., p. 242.
96. Ibid., Bālakāṇḍa, p. 88.
97. Ibid., Verse 95.
98. Vāl. Rāmā, Ayodhyākāṇḍa, Canto 84, 85, 86.
99. Ibid., Ayodhyākāṇḍa, pp. 182-188.
100. Ibid., Bālakāṇḍa, p. 97.
101. *'sītā dharaṇitanayā jānakī maithile'*
Ibid., Yuddhakāṇḍa, Verse 15.
102. Ibid., Ayodhyākāṇḍa, Verse 31.
103. Ibid., Verse 38.
104. Ibid., Araṇyakāṇḍa, Verse 13.
105. Ibid., Verse 29.
106. Ibid., Sundarakāṇḍa, Verse 17.
107. Ibid., Yuddhakāṇḍa, p. 557.
108. Ibid., Verse 94.
109. Ibid., Ayodhyākāṇḍa, p. 158.
110. Ibid., Sundarakāṇḍa, p. 394.
111. Ibid., Yuddhakāṇḍa, Verse 97.
112. Ibid., Bālakāṇḍa, Verse 110.

113. Ibid., Ayodhyākāṇḍa, p. 153.
114. Ibid., p. 154.
115. Ibid., p. 209.
116. Ibid., p. 128.
117. *tayorekasya saṁrambho Bharatasyābhiṣecanam / anyasya vanyavṛttyaiva vane rāmasya vartanam //*
Ibid., p. 129, Verse 11.
118. Ibid., Verse 37.
119. Ibid., Verse 71.
120. Ibid., Bālakāṇḍa, Verse 32.
121. Ibid., Ayodhyākāṇḍa, Verse 9.
122. *sā dahyamānā krodhena mantharā pāpadarśinī / śayānameva Kaikeyīmidaṁ vacanamidaṁabravīt //*
Vāl. Rāmā. Ayodhyākāṇḍa, Canto 7, Verse 13.
123. CR. Ayodhyākāṇḍa, pp. 126-128.
124. Ibid., Araṇyakāṇḍa, p. 288.
125. Ibid., Bālakāṇḍa, pp. 84-87.
126. Ibid., Ayodhyākāṇḍa, p. 224.
127. *'kuharamavagāhya kañcana kāñcanamayaṁ maya māyānirmitaṁ..... merusāvarṇiduhitrā svayaṁpravā*
Ibid., Kiṣkindhākāṇḍa, p. 341.
128. ..... *'prabhañjānatmajaṁ'*, Ibid., p. 296.
129. *'ithaṁ jāmbavatā parāparavidā saṁdhukṣita prābhavaḥ kṛtvā vṛdhimupeyuṣā svavapuṣā traivikramaṁ ..... vārāṁnidhiṁ mārutiḥ* / Ibid., Verse 48.
130. *'....... tato Hanūmān ... mahendraśailasya mānavegaḥ'*
Ibid., Sundarakāṇḍa, Verse 1.
131. Ibid., p. 412.
132. *kṛtvākarma yathādiṣtaṁ pūrvakāryavirodhiyaḥ / karotyabhyadhikaṁ kṛtyaṁ tamāhurdūtamuttamm //*
Bhaṭṭi. 8/128
133. *'soyam mandāndhahṛdayo raghuvīrapatnīṁ sīmantinīti hatanītiravāpa pāpaḥ / āmūlapallavitakomalasallakīti vaitānapāvakaśikhāmiva vāraneṇdraḥ //*
Cr. Sundarakāṇḍa, Verse 20.
134. Ibid., pp. 367-370.
135. Ibid., Sundarakāṇḍa, pp. 401-404.
136. Ibid., p. 412.
137. Ibid., Verse 48, 52.
138. Ibid., Kiṣkindhākāṇḍa, p. 300.
139. Ibid.
140. Ibid., p. 333.
141. Ibid., Verse 20.
142. Ibid., p. 321.

143. Ibid., pp. 311-312.
144. Ibid., p. 351.
145. *'acalamatha salīlamoṣadhīnāṁ harati hanūmati jāmbavanniyogāt / vicalitambhavadbalaṁ viślyaṁ vibudhamonoapi vidhūtaśokaśalyam //*
Ibid., Yuddhakāṇḍa, Verse 66.
146. Ibid., Kiṣkindhākāṇḍa, Verse 18.
147. Ibid., Verse 19.
148. Ibid., Bālakāṇḍa, pp. 23-31.
149. Ibid., Sundarakāṇḍa, Verse 44.
150. Ibid., Verse 45.
151. Ibid., Verse 46.
152. Vāl. Rāmā. Uttarakāṇḍa, Canto 10, Verses 10, 13, 16, 20.
153. CR. Bālakāṇḍa, pp. 25-29.
154. '..... ... *Kailāsavikṣepanam'*
Ibid., Yuddhakāṇḍa, p. 485.
155. Śiśu Canto. 1. Verses 48, 50.
Vāl. Rāmā. Uttarakāṇḍa Canto 12, Verse 32-37.
156. CR. Araṇyakāṇḍa, pp. 273-274.
157. Val. Rāmā. Bālakāṇḍa, Canto 15, Verses 6-38.
158. CR. Yuddhakāṇḍa, pp. 539-543.
159. *rākṣasāmstrāsayāmāsa kārtavīryajunastadā / ravaṇaṁ gṛhya nagaraṁ praviveśa puruhutsaṁnibhaḥ //*
Vāl. Rāmā. Uttarakāṇḍa, Canto 32-34, Verse 32.
160. *'sāgaraṁ cāmbaraprakhyambaraṁ sāgaropamam / Rāmarāvaṇayoryuddhaṁ Rāmarāvaṇayoriva /*
Vāl. Rāmā. Yuddhakāṇḍa, Canto. 107, Verses 51-52.
161. Śiśu, Canto 1, Verses 48-68.
CR. Bālakāṇḍa, Verses 19-21.
162. CR. Yuddhakāṇḍa, pp. 451-454.
163. Ibid., Verse 17.
164. *'abhayāgatomadapayāti cenmudhā*
rāghavo bhavanti laghavo na kiṁ sakhe !
anujoayamastu tanujoathavā ripoḥ
karuṇāpadaṁ hi śaraṇāgato janaḥ // Ibid., Verse 18.
165. Ibid., p. 474.
166. Vāl. Rāmā. Yuddhakāṇḍa, Canto 17.
167. Bhaṭṭi. Canto 12, Verses 22-54, 69-75, 82-86.
168. *'āryasya rakṣitumsūnanujaḥ sa ekaḥ*
prānānmuñcata paraṁ yudhikumbhakarṇaḥ /
tvajjīvahṛtsvayamahaṁ nijajīvaheto-
radyāpi hanta sahate hatako vidhirmām //
CR. Yuddhakāṇḍa, Verse 90.
169. Ibid., Sundarakāṇḍa, pp. 406-408.

170. Ibid., Verse 41.
171. *viyattale tadanu nilīya māyayā*
sa lakṣyan raghutanayaṁ salakṣmaṇam /
ajihmagānadhigatajihmagākṛtī
namarṣataḥ samiti vavarṣa Rāvaṇiḥ //
Ibid., Yuddhakāṇḍa, Verse 44.
172. Ibid., Sundarakāṇḍa, Verse 38.
173. Ibid., Bālakāṇḍa, Verses 41, 48.
174. Ibid., Araṇyakāṇḍa, Verse 17.
175. Ibid., Verse 18.
176. Ibid., Verse 19.
177. Ibid., pp. 266-275.
178. Ibid., Yuddhakāṇḍa, Verse 92.
179. Ibid., Verse 94.
180. Ibid., Araṇyakāṇḍa, Verse 13.
181. Ibid., Verse 31, 32.
182. Ibid., Kiṣkindhākāṇḍa, pp. 344-346.
183. *śṛṅgārahāsyakaruṇa raudra vīrabhayānakāḥ /*
bībhastoadbhuta etyeṣṭau rasāḥ śāntaṣṭathāmataḥ //
SD. III. 182.
184. *śṛṅgāravīraśāntanāmekoaṅgi rasa isyate /*
aṅgāni sarveapi rasāḥ sarve nāṭaka sandhayaḥ //
Ibid., VI, 317.
185. *Utsāhāadhyavasāyādvisaditvadvismayāmohāt /*
vividhadthavisesadviraraso nama sambhavati //
NŚ. IV. 67.
186. *'dānavīramdharmavīraṁ yuddhavīraṁ tathaiva ca'*
NŚ. VI. 79.
187. *'Sa ca vīro dānavīro dharmavīro yuddhavīro*
dayāvīrośćti caturvidhaḥ'
SD. III. p. 257.
188. CR. Bālakāṇḍa, Verse 103.
189. *'eka eva bhavedaṅgī śṛṅgārovīra eva vā'* SD. VI. 10.
190. *'tatra śṛṅgāronāma ratisthāyībhāvaprabhāva'*
NŚ. p. 73.
SD. III. 187.
191. NŚ. p. 73.
192. *'sa ca purvarāgamānapravāsakaruṇatmakascaturdhā syāt'*
SD. III. 187.
193. KŚ. p. 85.
194. SKB. NS. Edn. p. 625, Verse 182.
195. SD. III. 13.
196. CR. Araṇyakāṇḍa, Verse 17.
197. Ibid., pp. 244-246.
198. CR. Araṇyakāṇḍa, Verse 18.

199. *tamuttamāṁ trilokānāṁ padmahīnāmiva śrīyaṁ /*
vibhrājamānāṁ bapuṣā Rāvaṇaḥ praśaśamsa ha //
hrī śri kīrtiḥ śubhā lakṣmīrapsarā vā śubhānane /
mūtirvā tavaṁ varārohe ratirvā svairacārini //
cārusmite cārudati cārunetre vilāsinī /
naivaṁ rupā mayā nārī dṛṣṭapurvā mahītale //
rupamagrayaṁ ca lokeṣu saukumāryam vayaścate //
Vāl. Rāmā. Araṇyakāṇḍa, Canto. 45, Verse 15, 17, 23.
200. CR. Araṇyakāṇḍa, Verse 37.
201. Ibid., Verse 38.
202. Ibid., Verse 29.
203. NŚ. p. 76.
204. Ibid.
205. *mayūrīva mahānāgaṁ kekayā kekayātmajā /*
bhāratyā bharataṁ cakre parikṣubhitamānasam //
pariṇatiparuṣāṇāṁ pāpamanāṁ sannipātā /
nna hi bhavasi caturṇāṁ sā tvamasmākamambā //
tadiha tanayavatyaḥ saṁlapayiṣyanti kāmaṁ /
śtutipuṭaracitartesatvāṁ savitrīmakīrtcḥ //
CR. Ayodhyākāṇḍa, Verse 65, 66.
206. Ibid., Araṇyakāṇḍa, Verse 29.
207. '*atha bhayānako nāmabhayasthāyībhāvatmakaḥ*
.... *pasmāramaranādayaḥ*'
NŚ. p. 76.
208. '*bhayānako bhayasthāyībhāvo bhūtadhidivataḥ /*
strīnīcaprakṛtiḥ kṛṣṇo matastatvaviśārodaiḥ //
SD. III. 235.
209. CR. Bālakāṇḍa, Verse 48.
210. NŚ. p. 78.
'*adbhuto vismayasthāyībhāvo gandharva daivataḥ*'
SD. III. 242.
211. NŚ. 75, 76.
SD. III. 242-244.
212. CR. Bālakāṇḍa, Verse 50.
213. Ibid., Verse 105.
214. NŚ. IV. 62.
215. Ibid., p. 75.
216. CR. Kiṣkindhākāṇḍa, Verse 15.
217. Ibid., Verse 16.
218. Ibid., 18.
219. *krodhaṁ prabho saṁhara saṁhareti yāvadgiraḥ khe*
marutāṁ caranti /
tāval sa vahnibhavanetrajanmā bhasmāvaśeṣaṁ madanaṁ
cakāra //

tivrābhiṣaṅgaprabhāveṇa vṛttiṁ mohena saṁastambha
yatendriyāṇām /
ajñātabhaṛtṛvyasanā muhurtaṁ kṛtopakāreva
ratirbabhuva //
Kumāra III. 72. 73.

220. NŚ. p. 78.
'jugupsā sthāyibhāvastu bhībhatsaḥ kathyate rasaḥ
' SD. III. 239.
221. NŚ. VI. 73, 74.
SD. III. 240-241.
222. CR. Yuddhakāṇḍa, Verse 86.
223. *vaṁasāmyanuprāsaḥ svaravaisādṛsyeapi vyañjanamatā-trasadṛśatvaṁ vaṇasāmyam /*
rasādyanugataḥ prakṛṣṭoṇyāsoanuprāsaḥ'
KPŚ. IX. p. 346.
224. SD X. 3.
225. Ibid., 668.
226. CR. Kiṣkindhākāṇḍa, Verse 26.
227. SD. X. 4.
228. CR. Bālakāṇḍa, Verse 5.
229. SD. X. p. 671.
230. CR. Bālakāṇḍa, Verse 34.
231. *gadyānubandharasamiśritapadyasūkti*
rhṛdyā hi vādyakalayā kaliteva gītiḥ /
tasmāddadhātu kavimārgajusāṁ sukhāya
campūprabandharacanāṁ rasanā madīya //
CR. Bālakāṇḍa, Verse 3.
232. Ibid., Verse 7.
233. *śrautī yathevāvaśabda ivārtho vāvatiryadi /*
ārthī tulyasāmānadyāstulyārtho yatra vā vati //
SD. X. 16.
234. Ibid., p. 17.
235. CR. Bālakāṇḍa, Verse 22.
236. Ibid., Ayodhyākāṇḍa, p. 145.
237. Ibid., Yuddhakāṇḍa, Verse 42.
238. SD. X. 28.
239. CR. Bālakāṇḍa, Verse 20.
240. Ibid., p. 24.
241. SD. X. 78.
242. Bhaṭṭi. 2. 19.
243. CR. Bālakāṇḍa, Verse 2.
244. CR. Bālakāṇḍa (R), p. 4.
245. SD. X. 40.
246. CR. Bālakāṇḍa, Verse 46.
247. CR. Ayodhyākāṇḍa, Verse 45.

248. Ibid., Araṇyakāṇḍa, 244-245.
249. Ibid., Yuddhakāṇḍa, Verse 28.
250. Twenty five Sanskrit Inscription, pp. 10-13.
251. SD. X. p. 36.
252. CR. Bālakāṇḍa, Verse 4.
253. SD. X. 51.
254. CR. Ayodhyākāṇḍa, Verse 52.
255. Ibid., Sundarakāṇḍa, Verse 16.
256. Ibid., Verse 48.
257. Abh. 1-17.
258. Vāl. Rāmā. Araṇyakāṇḍa, Canto. 47, Verses 38-43.
259. CR. Bālakāṇḍa, Verse 15.
260. Ibid., Verse 18.
261. *'atra kramikasya stambhādividaraṇasya yaugapadyā-sambandheapi tatsambandhoratiśayoktiḥ'* /

Ibid., (R), p. 19.

262. Ibid., p. 23.
263. Ibid., Yuddhakāṇḍa, Verse 14.
264. Ibid., p. 313.
265. SD. X. 34.
266. Ibid., p. 25.
267. CR. Ayodhyākāṇḍa, Verse 26.
268. Pūrṇapātra : A pot duly filled with religious articles is placed by the side of the sacrificial site. This is called Pūrṇapātra.
269. SD. X. p. 25.
270. Ibid., 38.
271. *'pariṇatipuruṣāṇāṁ pāpamanāṁ sannipātā*
nna hi bhavasi caturṇāṁ sā tvamasmakambā /
tadiha tanayavatyaḥ saṁlapiṣyanti kāmaṁ
śrutipuṭaracitārtesatvāṁ savitrīmakīrteḥ //

CR. Ayodhyākāṇḍa, Verse 66.

272. SD. X. 62.
273. (a) *'tasya sthitvā kathamapi puraḥ kautukādhānaheto*
rantrvāṣpaściramanucaro rājarājasya dadhyau /
meghāloke bhavati sukhinoapyanyathāvṛtti cetaḥ
kaṇthāśleṣapraṇayinijane kiṁ punardūrasaṁsthe //

(b) *jātaṁ vaṁśe bhuvanavidite puṣkarāvarttakānām*
jānāmi tvāṁ prakṛtipuruṣaṁ kāmarupaṁ madhonaḥ /
tenārthitvaṁ tvayi vidhivaśaddūravandhurgatoahaṁ
yāñca moghā varmadhiguṇe nādhame labdhakāmā //

(c) *tvāmārudhaṁ pavanapadavīmudgṛhitālakāntā*
prekṣyante pathikavanitāḥ pratyayādaśvasatyaḥ /

kaḥ sannadhe virahavidhurāṁ tvayyupekṣet jāyām
na syādanyoapyahamiva janoḥ yaḥ parādhīnavṛttiḥ //
MD. Verses 3, 6, 9.

274. CR. Bālakāṇḍa, Verse 115.
275. Ibid., Yuddhakāṇḍa, Verse 2.
276. Ibid., 20.
277. SD. X. 66.
278. CR. Ayodhyākāṇḍa, Verse 60.
279. 'virupayoḥ saṅghaṭanā yā ca tadviṣamṇ matam/'
SD. X. 70
280. CR. Ayodhyākāṇḍa, Verse 25.
281. SD. X. 68
282. CR. Ayodhyākāṇḍa, Verse 27
283. Ibid, Kiṣkindhākāṇḍa, Verse 39.
284. SD. X. p. 60
285. CR. Kiṣkindhākāṇḍa, pp. 324-325.
286. Ibid, 1-20, 40, 100, 11-61,86, VI-5, 23, 43
287. Ibid, 1-7, 27, V. 36, 58
288. Ibid, III, 3, IV-11.
289. Ibid, VI. 87.
290. Ibid, V. 68.
291. Ibid, V. 69.
292. Ibid, V. 67.
293. Ibid, V. 29.
294. Ibid, VI. 77.
295. CR. Bālakāṇḍa, Verse 48.
296. *'apahṛtavibudhārtervāmanasyājamūrte*
rakhilabhuvanabhikṣorāśramānokahānām/
tatiriyamatinīlā vyāptadigvyomasīmā
svayamapi paritātuṁ lokamabhyudyateva//
Ibid., verse 46
297. Ibid, Verse 100.
298. *'Kalyānvādasukhitāṁ sahasaiva kāntāṁ*
kāntāracārakathayā kaluṣīcakāra /
ambhodanādamuditāṁ vipine mayūrīṁ
saṁtrāsayanniva dhanurdhvanina pulindaḥ //
Ibid., Ayodhyākāṇḍa, Verse 31.
299.
'tadānīmudanvadullaṅghanadṛhataranihitacaraṇaniṣpīḍanaṁ sohumakṣamaḥ kṣmābhṛdeṣa niḥśeṣaniḥsarannirjharau-dhatayā nirantaraniṣpatadbāṣpa varṣa iva itastato vitatajīmūtavṛndatayā pāriplavaśithiladhamilla iva,
.... *hariṇagaṇacaraṇakharatarakhurakoṭipāṭa*
..........*pāṭalitavikaṭakaṭakatayā kṣaritaśoṇita iva,*
.....' Ibid., Araṇyakāṇḍa, p. 353.

300. ...... *sphaṭikataṭopalapatanadalitakīcakasuṣirasaṁmūr-cchatpavanaphutkāraparipūritagaganatayā pravadhamānordhvaśavāsa iva vasasāmaviṣayaṁ dauḥsthamabhajat'.*

Ibid., p. 354.

301. Ibid., Bālakāṇḍa, Verse 104.
302. Ibid., Yuddhakāṇḍa, pp. 492-493.
303. Ibid.
304. American Literature, (1890-1965) Ed. by Oliver, S.E. Egbert, p. 458.
305. *jalāghātāttahāsogrāṁ phenanirmalahāsinim / kvacidveṇīkṛtajalāṁ kvacidāvartaśobhitām //*

Vāl. Rāmā Ayodhyākāṇḍa, Canto 50, Verse 16.

306. (a) *Kṣaumaṁ kenacidindupāndu taruṇā māṇgalyamāviṣkṛtam niṣthayut ścaraṇo parāga subhago lākṣārasaḥ kenacit / anyebhyo vanadevatākaratalaiḥ, rāparvabhāgotithi-tair dattānyabharaṇaṇi na kisalayobdheda pratidvandībhiḥ //*

(b) *ramyāntaraḥ kamulinī-haritaiḥ sarobhiḥ chūyā drumairniyamitārka mrīci-tāpaḥ / bhūyat kuśasaya rajomṛdureṇursyāḥ śāntāanukela pavanśca śivaśca panthāḥ //*

(c) *anumatagamanā śakuntalā tarubhiriyaṁvanavasa-bandhubhiḥ / parabhṛtabirutaṁ kalaṁ yathā prativacanikṛtam-ebhirātmanaḥ //*

(d) *udgīṃadarbhakavalā mṛgyaḥ parityaktanartanā mayurāḥ / apasṛtapāṇḍuputrāḥ muñcantyaśruṇīva latāḥ //*

Abh. IV, 5, 10, 11, 12.

307. *sā saṁbhavadbhiḥ kusumairlateva jyotibhirudhyadbhi-riva triyāmā saridivihaṅgairiva līyamānairāmucyamānabharaṇa cakāse//*

Kumāra VII, 21.

308. *Muralā-Suvicintitaṁ bhagavatyā Bhāgirathyā rājanītisthi-tasyā*
asya khalu taistairjagatāmabhyudaryikaih kāryyair-vyāpṛtasya rāmabhadrasya niyatāśittavikṣepaḥ/
avyagrasyaṁ panarasya śokamātradvitīyasya
pañcavaṭīpraveśo mahānanarthaḥ iti/
tat kathamidānīṁ sītādevyā rāmabhadra āśvāsanīya sayāt'?
Tamasā — Aho samvidhānakam, —

akorasaḥ karuṇa eva nimittabhadād
bhinnah pṛthak pṛthagivāsrayate vivarttān/
āvarttadbudutaraṅgamayān vikārān
ambhoyathā śalilameva hi tat samagram//
Tamasāvāsantyu (sitaramauprati)
avaniramarasindhu sārdhamasamadvidhābhiḥ
sa ca kulapatirādyaschandasāṁ yaḥ, yrayoktā/
sa ca muniranuyātārundhatiko vasiṣṭha
stva vitaratu bhadraṁ bhūyase maṅgalaya/

URC, p. 257, Verse 47, 48

309. CR. Bālakāṇḍa, Verse 78
310. Ibid., 79.
311. Ibid., verse 85
312. Ibid., Sundarakāṇḍa, p. 372
313. *'asminmahāpathadhiyā vadanaṁ vigāhya*
nirgantumkṣamatayā jaṭhare luṭhadbhiḥ/
vanyirgajairajagarāḥ piśitasanebhyo...//

Ibid., Araṇyakāṇḍa,
Verse 10.

314. Ibid., Sundarakāṇḍa, pp. 269, 364.
315. *'...guhena saha rāmamanviṣyan havyagandhinā gandhavahena dhūmagandhena... vanadevatābhirava-kīryamāṇabalikusumm .... atithijanasaparyāparyut-sukausaumitrisamāhṛtakandamūlaphala... rāmāśrmṁ bharataḥ sasambhrammbhajat'/*

Ibid., Ayodhyākāṇḍa, pp. 212-213.

316. *'avamasu kriḍitānekapāmarān girīn grāmāśca bahuta-rango paśobhitaḥ saritaḥ simnaśca vyuhapattrathāna pathaḥ pādapāṇśca langhayabn, sālasahitāḥ purirnārīśca sevamānaḥ śatrusīmantīnīraṭaviśca tikrāman, parivārīni bandhukulāni sarāṇisi ca bahumānayan, nāticirena ravirathaturaṅgaparihrta viṣamaśiraḥśikharasahramajasrammaragaṇagandhar-vasidharudhaskandhamadyaṁ vindyācalamanusacāra'.*

NC. 5, p. 275

317. *'tatastasyāṁ nāgapuṁnāgatālahintālatamālakṛtamāla saralabakulavanājulatilakāamalakakutajalikucakataka kakkolaṅkolalavaṇgavikaṇkataketakīkadambodumbare-kapithāaśvatthakurabakamarubakamākandakundatinduka candanasy andanacampakacāmpeyapanasavetasapalāśa-pāṭalā rasāla priyāluprayairanekairanokahanivahaiḥ parivṛttāyāṁ paribharamannbhrakaṣa........................... ....śiṁśapāmaruruha. 'mallīṁ cūtavanādiva snuhivane...................................//*

CR. Sundarakāṇḍa, pp. 372-373

318. *vasatastasya tu sukhaṁ Rāghavasya mahātmanaḥ/*
śaradyapāye hemantaṛturiṣṭaḥ pravartat//
ayaṁsa kālaḥ samprāptaḥ priyo yste priyaṁvadaḥ/
alaṁkṛta evabhāti yena saṁvatsaraḥ śubhaḥ//
nihāraparuṣo lokaḥ pṛthivi śasyaśālinī/
jalānyanupabhogyāni subhago havyavāhanaḥ/
navāgrayanpūjābhirabhyarcya pitṛdevataḥ/

Vāl. Rāmā. Arṇyakāṇḍa, 16
Verses1, 4, 5, 6.

ayaṁ sa kālaḥ saṁpraptaḥ samayoadya jalāgamaḥ/
saṁpasya tvaṁ nabho meghaiḥ saṁbṛaṁ girisaṁnibhaiḥ//
navamāsadhṛtaṁ garbhaṁ bhāskarasya gabhastibhiḥ/
pītvā rasaṁ samudrānaṁ dyauḥ prasūte rasāyanam//
śakyambaramāruhya meghasopānapantibhiḥ/
kūṭajārjunamālābhiralaṁkaṛtuṁ divākaraḥ//
sandhyārāgothitaistāmrairanteṣvapi ca pāndubhiḥ/
snighairbhrapatacchedairbadhavraṇamivāmbaram//
mandāmarutaniḥśvasaṁ saṇdhyācandanaranjitam/
āpāndujaladaṁ bhāti kāmāturamivāmbaram/
āsādharmapariklisṭa navavāripariplutā/
sīteva śoka saṁtāpa mahi bāṣpaṁ vimuñcatī//
meghodaravinirmuktāḥ karpuradalaśitalāḥ/
śākyamanjalibhiḥ pātuṁ vātāḥ ketagandhinaḥ//

Ibid., kiṣkindhākāṇḍa, 28, Verses 2-8.

319. *navapravāloudgamasasyaramyaḥ prafullalodhraḥpari-pakkaśāliḥ/*
vilīnapadmaḥ prapattuṣāro hemantakālaḥ samupāgatoḥ ayam//
manoharaiścandanarāgagaurestuṣārakundendunibhaiśca hāraiḥ/
vilāsinīnāṁ stanaśālinīnāṁ nālaṁkriyante stanamaṇḍalāni//
praphullanīlotpalaśobhitāni sonmādakādambavibhuṣitani/
prasannatoyāṁ suśītalāni sarāṁsi cetāṁsi haranti puṁsāṁ//

RS. 4/1 2.9

320. *vṛṣasyantī vṛṣaskandhaṁ rāghavaṁ Rāvaṇānujā/*
bhūyaḥ śūrpaṇakhā bheje śūrpakāratibādhita//

CR. Araṇyakāṇḍa, Verse 17.

321. Ibid., Araṇyakāṇḍa, pp. 244-246
322. Ibid., Kiṣkindhākāṇḍa, Verse 27.
323. Ibid., Verse 28
324. Ibid., Verse 29
325. *śaśikarāmbhodaraṁmttakuñjara*
staritpatākoaśaniśabdamardalaḥ/

samāgato rājavadudhatadyuti
rghanāgamaḥ kāmijanah priye// RS. 2.1

326. *'tiraskṛtataraṇitviṣi, vigaladvāriviprusi, śāntacātaka tṛṣi, nivānavāranavapuṣi, māninīmānagrahagrathimuṣi, janitajavāsakaśusi.... vidrānapaṇkajasarasi, ... prositakalahamsavayasi...... sphutakutajarajah puñjapiñjaritāṣṭadigbhāsi...mayūramadākṛti... vistaratsariti....hṛṣyatkṛpānayositi....... puṣyatketa. kīgandhapānamattamadhukṛti.... syāmānadaśadiśi....... .....pallavitavirudhi .... vikasitabakulavanarajni.... vijayamanamānojanmani jātejagajjivinim, jimūtasamaye kadācidambhasi divase mṛgayāvanapālakaḥ praviśya rājānaṁ vijñāmāsa.'*
NC. p. 57

327. *'mahendraśailasya khagendravegaḥ prasthādudāsthat prathamānavegaḥ'*
CR. Sundarakāṇḍa, Verse 1

328. *tadanīmudanvadullanghanadṛhataranihitacaraṇa niṣpīḍanaṁ sohomakṣamaḥ kṣmābhṛdeṣa nihśeṣaniḥsara eva.... saṁtrasyamānakuñjarajūthatayā......... sādvasadhāvamānahariṇagaṇacaranakharatarakhurako ṭipāṭanoddhūtādhāturdhūlīpālipāṭalitavikaṭakaṭaka-tayā kṣaritaśoṇita iva... vacasāmaviṣayaṁ dauḥsthyamabhajat/'*
Ibid., pp. 353-354

Chapter V

INDIA AS KNOWN TO THE AUTHORS OF THE CAMPŪRĀMĀYAṆA

(A)

Geographical accounts of India

The authors of the *Campūrāmāyaṇa* give a vivid geographical account of India in the course of narrating their story. Like Vālmīki they also refer to lands, cities, rivers hills and tribes of India together with its rich flora and fauna. Let us, discuss the point more clearly and in a systematic manner. Bhoja and Lakṣmaṇasūri mentioned the countries like Aṅga, Kosala, Kekaya and the famous cities of ancient India such as Vīśālā and Śṛṁgaverapura and also the rivers and mountains like Sarayū Gomatī, Citrakūṭa and Ṛṣyamūka.

(a) Aṅgadeśa

Aṅga was one of the very rich and prosperous country of India. According to the *Rāmāyaṇa* Aṅga was so named because of Lord Madana fled to this country to save himself from the wrath of Rudra and became an aṅga or bodiless by losing his anga here. It is an amusing explanation of the origin of the word.[1] Ancient Aṅga is said to have included the hermitage of the sage Ṛṣyaśṛṁga. In the Bālakāṇḍa of the *Campūrāmāyaṇa* it has been described that Ṛṣyaśṛṁga with his wife Śāntā came to Ayodhyā to perform the horse sacrifice and putrakāmeṣṭiyajña of king Daśaratha.[2] In the *Rāmāyaṇa* of Vālmīki the king of Aṅga was invited to the horse sacrifice of king Daśaratha. The sage Ṛṣyaśṛṁga, son of Vibhāṇḍaka came to Aṅga at the invitation of Lomapāda (Romapāda) who was the powerful king of the Aṅga country. King Lomapāda received him cordially and gave his daughter Śāntā in marriage to him because the sage succeeded in removing drought from his kingdom.[3] According to the *Mahābhārata*, Karṇa was placed on the throne of Aṅga at the instance of his ally Duryodhana.[4] The *Mahābhārata* describes that Arjuna visited the kingdom of Aṅga also during his pilgrimage.[5] In the battle of Kurukṣetra the heroes of Aṅga fought against Arjuna.[6] The modern name of Aṅga is Bhagalpur which is in Bihar.[7]

(b) Kosala

In the Bālakāṇḍa of the *Campūrāmāyaṇa* the author mentions that Kosala was a wealthy and prosperous country on the bank of the river Sarayū. Ayodhyā was the capital of this kingdom.[8] This city was built by Manu, the father of Ikṣvāku. During the times of Daśaratha this city was developed such and extent as to be on a par with any modern city.[9]

In the early Buddhist age, Kosala was an important kingdom. The ancient Kosala kingdom was divided into two parts the river Sarayū serving as the wedge between the two. The north of the Sarayū was called the Uttarakosala and the south was called Dakṣiṇa Kosala.[10] The capital cities of Kosala were Srāvastī and Sāketa. Bhīmasena once conquered Uttarakosala or north Kosala.[11] According to the Vanaparva of the *Mahābhārata* the Ṛṣabha tīrtha was in Kosala and those who bathed in this tīrtha were supposed to obtain the fruits of giving one thousand cows as alms.[12]

At the time of the marriage of Ambā, Bhīṣma defeated the king of Kosala.[13] The modern name of Kosala in Oudh.[14]

(c) Mithilā

The authors of the *Campūrāmāyaṇa* refer to the country of Mithilā, which was ruled by Janaka the father of Sītā.[15] Mithilā is a famous country of ancient India. Mithilā was the capital or Videha at one time.[16] Its modern name is

Tirhut. According to the *Rāmāyaṇa* it was the name of the capital as well as of the country itself. It has been identified with the modern Janakapura, a small town near the Nepal border in Bihar. The district of Mazaffarpur and Dārbhaṅgā meet on the north of it.[17] The *Rāmāyaṇa* states that Nimi's son Mithi founded the beautiful city of Mithilā. He came to be known as Janaka, because he was the founder of the city.[18] The *Viṣṇupurāṇa* gives a factual account of the origin of the name of Mithilā, Vasiṣṭha, having performed the sacrifice to Indra, went to Mithilā to perform a sacrifice on behalf of king Nimi. On reaching the place of Nimi he found Gautama engaged by the king for the same purpose. Vasiṣṭha found the king asleep. Being angry the sage cursed Nimi as 'king Nimi will be bodiless'. The king on awakening was equally angry. He cursed Vasiṣṭha saying that he would also perish as he had cursed a sleeping king.[19] Mithilā was named after Mithi and the kings were called Mithilas.[20]

Among the kings of Mithilā the most important was Janaka who performed the sacrifice at Mithilā. Though a king, Janaka was a famous sage.[21] According to the *Mahābhārata* once Pāṇḍu, father of Pāṇḍavas, attacked this country and conquered it.[22] Śrīkṛṣṇa, Arjuna and Bhīma once visited this country on their way to Magadha from Indraprastha.[23] Karṇa the king of Aṅgadeśa once conquered and captured the country of Mithilā.[24]

According to the *Rāmāyaṇa*, Śuka, the great sage with the permission of his father Vyāsa came to Mithilā and took dharmopadeśa from king Janaka.[25] Bhoja says that Viśvāmitra came to the court of Janaka with Rāma and Lakṣmaṇa. Rāma broke the bow of Śiva and was garlanded by Sītā as her husband.[26]

(d) Kekaya

Kekaya is another famous country of ancient India. The country was known as Kekaya as it was ruled by king Kekaya. The king and the people of the Kekaya country were called the Kekayas.[27] There is a reference to the Kekaya country in the *Campūrāmāyaṇa*[28] and in the *Rāmāyaṇa*[29] of

Vālmīki. Kaikeyi, the wife of King Daśaratha was a daughter of king of Kekaya. Her role in the *Rāmāyaṇa* and the *Campūrāmāyaṇa* is necely described.

(e) Laṇkā

The name of Laṇka as the abode of Rāvaṇa is appears in the *Rāmāyaṇa* and quite naturally in the *Campūrāmāyaṇa* also.[30] Laṇka is the Kingdom of Rāvaṇa. The present island of Śrilaṇkā was the Laṇkā of the Epic Laṇkā was situated on the top of the mountain Trikūṭa.[31] This Trikūṭa was a peak of Mahāmeru. Because of a fight between Vāsuki and Vāyu (Pavana) this peak broke away from the Mahāmeru and fell into the ocean.

Viśvakarmā constructed a magnificant city on the top of the mountain Trikūṭa for the use of Kuvera lived there adored and worshipped by all. Then Rāvaṇa conducted a victory march as an arch opponent of all living forces and drove away Kuvera from Laṇkā and took possession of Laṇka as the place of his abode. He took along with him all the demons residing in Pātālaloka.[32]

Hanūmān burnt the city of Laṇkā with the help of his burning tail. After the death of Rāvaṇa, Vibhīṣaṇa was crowned the king of Laṇkā.[33] Lakṣmaṇasūri describes Laṇkā as Siṁhala in the Yuddhakāṇḍa of the *Campūrāmāyaṇa.*[34]

The following accounts of Siṁhala occur in the *Mahābhārata.*

The low caste people of the Siṁhalas originated from the sides of Nandinī the cow of the Devas.[35] The king of Siṁhala had taken part in the Rājasūya sacrifice of Yudhiṣṭhira.[36] It is said in the *Mahābhārata* that the Kṣatriyas of the Siṁhala country presented to Yudhiṣṭhira pearls and such other costly articles.[37]

(f) Vatsa (Vatsabhūmi)

Among the countries of ancient India the name of Vatsa

also appears in the *Campūrāmāyaṇa*. It is mentioned in the *Campūrāmāyaṇa* that when Rāma went to the forest with Lakṣmaṇa and Sītā, he had crossed the Vatsa country.[38] We find some important accounts about this country from various sources. According to the *Mahābhārata*, Bhīmasena conquered this country during his campaign of India.[39] In the Kurukṣetra battle the people of Vatsa faught on the side of the Pāṇḍavas.[40]

(g) Aśvamedhapura

In the Ayodhyākāṇḍa of the *Campūrāmāyaṇa*, Bhoja casually mentioned Aśvamedhapura.[41] Aśvamedhapura was a country of ancient India which was ruled by a king called Rocamān.[42] According to the *Mahābhārata* Bhīmasena conquered him during his campaign of India.[43]

(h) Śṛṁgaverapura

The name of Śṛṁgaverapura appears in the *Rāmāyaṇa*[44] of Vālmīki and also in the *Campūrāmāyaṇa*.[45] Śṛṁgaverapura was known as Nīṣada also. It is a sacred place. Guha, ruler of Niṣadas ruled from this place, It was situated on the banks of the river Gaṅga.[46] When Rāma went to the residence of Guha along with Lakṣmaṇa and Sītā during the initial periods his banishment.

Cities mentioned in the Campūrāmāyaṇa

(a) Ayodhyā

Ayodhyā was a famous city of North India which enjoyed great importance and reputation under the kings of the solar dynasty. This city was also known as Sāketa.[47] Ayodhyā is mentioned in the *Rāmāyaṇa* as the past (previous) capital of Kosala.[48] All the kings of the Solar dynasty ruled the country from this famous city. According to the *Brahmāṇḍa purāṇa*, Vasiṣṭha, the preceptor of the Ikṣvāku family came to Ayodhyā during the reign of Kalmāṣapāda.[49] We learn from the *Skandapurāṇa* that the city of Ayodhyā possessed the shape of a fish.[50]

The *Rāmāyaṇa* describes Ayodhyā as a city, full of wealth and granaries of paddy. It was a spacious city enriched with all the amenities of urban life. It was fully protected. There were many skilful artisans and craftsman in Ayodhyā in the age of *Rāmāyaṇa*[51] The ·city was unassailable to the enemies, as it was surrounded by deep ditches.[52] The city of Ayodhyā rose to great eminence under Yuvanāśva and specially his son Māndhātā.[53] Till the time of Rāma the city of Ayodhyā maintained its great splendour. The supremacy of Ayodhyā gradually waned. The Haihayas overcame Ayodhyā and the foreign tribes settled there after him. Ayodhyā again became famous under Bhagīratha and Ambarīṣa.[54] The modern city of Ayodhyā is now a holy place of India reminding visitors of its past glory.

(b) Kauśāmbī

The name of the city Kauśāmbī mentioned in the *Campūrāmāyaṇa.*[55] According to the *Rāmāyaṇa* the city of Kauśāmbī was built by Kuśāmba the son of Kuśa.[56] The ancient city of Kauśāmbī is probably the same with Kosom at present.[57]

(c) Gokarṇa

It was mentioned in the *Rāmāyaṇa*[58] and in the *Campūrāmāyaṇa*[59] that Gokarṇa was a holy place where Bhagīratha practised penance to bring down Gaṅgā. It is situated on the extreme north of modern Keralā.

According to the *Mahābhārata*, Arjuna visited Gokarṇa while he was on his pilgrimage.[60] Gokarṇa was one of the abodes of Śiva, Brahmā, great sages and many terrestrial beings[61] The modern name of Gokarṇa is Rāmeśvaram.[62]

(d) Viśālā

Bhoja refers to the ancient city of Viśālā in the following passage of the *Campūrāmāyaṇa* :

alambuṣāyāmikṣvākorjātaḥ kaścinmahīpatiḥ/
viśāleti svanāmnātra viśālāṁ vidadhe purīm//[63]

According to him, one legendary king Viśāla who was born in the family of Ikṣvāku built the city. Vīśālā is a holy place on the bank of the river Gaṅgā. According to the *Rāmāyaṇa* a son named Viśālā was born to Ikṣvāku, by the Alambuṣā and that Viśāla who built the city named Viśāla. This Viśāla had a son named Hemacandra. This Viśālā city is found in the Rāma's journey with the sage Viśvāmitra in the Bālakāṇḍa of the *Rāmāyaṇa.*[64] The modern name of Viśālā is called Besārā.[65]

(e) Daṇḍakāraṇya

The Author of the *Campūrāmāyaṇa* makes a reference of Daṇḍakāraṇya in Araṇyakāṇḍa. Daṇḍakāraṇya is a forest in the Indo-gangetic valley.[66] According to the *Rāmāyaṇa*, Rāma killed many demons in the Daṇḍakāraṇya forest.[67]
The *Mahābhārata* describes it as a holy place. It is said these that a dip in the water of this forest would yield the result of donating a thousand cows.[68]

During exile Rāma made his cottage in this forest and stayed there for sometime. It was in this forest the nose of Śūrpaṇakhā was chopped off by Lakṣmaṇa and the army of fourteen thousand Rākṣasas who faught under the leadership of Khara, Duṣaṇa and Trīśirā was completely destroyed by Rāma. The elusive demon Mārīca was killed by Rāma. Sītā was kidnapped by Rāvaṇa and jaṭāu died in the hands Rāvaṇa in this very forest.[69]

(f) Pañcavaṭī

Pañcavaṭī is the sacred place where Rāmacandra lived for sometime with Sītā and Lakṣmaṇa during their exile in the forests.[70] There is a story about Pañcavaṭī in the *Kambarāmāyaṇa.*

Pañcavatī is on the southern bank of the Godavarī river. Five Vaṭavṛksas (banyan trees) stand here in a circle and therefore, the place got the name Pañcavaṭī. There is a legend about the origin of these banyan trees. Once five Gandharva youths surrounded sage Agastya in the forest in order to make a fun. They prevented him from moving towards any direction. The angry sage Agastya then cursed the Gandharva youth to stand in the same position as banyan tree. Before they changed into trees they begged the sage for deliverance from the curse. The sage told them that, when Rāma with his wife and brother would enter into the forest stay in an āśrama built in their midst, they would be delivered from the effect of the curse.

When Rāma and Lakṣmaṇa came to that forest decided to build āśrama in the centre of the circle formed by the five banyan trees. Lakṣmaṇa started to build a hermitage there. At first he cut down one of the trees standing tall and straight and to the surprise of all the fallen trunk of the trees disappeared and there appeared a dead body of demon youth Śambhukumāra, son of Śūrpaṇakhā. He was doing penance there. Rāma understood the significance of this sad episode.[71]

Rivers in the Campūrāmāyaṇa

The names of several rivers appears in the *Campūrāmāyaṇa* among which Gaṅgā, Sarayū, Mandākinī, Godavarī and Gomatī are some important river of India.

(a) Gaṅgā

The river Gaṅgā is the life-line of the people of North India. The river appears in the Himālaya, and flows through Uttarpradesh, Bihar, West Bengal and Bangladesh and fall into the Bay of Bengal. The *Rāmāyāṇa*[72] and the *Campūrāmāyaṇa*[73] describe the legendary origin of the river Gaṅgā. According to the description found in the *Rāmāyaṇa*, the river was brought down by the solar prince Bhagīratha to the earth.[74] Similarly, king Bhoja also gives a brief description about the legendary origin of the river Gaṅgā.[75]

(b) Sarayū

Sarayū is famous river in the *Rāmāyaṇa* and the Purāṇas. The city of Ayodhyā was situated on the bank of the Sarayū.[76] In the *Rāmāyaṇa*[77] of Vālmīki and in the *Campūrāmāyaṇa* it is described that Rāma and Lakṣmaṇa went to the forest for protecting the religious order of the sages then they crossed the river Sarayū on their way.[78] Seven subsidiary streams of the river Gaṅgā originate from the peaks of the Hīmālaya's and Sarayū is one of them.[79] According to the Sabhāparva of the *Mahābhārata*, Śrīkṛṣṇa, Arjuna and Bhīma crossed this river on their way to Girivraja.[80]

(c) Mandākinī

The name of the river Mandākinī is mentioned in the Bālakāṇḍa of the *Campūrāmāyaṇu*.[81] Mandākinī is a river which flows from near the Citrakūṭa mountain. It is said in the *Mahābhārata* that if a person bathes in this river he earns the merit of performing one aśvamedhayajña.[82] In the *Rāmāyaṇa*[83] of Vālmīki and in the *Campūrāmāyaṇa*[84] it is described that when Rāma and Lakṣmaṇa once entered into the forest with Viśvāmitra, they knew about the origin of the river. Mandākinī is described as the daughter of Himavān or Himālaya. It has been said in the *Mahābhārata* that if a person bathes in that river daily he will be the possession of Rājalakṣmī (Royal Fortune.)[85]

(d) Vedaśruti

Bhojarāja mentions the river Vedaśruti in the following passage of his *Campūrāmāyaṇa*.

> '*atha niśīthe dāśarathiḥ........... syandanena vedaśruti...... .../*'[86]

The name of Vedaśruti is famous in the Epics and Purāṇas. It is mentioned in the Ayodhyākāṇḍa of the *Rāmāyaṇa* Rāma crossed this river and entered the hermitage of sage Agastya.[87] The modern name of this river is Sot or Sati.[88]

(e) Gomatī

The river Gomatī is mentioned in the Bālakāṇḍa of the *Campūrāmāyaṇa* Gomatī is another holy river of India.[89] Rāma's journey as described in the Ayodhyākāṇḍa of the *Rāmāyaṇa* he has crossed the river Gomatī.[90]

It has been said in the *Mahābhārata* that the presiding deity of Gomatī river lives in the court of Varuṇa constantly worshiping him.[91] Yudhiṣṭhira came to this river during his pilgrimage.[92] The river is known as Gomatī at present.[93]

(f) Niṣyandikā or Ṣyandikā

Niṣyandikā or Ṣyandikā is another river which is mentioned in the *Campūrāmāyaṇa*.[94] This river is very famous is purāṇas. Niṣyandikā is a river which flows in Kosala. It is said in the *Rāmāyaṇa* of Vālmīki that while Rāma started to the forest he crossed the river Niṣyandikā on his way. The modern name of this river is Sai.[96]

(g) Godāvarī

Bhojarāja casually refers to the Godāvarī river in the *Campūrāmāyaṇa*.[97] Godāvarī is a famous river of South India. According to the *Rāmāyaṇa* of Vālmīki, Rāma, Lakṣmaṇa and Sītā stayed for a long time during their exile in pañcavatī on the bank of this river Godāvarī.[98] The river Godāvarī is described in the *Mahābhārata* as a member of the court of Varuṇa.[99] According to this Epic one who bathes in this river will derive the benefit of performing a Gomedhayajña. Not only that, after his death he will go to the land of Vāsuki.[100] Godāvarī is one of the most important rivers of India.[101] It is known by the same name at present.[102]

Mountains in the Campūrāmāyaṇa

We find in the *Campūrāmāyaṇa* the names of many mountains of India like Himālaya, Vindhya, Citrakūṭa, Ṛsyamūka, Mahendra and Maināka, The last one is a suboceanic mountain which remains submerged in the waters of the Indian ocean.

(a) Himālaya

In the *Campūrāmāyaṇa* Bhoja refers to the mountain Himālaya in the following passage :

> *purā manoramā nāma sumerorbhavatsutā/*
> *gṛhamedhī tayaivāsīccakravartīṁ dharābhṛtām//*[103]

Among the mountains Himavān is the most important one from the point of his personification.[104] It is the Lord of the mountains.[105] Himālaya is one of the six rain producing mountains stretching from the east of India to its west.[106] Bhagīratha performed tapasyā on the Himālaya.[107]

(b) Vindhya

Vindhya is one of the seven chief mountain chains of India which finds a place in the *Campūrāmāyaṇa*. This mountain which separates South India from North India is famous in various ways in the Purāṇas. According to the *Rāmāyaṇa*, sage Agastya humbled this mountain which gradually rose towards the sky.[108] The beauty of the Vindhya mountain is described in the *Nalacampū* of Trivkramabhaṭṭa.[109]

(c) Citrakūṭa

Citrakūṭa is another mountain of India which is famous in the Epics and the Purāṇas. This mountain stands on the bank of the river Mandākinī.[110] Rāma lived in this mountain with Sītā and Lakṣmaṇa for a period of time.[111] According to the *Mahābhārata*, it is said that Rājalakṣmī (Royal Fortune) will embrace those who fast on Citrakūṭa after a bath in the Mandākinī.[112] This mountain is in Banda district of Uttarpradesh in modern India.[113]

(d) Ṛṣyamūka

The *Campūrāmāyaṇa* mentions another mountain

namely Ṛṣyamūka.[114] The *Mahābhārata* states that Rāma and Lakṣmaṇa visited sage Mārkeṇḍeya on the top of this mountain. It was here that Rāma and Lakṣmaṇa met Sugrīva.[115] According to Varāhamihira, the mountain belongs to South India.[116]

(e) Mahendra

The mountain Mahendra plays an important part in the story of the *Campūrāmāyaṇa*[117] Bhojarāja describes that Hanūmān limped to the sky from Mahendra while attempting to cross the ocean.[118] The mountain is mentioned in the *Rāmāyaṇa.*[119] and the *Mahābhārata.*[120] It was the permanent abode of sage Paraśurāma. After slaughtering the Kṣatriyas, sage Paraśurāma chose Mahendra as his permanent abode.[121] The *Mahābhārata* says that once Arjuna visited the mountain Mahendra.[122] The *Mahābhārata* describes that if a man bathes in the Rāmatīrtha on this mountain he will earn the puṇya of performing an Aśvamedha or horse sacrifice.[123] Brahmā once went to this mountain and performed a yāga there.[124] Yudhiṣṭhira, during his pilgrimage, visited this mountain.[125] Hanūmān while searching Sītā, visited this mountain along with other monkeys.[126]

(f) Maināka

We have already said that Maināka is a sub-oceanic mountain. The name of Maināka appears in the *Rāmāyaṇa*[127] and in the *Campūrāmāyaṇa* .[128] There is a unbreakable tie between Maināka and the kings of the Ikṣvāku family[129] There is a story in the *Rāmāyaṇa,* that in the old days mountains had wings and could fly like birds. The sight of the floating mountains aroused great fear in the heart of the people and so Indra chopped off their wings by his thunderbolt. Only Maināka escaped because he concealed himself in the water of the sea.[130] Bhoja has casually mentioned the story in the Sundarakāṇḍa of the *Campūrāmāyaṇa.*[131]

The Tribes of India

There were a number of tirbes in ancient India like Niṣāda, Pulinda and Śabara which have been mentioned in the *Campūrāmāyaṇa* also.

(a) Niṣāda

Niṣāda was one of the wild aboriginal tribes of India. They were mostly hunters, fisherman and robbers. Poet Vālmīki has mentioned about this Niṣāda tribes in his Epic.[132]

The Niṣāda tribe used to leave in forest. According to Manu, Niṣāda is the son of a Brāhmaṇa by a Śūdra woman.[133]

In the Ayodhyākāṇḍa of the *Campūrāmāyaṇa* it has been mentioned that when Rāma lived in exile he met Guha the Niṣāda king.[134]

(b) Pulinda

The Pulinda tribe was a barbarious savage aboriginal tribed who lived in mountains. In the *Campūrāmāyaṇa* the author casually mentions about Pulindas. In the Ayodhyākāṇḍa the author describes that when Sītā heard about the banishment of Rāma she was frightened like a peacock being terrified by the twang of a bow of a Pulinda hunter.[135]

From the *Mahābhārata* we gather some information about the Pulinda tribe. According to *Mahābhārata* the Pulindas were Kṣatriyas, but they became Śudras by a curse of the Brāhmaṇas.[136]

Pulindas were born from the foam of the celestial cow Nandinī of the sage Vasiṣṭha when she was enraged by the rash behaviour of king Viśāmitra.[137] According to *Mahābhārata*. Bhīma fought against the pulindas and destroyed all their big cities.[138] According to *Mahābhārata* Pulindas were belong to the Mleccha tribe became ruler in Kaliyuga.[139]

(c) Śabara

In the *Campūrāmāyaṇa* poet Bhoja casually mentioned about the Śabara tribe also. Śabarī a powerful female hermit belonged to this particular tribes. As described in the Araṇya-kāṇḍa when Rāma and Lakṣmaṇa visited the hermitage of sage Mātaṇga in search of Sītā, Śabarī who lived in her āśrama offered hospitality to Rāma and Lakṣmaṇa and advised them to go to Pampā lake for searching Sītā.[140]

The *Mahābhārata* also mentions the Śabaras, It is said about that the Śabaras were born from the dung and urine of Nandinī, the cow of sage Vasiṣṭha.[141] In early days the Śabaras lived in the kingdom of Māndhātā, their profession being murder and looting.[142]

(B)

Flora and fauna in the Campūrāmāyaṇa

Bhoja writes an account of various kinds of trees, birds, and animals in his *Campūrāmāyaṇa*. The description of different types of trees is found in the Sundarakāṇḍa of the book. Thus, the authors, while drawing a picture of the Aśoka garden of Rāvaṇa. shows that the garden possessed many rare and valuable trees like Nāga (Colophyllum inophyllum), puṁnāga (Mesua ferrea), Tāla (Borassusflabellifer),Hintāla (Phoenix sylvestris), Kṛtamāla (Cassia fistula), Sarala (Pinus longifalia), Bakula (Mimosop elengii), Vañjula (Saraca indica), Tilaka (Acacia arabica), Āmalaka (Phyllanthus emblica), Kuṭaja (Holarrphena antidyasenterica), Likuca (Artocarpus lakoocha), Kaṭaka (Sapindus mukorossi), Lavaṇga (Eugenia caryophyllaea), Ketakī (Pandanus fascicularis), Kadamba (Anthocephalus cadamba), Udumbara (Ficus glomerata), Kapitha (Albizzia lebbeck), Aśvatha (Ficus religiosa), Kunda (Jasminum pubescens), Tinduka (Diospyros ebenum), Candana (Santalum album), Syandana (Sesamum indicum), Campaka (Michelia Champaca), Cāmpeya (Crocus sativus), Panasa (Artocarpus integrifalia) Vetasa (Calamus viminalis), Palāśa (Butea monosperm), Priyāla (Buchanania latifolia) and Siṁśapā (Delbergia latifolia).[143] In the Bālakāṇḍa of the

Campūrāmāyaṇa, Bhoja gives an appropriate description of the body of Lord Viṣṇu which is all blue. The poet compared the body of the Lord Viṣṇu to a blue Atasī flower.[144] While describing the rainy season the poet says that Arjuna trees (Terminalia arjuna) were fully blooming in the Ṛṣyamūka mountain.[145] Similarly, in the Araṇyakāṇḍa while describing the beauty of Pampā the poet says that mādhavīlatā (Quisqualis indica) were blooming on the bank of the lake Pampā..[146] Apart from these Bhoja and Lakṣmaṇasūri gives an account of various kinds of trees like Kumuda (Nymphacalotus),[147] Padma (Nelumbium speciosum),[148] Nyagradha (Ficus bengalensis),[149] Girimallikā (Holorrhena antidyasenterica),[150] and Sāla (Shorea robusta).[151]

Birds

India is a paradise of birds and beasts. The animal population has past dwindled as a result of thoughtless poaching by merciless hunters. In old days though the human assult of birds and beasts are a regular feature, there was a great wealth of animals, birds and beasts of different varieties.

In the *Campūrāmāyaṇa*, there are references to such rare or common Indian birds like Cakora (Clamator jacobinus),[152] Kapota (Streptopelia tranquebarica),[153] Mayūra (Pavocristatus linnaeus),[154] Gṛdhra (Gyps bengalensis),[155] Kaṇka,[156] Kāka (Carvus macrorhynchos waglen)[157], Haṁsa (Anser indicus),[158] Rathāṅga (Tadornaferr uginea), [159] Uluka (Bubozeylonesis)[160], Parabhṛta (Eudynamys scolopacea linnaeus)[161] etc.

Animals

The *Campūrāmāyaṇa* mentions such rare and precious animals as lion, tiger, elephant, wild buffalo, alligator, python, antelope, wild dog and wild pig. The population of these animals has past-dwindled as a result of errating poaching, proper human care and encroachment upon their habitant. These animals are found in the different parts of the country.

In the Araṇyakāṇḍa of the *Campūrāmāyaṇa*, lion was mentioned in the context of Virādha Rākṣasa. Commentator Rāmacandra Budhendra has compared the ferocity of Virādha Rākṣasa with the ferocity of a lion.[162]

The lions were available in different places of ancient India. Now a days also lions are found in the Gir forest of Gujrat.[163]

In the same Kāṇḍa Bhoja has mentioned about the ferocious animals as 'hiṁsraiḥ satvāirna' Commentator Rāmacandra Budhendra has explained it as '...hiṁsraiḥ ghātukaiḥ satvairjantubhirvyāghrādibḥ'.[165] This passage refers to wild tigers.

It may be mentioned here that when Rāma failed to find out Sītā he doubted that tigers might have eaten her up. Tigers were also available in different jungles of ancient India in large number. At present also tigers are found in Kanha and Bandhavgarh in Madhya Pradesh, Ranthambhore in Rājasthān and Corbett and Dudhwa in Uttar Pradesh, Mānas and Kāziraṇgā in Assam and Nagarahola and Bandipur in Karnāṭaka.[166]

Both Bhoja and Lakṣmaṇasūri another of the *Campūrāmāyaṇa* have mentioned elephants in their writings. In the Araṇyakāṇḍa Bhoja has mentioned about the death of Vātāpidānava by entering in the stomach of sage Agastya. As wild elephant digest by Phython. Similarly, the Vātāpidānava also being digest in the stomach of Agastya.[167]

Wild elephant were available in the time of king Bhoja. Those are also available at present in the jungles of Central India (in Orisa, Bihar and West Bengal), North India (in sub Himālayān tracts of Uttar Pradesh), North East India (in Arunachal Pradesh, Assam, Meghalaya, Mizoram, Nagaland, Tripura, few come into Manipur, Apart from India, elephants are found in Nepal, Śrīlaṇka and Bangladesh.[168]

In the same Kāṇḍa Bhoja has mentioned about wild Buffalo also.[169] Those wild buffalos are available at present also in the forest and grassland of Gaṅgā, Brahmaputra Valley, Narmadā and Godāvarī.[170]

In the Yuddhakāṇḍa of the *Campūrāmāyaṇa*, Lakṣmaṇasūri has described the alligator.[171] The alligators are found mainly in the water-logged delta of the Gaṅgā between the Dāmodar and the Hoogly is the home of the alligator.[172]

Again Bhoja described about the antelopes in the Sundarakāṇḍa. He described that while Hanūmān climbed the mountain Mahendra it trembled for which the antelopes are frightened and started running. Because of their swift and speedy running the mountain became red by the dust.[173] These antelopes are also available at present in India. They are found in Ranthambhore National Park in Rajasthan, Satpura National Parks in Maharastra. They Belta Tiger Reserve in Bihar in Corbett and Dudhwa, Mānasa and Kāziraṅgā and most of the forests different parts of India.[174]

Wild dogs and pigs are mentioned in the *Campūrāmāyaṇa*.[175] The wild pigs and dogs are found in many forest of India.

(C)

The Social life of India as reflected in the Campūrāmāyaṇa

The Indian society possesses some special characteristic which distinguish it from other societies of the world in a significant way. Though the present day social life of India has undergone a remarkable change on its surface under the impact of foreign cultures, the basic and deeper character of the society has not altered even after the gradual penetration of the western culture even in modern times. The independent features of the social life which Indian people have successfully preserved through centuries existed in their full form in the age of Bhoja.

One striking feature of the social life of Indian which has been repeatedly mentioned by the authors of the

Dharmaśāstras, *Purāṇas* and other literary sources is the presence of Varṇāśrama division.

(i) Varṇa and Āśrama

Indian society have recognised four distinct classes viz. Brāhmaṇa Kṣatriya, Vaiśya and Śūdra. The authors of the Dharmaśāstra like Manu and Yājñavalkya have assigned specific due to these caste.[176] The Brāhmaṇas were mainly engaged for performing religious and academic activities. The Kṣatriyas (were) have been asked to perform martial activities. The Vaiśyas were always engaged in trade, agriculture etc. While the duty of the Śūdras to served other caste.[177] In the age of the *Campūrāmāyaṇa* the Brāhmaṇas and Kṣatriyas plays a significant part of the society.[178] As the theme of the *Campūrāmāyaṇa* is borrowed from the *Rāmāyaṇa* of Vālmīki. It is difficult to point out categorically to the activities performed by the different caste. But it is needless to say that the Brāhmaṇas performed Yāgas and other religious activities while Kṣatriyas like Bhojarāja himself were engaged in the protecting the people from internal and external enemies. Priesthood was another duty exclusively reserved for the Brāhmaṇas. Any attempt of encroachment on this privilage of Brāhmaṇa by a person belonging to any other varṇas was vehemently residently resisted by the Brāhmaṇa community and condemned by the society. Thus the Brāhmaṇas refused to co-operate with Viśvāmitra, who though a Kṣatriya, was acting as a priest in the sacrifice of Triśaṇku.[179] In every kingdom there was a Brāhmaṇa purohita, who very often was also the king's chief counsellor. Sage Vasiṣṭha in Ayodhyā enjoyed very wide powers and high position.[180]

The second Varṇa was the kṣatriya Varṇa which was constituted of the martial section of the community. The status of a kṣatriya in the society, however, was next to that of a Brāhmaṇa, granting protection to the weak and the oppressed was the primary duty of the Kṣatriyas. In the Bālakāṇḍa of the *Campūrāmāyaṇa* king Daśaratha was hasitating to send Rāma with Viśvāmitra, but Vasiṣṭha reminded him that there was no duty of the Kṣatriyas more cherished than protection.[181] In the *Campūrāmāyaṇa* references to Vaiśyas are comparatively few. In the Ayodhākāṇḍa of this book it appears that they were engaged in trade, agriculture and cattle-rearing.[182]

The last Varṇa comprised of the Śūdras. They served the higher three Varṇas.[183] In the *Campūrāmāyaṇa* there is not the slightest indication of hatred by the higher three Varṇas towards the Śūdras. Śūdras were living in perfect goodwill with the rest of the people. Bhojarāja refers to the Varṇāśrama system in one passage of his work.

> *'Kṣtradharmoapi dharmyātpathaḥ pramādyāpi varṇāśramarakṣaṇataḥ samīcīnaḥ prāyeṇa puruṣaṁ niḥśreyase niyojayet'.*[184]

The four āśramas are recognised by the authors of the *Dharmaśāstras* viz. Brahmacārya,[185] Gārhasthya,[186] Vānaprastha[187] and Sannyāsa.[188] The reference of the Varṇāśrama passages clearly proves that these āśramas are definitely existing in the contemporary society. Brahmacārya refers to the student life gārhasthya refers to the weeded life of the householder. Vānaprastha denotes the life of a hermit started by a householder after quiting his worldly life, and sannyāsa refers to complete renunciation of the world. There are elaborate descriptions of these four stages of life in the writings of the eminent authors like Manu, Yajñavalkya and Vasiṣṭha.

Manu describes academic activities primarily meant for the Brāhmaṇas.[189] But it is interesting to note that Bhojarāja, who was a Kṣatriya, emerged as the most prolific writer of his age.

Religious life

It can be gathered from a critical study of the *Campūrāmāyaṇa* that people were engaged in both Vedic and non-vedic religious practices. The religions of India in those days ranged from the Vedic cult to the left path of the Vāmācāra Tāntrics. Viṣṇu occupies a dominent position in the religious society. Bhoja himself was a great devotee of

Viṣṇu. The reference to 'vāmācāra' in the *Campūrāmāyaṇa* clearly proves that the left path of the Tāntric cult flourished in the society side by side with other religious cult.

Vedic cult

Bhojarāja refers to Vedic sacrifices on different occasions. It does not necessarily signify that Vedic sacrifices like Aśvamedha or Vājapeya[190] were performed regularly in his days. But it is a fact that some Vedic sacrifices were always performed in India. This is true in the case of such daily Yāgas a Agnihotra and soma occasional Yāgas or Iṣṭis like putreṣṭi or putrakāmeṣṭi. It is always a difficult job to perform an Aśvamedha sacrifice which only powerful kings can initiate, but they are also not able to accomplish it without hindarances. In the *Campūrāmāyaṇa*, there is a reference to king Daśaratha performing an Aśvamedha Kratu in order to have an issue by the grace of gods. It is described in the following passage of the work.

> '*athasminnapatyatayā dūyamānamānase putrārthaṁ kratumāśvamedhaṁ vidhātuṁ mantribhiḥ saṁṁ mantrayamāṇe Daśarathe sumantraḥ prahṛṣṭamanā maharṣeraṅgade śasangatāvagrahanigrahaśauṇḍasya vibhāṇḍakasūnorvaśyaṁṛsyaśṛṇgasya prasādātpra-bhavo bhavitā kumārāṇāmiti sanatkumārodirītaṁ purāvṛttamasmai Daśarathāya kathayāmāsa.*'[192]

Bhoja describes the pitiable condition of sacrificial fires like Gārhapatya, who quitted their scheduled seats in the sacrificial alter and acted as cooks in the kitchen of Rāvaṇa.[193] The commentator Rāmacandra Budhendra, while explaining the relevent passage viz. 'etepi pāvakāḥ' etc. ennumarate the sacrificial fires as Gārhapatya, Āhavanīya and Dakṣiṇa which are the three divisions of fire in a Vedic sacrifice which are inflamed in different fire places.[194] The reference to the fires like 'Gārhapatya' in Bhoja's *Campūrāmāyaṇa* shows that the Vedic cult existed in its full form in the contemporary religious society.

Bhoja repeatedly uses the word 'avabhṛtha' in the sence of a 'Yāga'.[195] But 'avabhṛtha', in the Vedic tradition does not mean all sacrifices but 'avabhṛtha' was one important ritual performed in a Gavāmayana (Soma) Yāga where the fibres of Soma creeper after Somarasa is extracted is put in a container and the same should be upturned in the water.[196]

Viṣṇu's prominance in the religious society

Viṣṇu is a prominent Vedic God. The name of the God appears in a hymn of the first maṇḍala of the *Ṛgveda* where the god is described as the dweller of the celestial region viewed by only the learned seers.[197] Viṣṇu spreads his three strides over the universe.[198] The word 'Viṣṇu' is explained as an all pervasive god.[199] In the *Śuklayajurveda*, god Viṣṇu is described as the creator of the worlds.[200] He is a great friend of India in the Vedas.[201] But Viṣṇu emerges into the most exalted position in the Purāṇic age. The Purāṇic literature gives an elaborate account of various incarnations of Viṣṇu.[202] Thus, in the *Bhāgavatapurāṇa*[203] and the *Viṣṇupurāṇa*[204], Viṣṇu is recognised as the Supreme Being. Viṣṇu is variously known as Nārāyaṇa, Hari, Govinda, Mukanda etc.[205] Bhoja describes Viṣṇu as a dweller of Vaikuṇṭha, He remains associated with Goddess Laksmī. He has a blue colour resembling the beauty of Atasī flowers, Viṣṇu carries a bow called Śārṇga.[206] He relaxes on the serpent bed of Ananta in the Milky Ocean.[207] Bhoja ulogises God Viṣṇu as Nārāyaṇa who possesses a pair of extended blue eyes like lotus flower.[208] Such descriptions of Viṣṇu are regularly found in the Purāṇic and the post purāṇic period.

In the *Viṣṇupurāṇa* there is an eulogy of Lord Viṣṇu where Viṣṇu's highest abode is described.[209] Viṣṇu is also described in one passage as 'paramapada' or the highest God.[210] In the *Campūrāmāyaṇa* Bhojarāja refers to three incarnations of Viṣṇu viz. Vāmana or the Dwarf incarnation, [211] Nrsiṁha or Manlion who vanquished the demons.[212] and finally Rāma or Rāmacandra who is the hero of the *Rāmāyaṇa* and the *Campūrāmāyaṇa*. Nārāyaṇa or Viṣṇu tamed the mighty demon Vali who was a great devotee of the demon king with his three feet. While assuming the man-lion form the same God destroyed Hiraṇyakaśipu and saved his son Prahlāda from the tyranny of his father. These accounts are found in the Purāṇic literature.[213] Rāma killed Rāvaṇa and thus saved the worlds of man and divine beings from the constant oppression of this wicked demon of Laṇkā.[214] Though there is no direct reference to Viṣṇu worship in the *Campūrāmāyaṇa* it is clear from such poems as

(a) Prahlādasya vyasanamamitaṁ daityavargasya dambhaṁ
stambhaṁ vakṣaḥshthalamapi riporyaugapadyena bhettum/
baddhaśradhaṁ puruṣavapuṣā miśrite viśvadṛṣṭe
daṁṣṭrārocirvi śadabhuvane raṁhasā siṁhaveṣe//[215]

(b) nārāyāṇa nalināyatalocanāya
nāmāvaśeṣita mahābalivaibhavāya/
nanācarācaravidhāyakajanmadeśa
nābhīpuṭāya puruṣāya namaḥ parasmai//[216]

that the Viṣṇu cult emerged into great prominance in the Indian society in the age of Bhoja. In fact Bhoja himself was the devotee of the God Viṣṇu.

Śiva in the Campūrāmāyaṇa

Śiva was a great god of the Indians. Śiva occupies a prominent position by the side of Viṣṇu in the Purānic literature. Rāvaṇa, the Villain of the *Campūrāmāyaṇa* was a great devotee and worshipper of Śiva.[217] In the *Kūrmapurāṇa* it is said that Śiva created the heretical doctrines as advised by Viṣṇu.[218] Though Śiva occupies a very significant position in the religious life of India, he is only casually mentioned in the *Campūrāmāyaṇa*.[219] We do not gather any idea of Śiva worship or Śaivism from the *Campūrāmāyaṇa*, though it is coroborated by records that Bhoja refers to this god in the following verse of the *Campūrāmāyaṇa*.

tāṁ nadīṁ vibudhā labdhvā nākalokamanīnayan/
tapasyantīṁ girirgaurīṁ devāya mahate dadau//[220]

Śiva's name appears in the descripition of the emergence of the river Gaṅgā in the *Campūrāmāyaṇa*.

Bhoja was a prominent exponent of the Śaiva philosophy. He also wrote

(a) *avalepabharākrāntā suralokataraṅgiṇī/*
papāta pārvatīkāntajaṭākāntāragahvare//

(b) *alabdhanirgamā śambhoḥ kapardādamarāpagā/*
dadhau dūrvāśikhālagnatuṣārakaṇikopamām//

(c) *adṛṣṭvā tāṁ nadīṁ tatra tuṣṭāva parameśvaram/*
Bhagiratho vidheḥ krauyātparikṣīṇamanorathaḥ//[221]

Other gods in the Campūrāmāyaṇa

Bhoja pay obeissance to Heramba or 'Gaṇeśa' in the beginning of his work.[222] Heramba is famous as 'Vighnanāśaka' or the dispeller of all impediments for which his grace has become necessary for the poet to complete his literary work without any obstruction.[223] But there is no reference to 'Gaṇeṣa' worship in this Campūkāvya of Bhoja and Lakṣmaṇasūri.

Vāmācāra in the age of Bhoja

Bhoja casually mentions Vāmācārā in a passage of his work viz.

'kau yuvāṁ yuvānau, kutasyau, vāmācāravatpratibhāti vāmācāraḥ/ Cīraṁ vapuṣi jaṭāḥ śirasi, kare ca caṇḍakodaṇdaḥ / kvāyamākalpaḥ, kvaca kalpalatākalpeya manalpābharaṇā taruṇīti/'[224]

The commentator Rāmacandra Budhendra is unable to understand the meaning of the expression Vāmācāra.[225] Vāmācāra refers to the Tāntric cult of the Leftpath. The Tāntric religion is practically a new religion. There are two distinct paths in this religion viz. 'Dakṣiṇamārga' or 'Rightpath and the 'Vāma' or the Leftpath. The Right path of Tāntricism is a moderate school of the Tāntric sect. The Left path is an extreme one. Kaulas, Kāpālikas, Paśupātas and Cinas are all followers of the Vāmācāra. The five 'makāras or 'm' s viz. matsya, māṁsa, madya, mudrā and maithuna are essentially required in it.

The demon Virādha scoffs at Rāma and Lakṣmaṇa who are ascetics in their outward garb but they are associated with a beautiful woman. A woman is a must in the Vāmācāra religion.

The Tāntric religion developed to its fullform in the age of the *Campūrāmāyaṇa.* Bhojarāja refers to the Uccāṭanamantras by means of which the enemies can be driven away. The Tāntrics apply jārana, māraṇa, śoṣana, uccāṭana, vaśīkaraṇa etc. to tackle the enemies. Bhoja describes that the twanging sound of the bow of Lakṣmaṇa acted like the uccātana hymns of Tāntrics which disturbed the ghouls of Citrakūṭa (forest).[226]

Hermit life

Bhoja describes the hermitages of India where the dwellers were daily engaged in religious activities. Of course, the religious life of the Indian saints was the same for centuries, and they were not different in Bhoja's time. Bhoja refers to the sweet smell of clearified butter (ghṛta) oozing constantly from the sacrificial fire of the saints.[227] He also mentions in the passage, viz.

adṛśyarupābhivanadevatābhiravakīryamāṇabaliku-sumam'[228]

of his kāvya 'balikusuma' or flowers offered to gods at the time of their worship.[229] He draws an excellent picture of bark garments (Valkala) and deer skin (ajina) used by ascetics which were hanging from the branches of trees in the hermitage.[230] In one passage of the Araṇyakāṇḍa, he refers to the religious practice of performing japas in order to drive away the wicked female ghouls.[231]

It is clear from the above descriptions that Bhoja has tried to present a vivid picture of the religious life of the people of his age. The author, in the course of describing the forest life led by Rāma, Lakṣmaṇa and Sītā, incidentally mentions that Lakṣmaṇa was 'atithijanasaparyāparyutsuka' or eager to serve his guests (with fruits and roots).[232] Now, 'atithijanasaparyā' is not an isolated case in the case of Lakṣmaṇa, but it was one of the five compulsory duties of a householder to worship his guests by all possible means. This rule prevailed certainly in the days of Bhojarāja also. The Indian people are always hospitable by nature.[233] Rāmacandra Budhendra gives us a tentative idea of offering hospitality in his comentary on the verse viz.

> *'tathātithyaṁ cakre Bharatavalabhājāṁ tanubhṛtāṁ Bharadvājaḥ soayaṁ*
> *bhrukutibhaṭakalpakhilasuraḥ/*
> *tapastaptvā ghoraṁ divi sumanasastatphalabhujo yathā teṣāṁ toṣāṁ*
> *kṣaṇamabhilaṣeyurmunikṛtam//*[234]

He shows that the host usually offers objects of toilet, water for taking bath, clothes and garlands, ornaments,[235] sweetables and drinkis to the guest.[236] Bhoja repeatedly talks about the hospitality shown by different sages to Rāmacandra while Rāma was living in the forests.[237]

Education

(a) System of education

In ancient India, the Gurukula system of education prevalied throughout the country. There were some centres of higher studies in certain cities like Nālandā and Kānyakubja. Though we do not find any direct reference to the Gurukula system of education in the *Campūrāmāyaṇa*, it was existent in the days of Bhojarāja also. This system was substituted by the modern system of study introduced by the British rulers.

(b) Subjects studied

A number of subjects were studied in the age of Bhoja. We learn from the *Campūrāmāyaṇa* that astrology, Sanskrit and Prākṛta grammar and Kāvyas were studied in the age of Bhoja. It must be admitted here that we gather only a limited account of the different subjects which were studied in those days from the *Campūrāmāyaṇa* of king Bhoja than his personal history. We have shown in the introduction that Bhoja was a great authority in innumerable lores. In the Bālakāṇḍa of the book Bhoja gives a detailed heroscope of Rāmacandra in the following verse.

> *'uccasthe grahapañcake suragurau sendaunavamyāṁ tithau*
> *lagne karkaṭake punarvasuyute meṣaṁ gate pūṣaṇi/*
> *nirdaghuṁ nikhilāḥ palāśasamidho medhyādayodhyāraṇe*
> *rāvirbhūtamabhūta pūrvamaparaṁ yatkiñcidekaṁ mahaḥ//*[238]

Bhoja had extensive knowledge of astrology. He says that when five planets occupied their exalted position in the zodiac, and Jupiter was in conjunction with the moon, Rāma was born. He suggested that when Rāma was born, Jupiter was occupying the Karkaṭarāsi (Cancer), Mars was in Makara, Venus in Mina, Sun was in Meṣa (Aries) and Saturn occupied Tulā (Libra). The combination of Jupiter with Moon created Jīvayoga. This is the reason for which Rāma lived a long life, and he was a master of many (thousand) people.

Study of Grammar

Bhoja was an eminent Sanskrit grammarian. He was great follower of Pāṇini. Bhoja uses a number of rare words like 'pacelima', [239] 'rājanvatī', [240] and sthandilaśāyi.[241] In order to use or explain these words an intensive and extensive study of Pāṇini's grammar is essentially necessary. The Commentator quotes all the relevant rules of Pāṇini in interpreting these words from the grammatical point of view.[242] Bhoja refers to Prākṛta vyākaraṇa in the passage 'prākarṭa vyākaraṇaṁiva prakaṭitavarṇavyatyāsaṁ'.[243] The Prākṛta language was spoken by a large section of people of India. It had an extensive, scientifically worked out grammatical system. Vararuci presents a systematic Prākṛta grammar in the form of the famous *Prākṛta-prakāśa.* In later times kramadīśvara, author of the '*Saṁkṣiptasāra*, gives an account of the Prākṛta language by devoting a section of his grammar to the study of the Prākṛta language.[244] Bhoja refers to 'varṇavyatyāsa' in Prākṛta grammar in a passage of his work.[245] Such 'Varṇvyatyāsas' or mutation of letters are found in such prākṛta words a 'vicchuo' (Sanskrit vṛścika)[246] moro (Sanskrit-Mayūra)[247]

The Study of Kāvya

The Kāvya literature thrived in India since the time of the *Rāmāyaṇa*. The four great Mahākāvyas of Kālidāsa, Bhārvi and Māgha were written several countries before Bhoja wrote his Campūkāvya. Bhoja describes a poetical, that is, a kāvya as consisting of several sargas.[248] The *Rāmāyaṇa* of Vālmīki as divided into Kāṇḍas while its subdivisions are called sargas. Bhoja, in fact, refers to the Kāvya or Mahākāvya in his description of a 'padyaprabandha' when he says 'padyaprabandhamiva darśitasvarga-bhedam'.[249] It is needless to state that Bhoja was accuinted with poetical composition divided into sargas. Kāvyas were studied together with the science of prosody by at least a section of people likc Blıoja himself.

The study of Philosophy

Bhoja was an eminent writer of Śaiva philosophy. We have already mentioned his Tattvaprakāśa, a work on Śaivadarśana which is quoted by the renowned philosopher Mādhava in his '*Sarvadarśanasaṁgraha*'.[250] However, Bhoja does not discuss Indian philosophy in his *Campūrāmāyaṇa* except for a reference to the Rajo Guṇa, one of the three qualities mentioned in the Sāṁkhya philosophy in a description of Ahalyā found in the following poem :

Duḥkhe sukhe ca raja eva babhūva hetustādṛgvidhe
mahati Gautamadharmapatnyāḥ/
yasmād guṇena rajasā vikṛtiṁ gatā sā
Rāmasya pādarajasā prakṛtiṁ prapede.//[251]

Arts and Architecture

Lakṣmaṇasūri refers to the 'Sakalāḥ kalā' or all types of arts in the first verse of the Yuddhakāṇḍa of the *Campūrāmāyaṇa*.[252] Rāmacandra Budhendra explains these (sixty-four) arts which include the art of acting, singing, dancing the faculty of writing poetry, the art of playing dice etc. The Tāntric activities viz. stambhana, vaśīkaraṇa uccāṭana and māraṇa are incorporated in the list of sixty-four arts.[253]

In the *Campūrāmāyaṇa*, there is a casual reference to 'lasikālāsyopadeśa', Now, 'lāsya' refers to a gaitful dance and 'lasikā' means a (trained) dancer, There is also a significant word. viz. 'desikā'. Rāmacandra Budhendra explains the word 'lāsikā' as a dancer, but he says that 'desikā' means directors of the dramatical art.[254] Rāmacandra was well acquainted with the arts of dancing[255] and acting[256] which were duly cultured by a section of people in his days. In fact these two arts were prevalent in the Indian society since very ancient times and there was no interruption to them at any time.

Bhoja was conversant with the architectural science. He gives a vivid account of different type of palaces built by applying an extensive and intricate technics of Indian Vāstūśilpa in his *Samarāṅgaṇasūtradhāra.*[257] But Bhoja does not describe these palaces in his *Campūrāmāyaṇa.* On the other he gives a panoramic account of the costly and excellent royal palaces of Rāvaṇa which were studded with māṇikya gems.[258] Luxurious mansions in the city of Laṇkā were used as royal baths. These mansions had many golden pillars which were decorated with dolls made of moonstones in order to keep water cool. While refering to royal palaces of those days, it should be noted here that the royal palaces were associated with swimming pools.[259]

Food and drinks

Rice and roti are the two staple foods of the people of India. Rice was eaten since very ancient times in India in all parts of the country. Rice was duly cultivated in India in the age of Bhojarāja as evidenced by a description in the Araṇyakāṇḍa of *Campūrāmayaṇa*. The authors refers to paddy fields which were covered by ripe śāli plants in this Kāṇḍa.[260] The fields were duly girdled by a large number of dykes which were prepared to preserve the water in the paddy fields.[261]

Bhojarāja describes the country of Vatsa as 'vitīrṇasurasaritpūraḥ saṁpūrṇasasye vatsābhidhāne janapade .... niśāmanaiṣīt.'[262] A similar description of the Vatsa country is found in the following passage of the *Rāmāyaṇa* also viz.

'tataḥ saṁrdhañca śubhasasyaśālinaḥ
kṣaneṇa vatsan muditānupāgamat/[263]

Rāmacandra Budhendra, while explaining the relevent passage of the Ayodhyākāṇḍa of the *Campūrāmāyaṇa* states that the country of Vatsa was rich in paddy and other cereals which were produced with the help of the water of the Gaṅgā.[264]

Roti or Chapati became a food of a large section of people of this country probably in a later period. References to this particular food is found in the *Śubdānuśāsana* of Hemacandra,[265] and the *Bhāvaprakāśa* of Bhāvamiśra.[266] Bhojarāja does not mention this particular food in his work.

Tea or coffee or such soft drinks of our days were not known to the people in the age of the *Campūrāmāyaṇa*. Pānakarasa was an aristocratic drink in ancient India, particularly in the Buddhist period. Guṇaratna writes that Buddhists used to drink Pānaka in the afternoon as they were not allowed to take solid food by Buddhist laws.[267] Wine was drunk by a section of people since the Vedic age, In the *Rāmāyaṇa* of Vālmīki there is a reference to Maireya wine. Sītā promised to worship the river Gaṅgā with a thousand pots of wine if she would return to Ayodhyā with her husband and Lakṣmaṇa after period of banishment was over.[268]

In the *Campūrāmāyaṇa* there is a reference to '*Vīrapāṇa*' in the Araṇyakāṇḍa.[269] The commentator Rāmacandra Budhendra explains 'Vīrapāṇa' as : 'Vīrānām avaśyakaranīyaṁ madhupānam' or the hero's compulsory drinking of wine while going out to a fight a battle kept ready for the fighters in those days with the aim of producing vigour and courage in their bodies and minds.[270] The *Amarakoṣa* describes 'vīrapāṇa' as 'vīrapāṇaṁ tu yat pānaṁ vṛtte bhāvini va raṇe.[271] Which adequately explains the meaning of the term. Of course, there is no reference to the rugular habit of drinking by men and women in normal times in the *Campūrāmāyaṇa*. It is said there that 'vīrapāṇa' was made in a pān made of leafs.[272] There is a similar description of Raghu's warriors drinking cocoanut wine in the *Raghuvaṁśa* of Kālidāsa in leaf pots.[273]

In the Sundarakāṇḍa of the *Campūrāmāyaṇa*, Bhoja describes that monkey drank (honey) with great joy when they learnt that Hanūmān could Sītā in the city of Laṇkā.[274]

Dress, ornaments and cosmetics

In the history of mankind dress came to be recognised as an important mark of civilized living. The inventive faculty of man took into consideration the requirements of different climates and created countless varieties of dress materials and styles.

It is clear from a passage of the *Campūrāmāyaṇa* that there was a section of extremely poor people who begged alms from door to door. They were never favoured by the Goddess of wealth.[275] But there was a priviledged section in the society who always received the grace of this elusive goddess. These people used costly garments and cosmetics. Thus, in the description of Autumn in the *Campūrāmāyaṇa*, we hear that some wealthy people covered their bodies in winter with rugs made of soft hair grown in the stomach of hare.[276] It can be easily imagined how costly these garments were, and how much of invaluable natural wealth was wasted in the name of enjoying comfort. It is the extravagance of merciless mankind which has contributed to the dwindling of many rare fauna in the whole world. It reminds us of the erratic behaviour of a section of modern people who hunt Kangarros and serve their meat to domestic dogs. Many rich people and particularly kings painted their bodies with black agaru and saffron (Kāśmīraṅgarāga) in order to remove the tormenting heat of their body in the age of the *Campūrāmāyaṇa*.[277]

In the *Campūrāmāyaṇa* the author describes that people

used golden ornaments. Bhoja employs various synonyms of gold viz. Kāñcana,[278] Kārtasvara,[279] Hāṭaka[280] and Hema[281] etc. Among the precious stones he mentions Indranīla,[282] Candrakānta[283], (moonstone), Marakata,[284] Sphaṭika[285] (Crystal), and Muktā,[286] The skilled artisans of that period probably made beautiful articles of decoration with this material to enhance the beauty of person and palace.

The ornaments worn on the head were known as 'cūḍāmaṇi', In the Yuddhakāṇḍa of the *Campūrāmāyaṇa*, we find a description of Rāvaṇa wearing cūḍāmaṇi on his head. Reference to 'Cūḍāmaṇi' is met with in the Sundarakāṇḍa of the *Campūrāmāyaṇa* also.[288]

References

1. *kandarpo mūrtimānāsītkāma ityucyate budhaiḥ/*
   tapasyantamiha sthānuṁ niyamena samāhitam//
   kṛtodvāhaṁ tu deveśaṁ gacchantaṁ samarudraṇam/
   dharṣayāmāsa durmedhā humkṛtaśca mahātmanā//
   avadhyātaśca rudreṇa cakṣusā raghunandana/
   vyaśīryanta śarīrātsvātsarvagātrāni durmateḥ//
   tatra gātraṁ hataṁ tasya nirdagdhasya mahātmanaḥ/
   aśarīaḥ kṛtaḥ kāmaḥ kodhāddeveśvarena ha//
   anaṅga iti vikhyātastadā prabhṛti rāghava/
   ca cāṅgaviṣayaḥ śrīmānyatrāṅgagam sa mumuca ha//
   Vāl. Rāmā. Bālakāṇḍa, 23, 10-14.
2. *'Aṇgadeśa... ṛṣyaśṛṁga... Śāntākutumbiaṁ*
   sambandinaṁ munimānīya vasiṣṭhadiṣṭhamaśvame—
   dhādhvaraṁ sarayūrodhasi vidhāya tatra
   putriyāmiṣṭiṁ vidhivatkartumārabhata/'
   CR. Bālakāṇḍa, pp. 15-16.
3. *kāsyapasya ca putroasti vibhāṇḍaka iti śrutaḥ/*
   Ṛṣyaśṛṁga iti khyātastasya putro bhaviṣyati/
   Aṅgeṣu prathitorājā bhaviṣyati mahābalaḥ/
   tasya vyatikramādrājño bhaviṣyati sudāruṇā/
   anāvṛṣṭiḥ sughorā vai sarvalokabhayāvahā/
   anāvṛṣṭyāṁ tu vṛttyāṁ rājña duḥkasamanvitaḥ//
   Vāl. Rāmā, Canto 9, 3, 4, 8, 9.
4. *abhiṣiktoaṅgarājye sa śrīyā yukto Mahāvalaḥ*
   sacchatravātavyajano jayaśabdottarena ca//
   uvāca kauravaṁ rājanvacanaṁ sa vṛṣastadā/
   asya rājyapradānasya sadṛśaṁ kiṁ dadāni te//
   Mbh. Ādiparva, Ch. 136, 38, 39.

5. *Aṅgavaṅgakaliṅgaṣu yāhi tirthāni kānicit/*
jagāma tāni sarvāni puṇyā puṇyānyāytanānica//
Ibid., Ch. 215. 9.
6. *atha dvipaiderbaripudbipābhai derbāidarpāyamaha matyudagram/*
kaliṅgavaṅgāṅgānisadavira jighāmsabaḥ pāndavammyudhāban//
Ibid. Karṇaparva. Ch. 17. 12
7. Ancient Geo. of India. p. 108.
8. *'asti praśastā janalocanānāmānandasaṁdāyiṣu kosaleṣu/*
ājñāsamutsāritadānavānāṁ rājñāmayodhyeti purī raghunām//
CR. Bālakāṇḍa, Verse 11
kosalonāmamuditaḥ sphito janapado mahān/
niviṣṭaḥ sarayūtīre prabhūtadhanadhānyavān//
Vāl. Rāmā. Bālakāṇḍa, Canto 5, Verse 5.
9. *Ayodhyānāmanajarī tatrāsīllokaviśrutā//*
manunā mānavendreṇa yā purī nirmitā svayam//
tāṁ tu rājā daśaratho mahārāṣtravivardhanaḥ/
purimāvāsayāmāsa divi devapatiryathā//
Ibid., Verse 6, 9
10. HGAI, 20
11. *tato gopālakakṣṁ ca sottarānapi kosalān/*
mallānāmadhipaṁ caiva prāthivaṁ cājayatprabhuḥ//
Mbh. Sabhāparva, Ch. 30. Verse 3.
12. *ṛṣabhaṁ tīrthamāsādya kosalayāṁ narādhipa/*
bājapeyambāproti trirātroposito naraḥ//
gosahasraphalaṁ vindhyātkulaṁ caiva samudharet/
kosalāṁ tu samāsādya kālatīrthamupaspṛśet//
Ibid, Vanaparva, Ch. 85, Verses 10, 11
13. *ahaṁ vicitravīryasya dve kanye samudāvaham*
jitvā ca māgadhānsarvān kāśīnatha ca kosalān//
Ibid, Anuśāsanaparva, Ch. 44, Verse 38.
14. Ancient Geo. of India, p. 110
15. *'..........tadanu Janakarājadhānīṁ...nagaryāmārabdhayajñasya janakasya bhāgadheyātsītā nāmadheyabhājanamajījanatkanyāratnaṁ ratnagarbhā bhagavatī'.*
CR. Bālakāṇḍa, pp. 96-97.
16. *'avammuktvā muniśreṣṭhaṁ vedeho Mithilādhipaḥ'*
Vāl, Rāmā. Bālakāṇḍa, Canto 65, Verse 39
17. Geo. of early Buddhism, p. 131
Ancient Geo of India, Cunnighum, p. 718
ed. Mazumder, S. N.
18. *'Nimi paramadharmātmā sarvastvavatāṁ varaḥ/*

tasya putro Mithirnāma Janakomithiputrakaḥ/
prathojanakorājā Janakādpyudavasuḥ//
Vāl. Rāmā. Bālakāṇḍa, Canto 71, Verses 3, 4,

19. VP. P. 388
20. *anujasya vikukṣestu nimervaṁśaṁ nibodhat/*
yoasau niveśayāmāsa puraṁ devapuropamm//
jayaṁtamiti vikhyātaṁ gautamasyāśramāntikam/
yasyānvavāye yajñe vai janako nṛpasattamaḥ//
nirmirnāma sudharmātmā sarvasattvanamaskṛtaḥ/
āsītputro mahārāja cekṣvakurbhūritejasaḥ//
sa śāpena vasiṣṭhasya videha samapadyat/
tasya putro Mithirnāma Janitaḥ parvabhistribhiḥ/
araṅyāṁ mathyamānāyā pradurbhūtomahayaśāḥ//
nāmnā mithiriti khyāto jananājjanako abhavat//
mithirnāma mahāvīryo yenasau mithilāabhavat/
rājāasu nāma janako janakāccāpyudavasuḥ//
Bra. Purāṇa Verses 1-6, pp. 135-136
21. *upāssva kaunteya sahānujasatvaṁ*
tasyāśramaṁ puṇyatamṁ praviśya/
aṣṭāvakraṁ yasya dauhitramāhu
yoasau bandiṁ janakasyātha yajña//
Mbh. Vanaparva Ch. 132. Verse 5.
22. *tataḥ kośaṁ samādāya vāhanāni ca bhūriśaḥ/*
pāṇḍunā mithilāṁ gatvā videhaḥ samarejitaḥ//
Ibid Ādiparva, Ch. 113, Verse 28.
23. *Uttīrya sarayūṁ ramyāṁ dṛṣtvā pūrvāṁśca kosalān/*
atītya jagmurmithilāṁ mālāṁ carmanvatīṁ nadīm//
Ibid, Sabhāparva, Ch, 20, Verse 28.
24. *'aṅgān vaṅgān kaliṅgāścasundikān mithilānatha'*
Ibid, Vanaparva, Ch. 254, Verse 8.
25. Ibid, *Śāntiparva*, Ch. 325, Verse 5.
26. *Rāmākarṣaṇabhagnakārmukabhuvā dhvānena rudorudhā*
dṛptakṣatrayaśaḥ sitacchadakule jīmūtanādāyitam//
Vīraśrīprathamapraveśasamaye puṇyāhaghoṣāyitaṁ
sītāyāḥ kila mānase pariṇaye māṅgalyatūryāyitam//
CR. Bālakāṇḍa, Verse 104
27. Bhā, 9th Skandha.
28. *'pādādardhaṁpraṇayamadhuraṁ kekayedrasya putryai'*
kekeyendrasya kekayadeśādhīśvarasya'
CR. Bālakāṇḍa p. 35
29. *rukmaniṣkasahasre dve ṣodaśāsvaśatāni ca/*
satkṛtya kekayīputraṁ kakakī dhanamādiśat//
sa dattaṁ kekayendreṇa dhanaṁ tannabhyanandat/
Bharataḥ kekayīputro gamanatvarayātadā//
Vāl. Rāmā Ayodhyakāṇḍa, Canto 70. 21. 24.

30. *'......trikūṭaśṛṅgāmlaṅkāmabhigantumaṅgada........ .... samanīnahat.'* CR. Yuddhakāṇḍa, p. 441
31. *'Trikūṭasya tate Laṅkāṁ sthitaḥ svasthodadarśaha/* Vāl. Rāmā. Sundarakāṇḍa, Canto 2, Verse 1.
32. Vāl. Rāma. Uttarawkāṇḍa, Canto 15, 16.
33. *Laṅkāṁ samastāṁ saṁpīḍya laṇgulāgniṁ kapiḥ/* Vāl. Rāmā. Sundarakāṇḍa, Canto 54, Verse 49
tato hatvā daśagrīvāṁ laṅkāṁ rāmo mahāyaśāḥ/
vibhiṣaṇāya pradadau prabhuh parapurañjayaḥ//
Mbh. Vanaparva, Ch. 291, Verse 5, 6.
34. *'tatkṣaṇaṁ Lakṣmaṇāgrajaḥ sugrīveṇa saha suvela calakūṭamadhiruḥa... siṁhaladvīpakamalakarṇikām'* CR. Yuddhakāṇḍa, p. 478
35. *mūtrataścāsrgātkāṁścicchabarāmsciva pārśvataḥ/*
puṇdrānkirātannyabanānsiṁhalanbarbarānkhasān//
Mbh. Ādiparva, Ch. 175, Verse 37.
36. 'drāviḍaḥ siṁhalāsciva rājākāśmīrakastathā' Ibid. Sabhāparva Ch. 34. Verse 12.
37. *samudrasāraṁ vaiduryaṁ muktāsaṁghāṁstathiva ca/*
śataśśca kuryāstatra siṁhalāḥ samupāharan//
Ibid, Ch. 52, Verse 35
38. vatsābhidhāne janapade' CR. Ayodhyākāṇḍa p. 185
39. *'vatsabhūmiṁ ca kaunteyo vijjñe valavānbalāt'* Mbh. *Sabhāparva*, Ch. 30, Verse 10.
40. Mbh. *Udyogaparva*, Ch. 53. Verse 1.
41. CR. *Ayodhyākāṇḍa*, Verse 1.
42. *soaśvamedheśvaraṁ rājanrocamānaṁ sahānugam/*
jigāya samare viro valena valinām varaḥ//
Mbh. *Sabhāparva*, Ch. 29, Verse 8.
43. *sa taṁ nirjitya kaunteyo nātitiveṇa karmaṇā/*
purvadeśaṁ mahāvīryo vijigye kurunandanaḥ//
Ibid., Verse 9.
44. *'samudramahiṣiṁ Gaṅgāṁ sārasakrauñcanāditām/*
āsasāda mahābāhuḥ śṛṅgaverapuraṁ prati//
Vāl. Rāmā. Ayodhyākāṇḍa, Canto 50, Verse 26.
45. *Gaṅgātaraṅgasaṁgatamūlaṁ gaganagaṅgāliṅgata/*
śṛṅgaṁ śṛṅgaverapuralaṁkāramiṅgudīpādapamu-pāgamat//
CR. Ayodhyākāṇḍa, p. 176
46. Ibid.
47. *'sāketasaukhyaściramaramata Rāmaścitrakūṭasthalīṣu* CR. Ayodhyākāṇḍa p. 187
48. *Kosalo nāma muditaḥ sphīto janapadomahān/*
niviṣṭaḥ sarayūtīre prabhūtadhanadhānyavān//

Ayodhyā nāma nagarī tatrāsīllokaviśrutā/
Vāl.Rāmā.Bālakāṇḍa, Canto. Verse 6,7

49. *Vasiṣṭhastu mahātejaḥ kṣetre kalmāṣapādake/*
aśmakaṁ janayāmāsa tvikṣvākukulavṛdhaye//
Bra. purāṇa, p. 135, Verse 176.

50. HGAI, p. 85

51. *āyatā daśa ca dve cayojanāni mahāpuri/*
śrīmati trīnī vistīṃā suvibhaktāmahapathā//
rājamārgeṇa mahatā suvibhaktena śobhitā//
muktapuṣpavakīṃena jalasiktena nityaśaḥ//
kapātoranvatīm suvibhaktāntarāpaṇām/
savayantrāyudhavatīmuṣtitāṁ sarvaśilpibhiḥ//
Vāl. Rāmā. Bālakāṇḍa Canto. 5, Verses 7-10.

52. *durgagambhīraparikhāṁ durgānmanyairdurāsadam/*
vājivaranasaṁpūṃāṁ gobhiruṣṭiḥ kharaistathā//
Ibid, Verse 13

53. *Māndhātā rājaśārduastriṣu lokeṣu viśrutaḥ/*
kathaṁ jāto mahābrahmaṇyovanāśvo nṛpottamaḥ//
Mbh. Vanaparva, Ch. 126, Verse 1

54. Ancient Indian Historical Tradition, p. 314.

55. '.....*kuśambāpramukhai..kauśāmbī....mohodaya-dharmāraṇyagirivrākhyānāṁ purīnāṁ krtṛbhiḥ putrīṁ babhūva.*'
CR. Bālakāṇḍa, p. 63

56. '*kauśāmbastu mahāstejāḥ kauśāmbīmakarotpurīm/*'
Vāl. Rāmā, Bālakāṇḍa,
Canto 32, Verse 6

57. Ancient Geo. of India, p. 110.

58. *Vāl. Rāmā. Bālakāṇḍa*, Ch,. 42

59. *tato Gokaṃamāsādya tapasyati Bhagīrathe/*
devo devāpagaṁ vohumanvamaṁsta dayānidhi//
CR. Bālakāṇḍa, Verse 77.

60. *viproyogena saṁtāpaṁ mā kṛthāsatvamanindite/*
citrāṁgadāmebamuktvā Gokaṃamabhitogamat//
ādyaṁ paśupatḥ sthānaṁ darśanādeva muktidam/
yatra pāpai manjuḥ prānyotyabhayadṁpadam//
Mbh. Ādiparva, Ch. 217,
Verses 34, 35

61. *atha Gokaṃaṁ āsādya triṣu lokeṣu viśrutam/*
samudra madhye rājendra sarvalokanamaskṛtam/
yatra Brahmādayodevā ṛṣayasya tapodhanāḥ/
bhūtaykṣapiśācaśca kinnarāḥ samahorgāḥ//
Ibid, Vanaparva, Ch. 85. Verses 24, 25

62. Ancient Geo. of India, p. 111

63. CR. Bālakāṇḍa, Verse 89.

64. *Gaṅgākule niviṣṭāste viśālāṁ dadṛsuḥ purīm/*

tato munivarastūrṇaṁ jagāma saharāghavaḥ//
atharāmo mahāprajño viśvāmitraṁ mahāmunim/
prapacch prāñjalibhutvā viśālāmuttanaṁ purīm//
Vāl. Rāmā.Bālakāṇḍa, Canto 45, Verse 9,11

65. Ancient Geo. of India, p. 108.
66. CR. Araṇyakāṇḍa, p. 258
67. *Jagrāha paramakrudhaścaturdaśa śilāsitān/*
gṛhitvā dhanurāyamya lakṣyānuddiśya rākṣasān//
Vāl. Rāmā, Araṇyakāṇḍa, Canto 20, Verse 19.
68. *daṇḍakāraṇyamāsādya puṇyaṁ rājannupaspṛśet/*
gosahasraphalaṁ tasya snātamātrasya Bhārata//
Mbh. Vanaparva, Ch. 85. Verse 41.
69. Vāl. Rāmā. Araṇyakāṇḍa, Canto 17-29, CR. Araṇyakāṇḍa
70. *atha pañcavatīṁ gacchanntarā raghunandanaḥ/*
kamcitkālaṁ ca dharmātmā sītayā Lakṣmaṇena ca/
anvāsyamāno nyavasatsvargaloke yathāmaraḥ//
Vāl. *Rāmā Araṇyakāṇḍa*, Canto, 14, Verse 1
Ibid, 15, Verse 31
71. Purāṇic, Ency. pp. 561-562
72. Vāl. Rāmā. Bālakāṇḍa, Canto. 41-43
73. CR. Bālakāṇḍa, Verses 63-87
74. Vāl. Rāmā. Bālakāṇḍa, Canto 41-43
75. *tayā taṭinyā jāhnavyā prapayattridivaṁ pitṝṇ/*
bhagīrathaḥ puraṁ prāpa paripuṇamanorathaḥ//
CR. Bālakāṇḍa, Verse 88
76. *niviṣṭaḥ sarayūtīre prabhutadhanadhānyavān/*
Ayodhyā nāmanagarī tatrāsillokaviśrutā//
Vāl. Rāmā. Bālakāṇḍa, Canto. 5. Verses 5,6
77. *'saraḥpravṛttā sarayūḥ puṇyā brahmasaraśeyutā/'*
Ibid, Canto 24, Verse 10.
78. *'tadanu mānasasaraḥprasṛtāṁ sarayūmatikramya...'*
CR. Bālakāṇḍa, p. 49
79. *Purā himavatściṣā hemaśṛṅgādviniḥsṛtā/*
Gaṅgā gatvā samudrāmbhaḥ saptadhā samapadyat//
Gaṅgā ca yamunāṁ caiva plakṣajātaṁ sarasvatīm/
rathasthāṁ sarayūṁ caiva gomatīṁ gaṇḍakīṁ tathā//
Mbh. Ādiparva, Ch. 170, Verses 19, 20.
80. *Uttīrya sarayūṁ ramyāṁ dṛṣṭvāpurvaṁśca kosalān/*
atitya jagmurmithilāṁ mālāṁ carmaṇvatīṁ nadīm.//
Ibid, Sabhāparva, 2, Verse 28.

81. *kanyādvayamumuṣyāsidekā mandākinī tayoḥ/*
anyā bhagavatī sākṣāccandracūḍkutmbinī//
CR. Bālakāṇḍa, Verse 55.
82. *'apāṁ hada upaspṛśya vājimedha phalamlabhat/'*
Mbh. Anuśāsanaparva, Ch. 25, Verse 13.
83. *śaitendro himavānrāma dhātūnāmakaromahā/*
tasya kanyā dvayaṁ Rāma rupeṇapratimam bhuvi//
Vāl. Rāmā, Bālakāṇḍa, Canto 35, Verse 13.
84. CR. Bālakāṇḍa, Verses 56, 57
85. *Citrakūṭe janasthāne tathāmandākinījale/*
Vigāhya vai nirāhāro rājalakṣmyā niṣevyate//
Mbh. Anuśāsanaparva, Canto, Verse 29.
86. CR. Ayodhyākāṇḍa, p. 176
87. *'tato vedaśrutiṁ nāma śivavārivahāṁ nadīm/*
uttiryabhimukhaḥ prāyagastyādhyuṣṭāṁ diśam//
Vāl. Rāmā. Ayodhyākāṇḍa, Canto 49, Verse 9
88. Ancient Geo. of India. p. 12
89. CR. Ayodhyākāṇḍa, Canto 49, Verse 10.
90. *gatvā tu suciraṁ kālaṁ tataḥ sītavahām nadīm/*
gomatīṁ goyutānupaṁataratsāgaraṁjagāma//
Vāl. Ramā Ayodhyākaṇḍa, Canto, 49, Verse 10.
91. *laṁghatī gomatī caiva sandhyā trīḥsrotasītathā/*
atāścanyāśca rajendra sutīrtha lokaviśrutāḥ//
Mbh. Sabhāparva,
Ch. 9, Verse 23
92. *tatastīrtheṣu puṇyeṣu gomatyāḥ pāṇḍavānṛpa/*
kṛtābhiṣekāḥ pradadurgāśca vittaṁ ca Bhārata//
Ibid, Vanaparva, Ch. 95, Verse 2
93. Ancient Geo. of India, p. 12
94. 'niṣyandikānāma nadī...' CR. Ayodhyākāṇḍa p. 176
95. *Gomatīṁ cāpyatikramya rāghavaḥ śrīghragai rhayi/*
mayūra haṁsabhirutāṁ tatāra syandikāṁ nadīm//
Vāl. Rāmā. Ayodhyākāṇḍa, Canto 49, Verse 11.
96. Ancient Geo. of India, p. 12
97. *'tataḥ paramamaharṣeṇa maharṣinā praṇītābhirāsībhiḥ saha..... tadājñaya Godāvarī tatanikaṭaprakaṭitām/*
CR. Araṇyakāṇḍa, p. 242
98. *'sa kadācitprabhātayāṁ śarvayāṁ raghunandanaḥ/*
prayāyābabhiṣekarthaṁ ramyāṁ Godāvarī nadīṁ//
prahabaḥ kalaśahastastu sītāyā saha vīryavān/
pṛṣṭhatoanubranbhrātā saumitriridamvravīt//
Vāl. Rāmā. Araṇyakāṇḍa
Canto 16, Verses 2,3.
99. *'te tasyāṁ varuṇaṁ devaṁ dhamapaśadharm sadā/*
'upāsate mahātmānaṁ sarve sucaritavratāḥ//

Godāvarī kṛṣṇaveṇā kāverī ca saridvarā//
Mbh. Sabhāparva,
Ch. 9. Verses, 17, 20.

100. *tato Godāvarīṁ prāpya nityaṁ sidhaniṣevitāṁ/*
gavāṁmedhamāpnoti vāsukerlokamuttamm//
Ibid, Vanaparva, Ch. 85, Verse 33.
101. Mbh. Bhīṣmaparva, Ch. 9, Verse 14.
102. Ibid, Anuśāsanaparva, Ch. 25, Verse 12
103. CR. Bālakāṇḍa, Verse 55.
104. 'dhairyeṇa Himavāniva.'
Vāl. Rāmā, Bālakāṇḍa, Canto 1, Verse 17.
105. *'dhairābhṛtāṁ parvatānāṁ cakravartī samrāt Himavān'*
CR. Bālakāṇḍa, p. 67
106. *pragāyātā mahārāja ṣadete varṣaparvatāḥ*
avagātā hyubhayatḥ samudrau pūrvapaścimau//
Mbh. Bhīṣmaparva, Ch. 6, Verse 3.
107. *sarājyaṁ saciva nyasya hṛdayena vidūyatā/*
jagāma himavatpārśvaṁ tapastaptuṁ nareśvara//
Ibid., Vanaparva, Ch. 108, Verse 3.
108. *nāmnā ceyaṁ bhagavato dakṣinā dikpradakṣiṇā*
prathitā triṣu lokeṣu durhaṣā krūrakarmabhiḥ//
mārgaṁ nirodhuṁ satataṁ bhāskarasyācalaottamaḥ/
saṁdeśaṁ pālayaṁstasya vindhyaśailo na vardhate//
Vāl. Rāmā. Araṇyakāṇḍa, Canto 11, Verses 84, 85
109. *mādyaddantikapolapālivigaladdānāmbusiktadrumāḥ*
krīḍatkrodakulārdhacarvitapatanmustārasāmoditāḥ/
antaḥsusthitapānthamantharamarullolallatāmaṇḍapaḥ
kasyaitā na haranti hanta hṛdaya vindya-sthalībhū-
mayaḥ//
NC. 5. 34
110. *tato girivaraśreṣṭha citrakūṭe viśāṁpate/*
mandākinīṁ samāsādya sarvapāpaprānāśinīm//
Mbh. Vanaparva, Ch. 85, Verse 58.
111. *'iti taddinśatakalpaṁ tatra nītvā munernirddeśena*
sarve citrakūṭavanaoddeśamviśan.'
CR. Ayodhyākāṇḍa, p. 212.
112. *'Citrakūṭe janasthāne tathā Mandākinījale/*
vigāhyavai nirāhāro rājalakṣmyā niṣevyate//
Mbh. Anuśāsanaparva, Ch. 25, Verse 29.
113. Ancient Geo. of India, p. 12
114. CR. Kiṣkindhākāṇḍa, p. 300
115. Mbh. Vanaparva, Ch. Verses 7-9
116. BS. 13, 14
117. *'tato Hanūmāndaśakaṇṭhonītāṁ sītāṁ vicetum pathi*
cāranānāma/

mahendraśailasya khagendravegaḥ prasthādudasthāt-
prathamānavegaḥ//
CR. Sundarakāṇḍa, Verse 1.

118. Ibid.
119. *'sa sūryāya mahendrāya pavanāya svayaṁdbhuve/*
bhūtebyaścañjaliṁ kṛtvā cakāra gamanematim//
Vāl. Rāmā. Sundarakāṇḍa,
Ch. 1, Verse 8/
120. *'vṛtaḥ prāyanmahābāhumahendraṁ parvatottamm/*
tato mahendramāsādya bhāradvājomahātapā//
Mbh. Ādiparva, Ch. 130, Verse 53.
121. *'mahendra parvataṁ dṛṣṭvā tāpasairupaśobhitām/*
samudratīreṇa śanirmanipuramjagāma ha//
Ibid, Ch. 215, Verse 13.
122. *drumaḥ kiṁpuruṣeśaśca upāste dhanadeśvaram/*
rākṣasādhipatiściva mahendro gandhamādanaḥ//
saha yakṣaiḥ sagandharvaiḥ saha sarveniśācaraiḥ//
Ibid, Sabhāparva, Ch. 10, Verses 29, 30
123. *tato mahendramāsādya jāmadagnya niṣevitām/*
Rāmatīrthe naraḥ snvātvā aśvamedhafalinlabhat//
Ibid, Vanaparva,
Ch. 85, Verses 16,17
124. *hiraṇyabinduḥ kathito girau kālaṁjare mahān/*
āgastyayaṁparvato ramyāḥ puṇyo givivaraḥśivaḥ//
Ibid, Ch. 87. Verses 21, 22.
125. *tataḥ kṛtasvasatyayano mahātmanā*
yudhiṣṭhiraḥ sāgarambhyagacchat/
kṛtvā ca ta echāsanamasya sarvaṁ
mahendramāsādya niśāmuvāca//
Ibid, Ch. 114, Verse 30.
126. Vāl. Rāmā. Sundarakāṇḍa, Canto 1
CR. Sundarakāṇḍa, pp. 353-354
127. Vāl. Rāmā. Sundarakāṇḍa, Canto. 1.
128. CR. Sundarakāṇḍa, Verses, 4.5.
129. *sāgareṇa kṛtajñena tavādhaśrāntaye/*
mārute! preritoasamadya saumya! viśramya gamayatām//
Ibid, Verse 5.
130. *purvaṁ kṛtayuge tata parvatāḥ pakṣinoabhavat/*
teapi jagmurdiśaḥ sarvā garuḍā iva veginaḥ//
tatasteṣu prayāteṣu devasaṅghāḥ saharṣibhiḥ/
bhūtāni ca bhayaṁ jagmusteṣāṁ patanaśaṇkayā//
tataḥ krudhaḥ sahasrākṣaḥ pavatānāṁ śatakratuḥ/
pakṣāṁściccheda vrajeṇa tataḥ satasahaśrasaḥ//
Vāl. Rāmā. Sundarakāṇḍa,
Canto. 1. Verses 115-117

131. CR. Sundarakāṇḍa, Verse 3
132. *'mā niṣādapratisthāṁ tvamagamaḥ śāsvatīḥ samāḥ/'*
Vāl. Rāmā. Bālakāṇḍa Canto 2, Verse 15
133. *Brāhmaṇādvaiśyakanyāyāmbaṣtho māma jāyate/*
niṣadaḥ sūdrakanyāyāṁ yaḥ pāraśava ucyate//
Manu X. 8.
134. *atyujjṛmbhitaharṣaśokajanitairbāṣpairniṣādādhipaḥ*
śitāśitaguṇānvitairviralaiḥsampṛktavaktroabhavat//
CR Ayodhyākāṇḍa, 48
135. *kalyāṇavādasukhitāṁ sahasaiva kāntāṁ*
kāntāracārakathayā kaluṣīcakāra
ambhodanādamuditāṁ vipine mayurīṁ
saṁtṛāsayanniva dhanurdhvaninā pulindaḥ//
Ibid, verse 31
136. *drāviḍāśca kaliṅgāśca pulindāścāpyusinarāḥ//*
kalisarpā mahiṣakāstāstaḥ kṣatriyajātayaḥ//
Mbh. Vanaparva 188/34, 35.
137. *Cibukāṁaśca pulindāṁśca cināhūṇānsakeralān/*
sasarja fenataḥ sa gaurmleechānbahuvidhānape//
Ibid, Ādiparva, 175. 38
138. *pūrvadeśaṁ mahāvīryo vijigye kurunandanaḥ/*
tato dakṣiṇamāgamya pulinda nagarṁ mahat//
Ibid, Sabhāparva 29.9.10.
139. *bahavo mleccharājānaṛ pṛthivyāṁ manujādhip/*
andhrāh śakāḥ pulindāśca yavanaśca narādhipaḥ//
Ibid. Vanaparva 188-34, 35
140. CR. Araṇyakāṇḍa, pp. 288-289.
141. *yonideśacca yavavanān śakṛtaḥ śabarānbahun/*
mūtrataścāsṛjātakāmścitcchabaraṁściva pārśvataḥ//
Mbh. Ādiparva, Ch. 175, 36, 37.
142. *yavanaḥ kirātaḥ gāndharascināḥ śabarabarbarāḥ/*
madvidhiśca kathaṁ sthāpyāḥ sarve vai dasyu jīvinaḥ//
Ibid, Śāntiparva, Ch. 65, 13-15.
143. CR. Sundarakāṇḍa, p. 372
144. *'Laksmividyullasītamatasigucchsacchāyakaṁ'*
Ibid, Bālakāṇḍa, Verse 13
145. Ibid, Kiṣkindhākāṇḍa, p. 322
146. Ibid, p. 291
147. Ibid, Yuddhakāṇḍa, p. 517
148. Ibid, Bālakāṇḍa, p. 96
149. Ibid, Ayodhyākāṇḍa, p. 190
150. Ibid, Kiṣkindhākāṇḍa, p. 325
151. Ibid, Bālakāṇḍa, p. 23
152. Ibid, Ayodhyākāṇḍa, Verse 6.
153. Ibid, Verse 17.

154. Ibid, Verse 31.
155. Ibid, *Araṇyakāṇḍa*, p. 260
156. Ibid,
157. Ibid,
158. Ibid, *Kiṣkindhākāṇḍa*, p. 322
159. Ibid, *Sundarakāṇḍa*, p. 364
160. Ibid, *Araṇakāṇḍa*, p. 245
161. Ibid, *Ayodhyākāyṇḍa*, p. 147
162. '*rocena krodhena.........siṁhādināṁ.........*' CR. p. 158.
163. Iw. p. 77
164. CR. p. 299
165. Ibid,
166. Iw. p. 72.
167. '*vanyairajagarāḥ piśitāśanebhyo vātāpidānavadaśāmupadeśayanti.*'
CR. Araṇyakāṇḍa, Verse 10.
168. Iw. p. 83.
169. '*vipinamahiṣavesaiḥ*'
CR. p. 239
170. Iw. p. 213.
171. CR. p. 463
172. Iw. p. 22
173. CR. pp. 353-354
174. Iw. p. 91
175. '*khararaghuvarayo raṇaṁ samāptaṁ kharanakhārayudha-yoriva kṣaṇeno*'.
CR. p. 263
176. '*lokānāṁ tu vivṛdhyarthaṁ mukhabāhurupādataḥ/*
brāhmaṇaṁ kṣatriyaṁ vaiśyaṁ sūdraṁ ca niravartayat//
Manu.1/31
177. *adhyāpanamadhyanaṁ yājanaṁ yājanaṁ tathā/*
dāaṁ pratigrahaṁ civa brāhmaṇanāmakalpayat//
prajānāṁ rakṣanaṁ dānamijyādhyayānameva ca/
viṣayeṣvaprasaktiśca kṣatiyasya samāsataḥ//
paśunāṁ rakṣanaṁ dānamijyādhyayanameva ca/
vaṇikapthaṁ kuśīdaṁ ca vaiśyasya kṛṣimeva ca//
ekameva tu śūdrasya prabhuḥ karma samādiśat/
ateṣāmeva vaṃāmām śuśrūṣāmanasūyayā//
Ibid, 1.88-91
178. '*kṣatradharmoapi dharmyātpatha pramādyāpi vaṃāśrama rakṣaṇataḥ samīcinaḥ prāyena puruṣaṁ niḥśyase niyojayet.*'
CR. Ayodhyākāṇḍa, p. 149.
179. '*athasāvitraḥ kṣatriyastriśaṇkuḥ saśrīraḥ svargasidhimabhyarthayamāno......śaraṇamabhajat*'.

tatoavalambyāsya niyogaśaṅkuṁ lebhe triśaṅkurgagane pratiṣṭhām'/ Ibid, Bālakāṇḍa, pp. 90-92

180. Ibid, p. 46
181. *paryāptabhāgyāya bhavānamuṣmai kuryātsarpayāṁ kuśikātmajāya/ niryāṭudhānaṁ vasudhāṁ vidhātuṁ niryātu rāmaḥ saha Lakṣmaṇena//* Ibid, Verse 34.
182. *ahaṁ vaiśyasya śūdrāyāṁ jātatasmānna saṁbhavet/ brahmahatyeti māmuktvā svargato durgato muniḥ//* Ibid, Ayodhyākāṇḍa, Verse 58
183. *'akmeva tu śūdrasya prabhuḥ karma samādiśat/ ateṣāmeva varṇāṇāṁ śuśtrūṣāmansūyayā//* Manu. 1.91.
184. CR. Ayodhyākāṇḍa, p. 149.
185. *'Saṭtriṁsadābdikaṁ caryaṁ gurau traivedikaṁ vratam/ tadārrdhikaṁ pādikaṁ vāgrahanāntikamevavā//* Manu. 3.1
186. *vedānadhītya vedau vā vedaṁ vāpi yathākramm/ aviplutabrahmacaryo gṛhasthāśramamāvaset//* Ibid, 3.2.
187. *avaṁ gṛhāśrame sthitvā vidhivatsnātako dvijaḥ/ vane vasettu niyato yathavadvijitendriyaḥ/* Ibid, 6.1
188. *ataḥparaṁ pravakṣāmi dharaṁ vaikhānasāśramm/ vanyamūlaphalānāṁ ca vidhiṁ grahaṇamokṣṇe//* Ibid.
189. Ibid. 1.88.
190. *'athasminnanaptyatayā dūyamānamānase putrārthaṁ kratumaśvamedhaṁ vidhātum/* CR. Bālakāṇḍa, p. 15
191. *'.......aśvamedhādhvaraṁ....... vidhāya tatra putrī yāmistiṁ vidhivatkartumārabhat'* Ibid, p. 16
192. Ibid, p. 15
193. *'eteapi pavaka ruhisaṅkāvahāṁ hutavahakhyāṁ vahantastadgṛhe Gārhapatyapurogāḥ paurogavadhuraṁ dadhate'* Ibid (R), p. 22.
194. *'gārhapatyāhavanīyadakṣiṇanāgnyanvāhāryavathyādi-rupā agnayoapi,* Ibid.
195. CR. *Bālakāṇḍa*, p. 45, 62
196. *'avabhṛtheti majjayatīti/ṛjiṣa kumbhaṁ jale praveśayet / yajña daivataṁ / avācināni pātrāni jalamadhye mriyante yasminyajñaviśeṣe soabhavṛthaḥ/'* Śuklayaju. p. 141

197. *'tadviṣṇoḥ paraṁ padaṁ sodā paśyanti sūrayaḥ panditāḥ vedāntajñānarahasyavivṛtasaṁputaḥ...divīva dyulokamadhyagatamiva'.* Ibid, p. 99

198. *'idaṁ, viṣṇurvicakrame tredhā nidadhe padam'*
Ibid, p. 94

199. *'sarvavyāpin jagadrupa gagatsrasṭa janārddana/*
pāhi viprānimāmasmād duḥsahānambhrapāvakāt//
yathā sarveṣu bhūteṣu sarvavyāpi jagadguruḥ/
viṣṇureva tathā sarve jīvantvete puruhitāḥ//
VP. 1.18–36, 37

200. *'viṣṇornukaṁ vīryāni pravocaḥ yaḥ pāthivāni vimame rajamsi/*
yo askabhāyaduttaṁ sadhasthaṁ vicakramānastredhorugāyo viṣṇave tvā//'
Śuklayuju, p. 85

201. 'indrasya yujyaḥ sakhā'. Ibid, p. 98.

202. *'akarot sa tanūmanyāṅ kalpādiṣu yathāpurā.*
matsyakurmādikaṁ tadvarāhaṁ vapurāsthitaḥ//
VP. 1.4.8
matsyaṁ kurmaṁ varāhaṁ ca narasiṁhaṁ ca vāmanam//
rāmaṁ rāmaṁ ca kṛṣṇam ca buddhaṁ civa kalkinām//
avaṁ daśāvatārāṁśca pūjayedbhaktisaṁyutaḥ//
Varāh Purāṇ 211. 68, 69

203. Bhā p. 1.3.6-25
2.7.1-38
11.4.17-22

204. *'sarvaśaktimayo viṣṇuḥ svarupaṁ brahmaṇoparam/*
mūrttaṁ yodyogibhiḥ puraṁ yogārambheṣu cintyate//
VP. 1.22.59

205. *'āpo narā iti proktā āpo vai narasūnavaḥ/*
ayanaṁ tasya tāḥ pūrvaṁ tena nārāyaṇaḥ smṛtaḥ//
sambhakṣayitvā sakalaṁ jagatyekāṇavikrte/
śeṣe tvameva govinda cintyamāno maniṣibhiḥ//
VP. 1.4.6. 16
jotsnā lakṣmīḥ pradīpoasau sarvaḥ sarveśvaro hariḥ/
Ibid, 8.28
'sṛṣṭi sthiti vināśāmca bhagāvanmadhusudanaḥ'
Ibid, 7.37

206. *'santāpadhnaṁ sakalajagatāṁ śāṃgacāpāthirāmaṁ Lakṣmīvidyullasitamatasīgucchasacchākāyam//*
Vaikuṇṭhākhyaṁ munijanamanaśchātakānaṁ śaraṇyaṁ kāruṇyāpa tridaśapariṣatkālameghaṁ dadarśa',
CR. Bālakāṇḍa, Verse 13

207. *'kṣīrāmbhodherjaṭharamabhito dehabhāsā prarohaiḥ*
kālonmīlatkuvalayadaladhaitamāpādayantam/

ātanvānaṁ bhujagaśayane kāmapi kṣaumagaure
nidrāmudrāṁ nikhilajagatīrakṣaṇe jāgarukām//[2]
Ibid, Verse 14.

208. *'Nārāyaṇaya nalināyatalocanāya'*
Ibid, p. 19. Verse 16

209. *'viśuddhabodhavānnityaṁ ajaṁ akṣayaṁ avayaṁ*
avyaktakaṁ avikāraṁ yat tad viṣṇohparamampadam,
na sthūlaṁ na ca sukṣmaṁ yanna viśeṣaṇagocaram
tad padaṁ paramaṁ viṣṇoḥ pranamāmaḥ sadāmalam'.
VP. 1.9. 51-52

210. *'ekaṁ tavaṁ agryaṁ paramampadaṁ yat paśyanti*
tavāṁsurayo jñānādrśyam'. Ibid.5.1.45

211. *'nāmāvaśeṣitamahābalivaibhavāya'*
CR. Bālakāṇḍa, Verse 16

212. *'prahlādasya vyasanamamitaṁ dityavargasyadambhaṁ*
stambhaṁ vakṣaḥsthalampi riporyagapadyena
bhettum/
baddhaśradhaṁ puruṣavapuṣā miśrite viśvadṛṣṭe
daṁṣṭrārociviṁsadabhuvane raṁhasā siṁhaveṣe//
Ibid, Verse 15.

213. VP. 1.20.

214. *'kiṁtu sarasijāsanaśāsanamapyamoghīkurvannurvītale*
putrīyataḥ sutrāmmitrasya Daśarathasya mānorathamapi
pūrayitumādṛtamānuṣaveṣaḥ sannahameva taṁ
haniṣyāmiti vyāhṛtyāntradhāt.
tataḥ sā pariṣadanimiṣāṇāmunmiṣitaharṣā
hṛṣīkeśādeśātpraśamitadurdaśāni nirdaśānanāni
caturdaśabhuvanāni buddhvā dugdhasāgarānniragāt'
CR. Bālakāṇḍa, pp. 32-33

215. Ibid, Verse 15.

216. Ibid, Verse 16

217. Ibid, *Yuddhakāṇḍa*, Verse 16

218. *avaṁ sambodhito rudro māghavena murārinā*
cakāre mohaśāstrāṇi keśavoapi śiveritaḥ//
sṛṣtvā tānucatucaturdevo kurvāṇaḥ śāstracoditam
patantu niraye ghore bahun kalpan punaḥ punaḥ//
Kup. pp. 95-112, 114

219. CR. *Sundarakāṇḍa*, Verse 43

220. Ibid, *Bālakāṇḍa*, Verse 57

221. Ibid, Verses 82-84

222. *'Lakṣīṁ tanotu nitarāmitarānapekṣa*
maṇgridvayaṁ nigamaśākhiśihāpravālam/
hairambammburuhadambara cauryanighnaṁ
vighnādribhedaśatadhāradhurandharaṁ naḥ//
Ibid, Verse 1.

223. '.....*atragaṇeśacaraṇadvayasyavedāntapratipādya.. vighnādribhedaśatadhāradhurandharmiti........... vighnavināśapūrvakaṁ sevakajanasakalābhīpsitadāna-sāmarthyamāveditam*'. Ibid, p. 2
224. Ibid, (R) 148
225. '*ācāraḥ pravṛttirvāmācāravadvakracaravat*' Ibid, p. 228.
226. '....*śeṣapiśitāśanapiśācoccāṭana mantrāyamāṇa Lakṣmaṇacāpaghoṣaśravaṇasamucita*............../'
Ibid, Ayodhyākāṇḍa, p. 212
227. '*havyagandhinā gandhavahena dhūmaganahena cadurādeva vibhāvya-mānam.*' Ibid.
228. Ibid, p. 212
229. '*avakīryamāṇabalikusumam*'. *avakīryamāṇāni nikṣipyamāṇīni balikusumāni pūjopahārapuṣpāniyatra tādṛśam* Ibid, p. 213
230. '*vaikhānasakutumbinibirīsabhūbhāgamanokaha śākhāvalambamānavalkalājinataruśākhā*' *Ibid.*212, 213.
231. '*śītikapiśācikānirharaṇāya nipuṇaṁ mantrajapamiva kurvantam*'. Ibid, Araṇyakāṇḍa, p. 245
232. Ibid, Ayodhyākāṇḍa, p. 213
233. '*ghoraṁ duṣkaraṁ tapo vratopavāsadirupam taptvā kṛtvā sumanaso devāḥ santaḥ/ataeva divisvarge tatphalabhujastasya tapasaḥ phalabhujo rambhāsambhogādiphalabhoktāraḥ puruṣā munikṛtaṁ Bharadvājen vihitaṁ teṣāṁ Bharata campūcarānāṁ toṣamānandaṁ kṣaṇaṁ kṣanamatraṁ yathābhilaseyuḥ/ kṣanamātramapīdṛkparitoṣoasmākaṁ saṁbhavedyadi tarhi kṛtārthā bhavemiti yāthā vāñchyestathā cakāretyethaḥ/ sarveapi camūcarā munikṛtatithyavaśātsvargasukhādapyadhikaṁ sukhamanubhūvrityarthaḥ/*' Ibid (R), p 146
234. Ibid, Verse 76
235. '*Sītāmapyanasūyābhidhānasya patnī svabhūṣanistoṣayat*'
Ibid. p. 224
236. '*ātithyaṁ samadhuparkaṁ kartumiva*', Ibid, p. 181.
237. '*atremaharṣerjagrāhāsya pramuditadhiyaḥ premaparyāṁ saparyāṁ* Ibid, p. 223
'*āśramabhāgānabhitaścaratorātithya*'
Ibid, Araṇyakāṇḍa, p. 226
238. CR. *Bālakāṇḍa*, Verse 29.
239. CR. *Bālakāṇḍa*, Verse 28.
240. Ibid. *Ayodhyākāṇḍa*, p. 184
Ibid, *Bālakāṇḍa*, Verse 106
241. CR. *Ayodhyākāṇḍa*, p. 219
242. '*pac dhatoḥ ke-limar pratyaḥ karmakarttari*'
CR. p. 11

243. CR. Bālakāṇḍa, p. 43
244. SS. 'Prākṛtapādaḥ', pp. 1404-1405.
245. *'prakṛtavyākaraṇeapi varṇavyatyāsaḥ prasidha eva yathā /tālavyaśakāramūrdhaṇyaṣakārayoḥ prāyaśo dantyasakārabhāvaḥ'* CR. Bālakāṇḍa, p. 44
246. 'Udikṣuvṛścaikayaḥ', Prā p. 8
247. 'mayūramayukhayorvā vā', Ibid, p. 5
248. 'sargabandho mahākāvyam' SD. VI, 315
249. CR. Bālakāṇḍa, p. 43.
250. SDS, Śaivadarśanam, p. 334, 336, 338, 243.
251. CR. Bālakāṇḍa, Verse 94
252. Ibid, Yuddhakāṇḍa, Verse 1.
253. *'vācaḥ stambho vayaḥstambho vaśyākarṣaṇameva ca/ vidveṣaṇoccāṭanaṁ ca māraṇaṁ kālavañcanam//*
Ibid, p. 59
254. *'lāsikaḥ nartakyaḥ tāsāṁ lāsyopadeśe nṛtyakalāśikṣaṇe deśikāyamānāḥ deśikāḥ guravaḥ.*
CR. Araṇyakāṇḍa, pp. 288-289
255. *'varṣānaṭī gaganaraṅgatalāt prayātā'*
Ibid, Kiṣkindhākāṇḍa, Verse 33
256. *'viśleṣavedanā pūrvaraṅge rathāṅgavihaṅga'*
Ibid, Sundarakāṇḍa, p. 364
māyāmṛge samaranāṭakasūtradhāre Ibid, Verse 52
'Laṇkāpraveśanavanāṭakasūtradhāraḥ' Ibid, Verse 12
257. Samarā, Ch. 56
258. *'asti praśastavibhavairvibudhairlaṅghyā*
Laṅketi nāma rajanīcararājadhāni/
māṇikyamandirabhuvāṁ mahasāṁ prarohaistejastrayāya
dinadīpadaśā diśantī//
CR. Bālakāṇḍa, Verse 18
259. *'majjanagṛhābhimukhe daśamukhe tatratyavicitratara śātakumbhastambhāgrapratyagrapratyuptasphatika śilāśālabhañjikāpuñjakaratalakalitanijopalamayakalaś- -amukhadacchācchāmavicchinnadhārāmbudhārāṁ, nijakarābhimarśāpādayaṁstasya prasāda/'* Ibid, p. 26
260. *'upacīyamānamonobhavavaibhavaḥ pākakapiśa kalamamañjarī.*
Ibid, *Araṇyakāṇḍa*, p. 244
261. *'nirodhāhituṇḍikāyita,'* Ibid, *Kiṣkindhākāṇḍa*, p. 320
262. Ibid, *Ayodhyākāṇḍa*, p. 185
263. *Vāl. Rāmā, Ayodhyākāṇḍa*, Canto 52, Verse 101.
264. CR. *Ayodhyākāṇḍa*, p. 185
265. *'ghṛtapradhanarotiḥ ghṛtarotiḥ'* SS. p. 158
266. *'atha polikā (bhede ki roti) tasyāḥ sādhanaṁ guṇāścaha'*
BHP, Ch. 12, p. 727

267. *mṛdvī śayyā prātaruthāya peyā bhaktaṁ madhye pānakaṁ caparahne/*
drākṣākhaṇḍaṇṁ śarkarā cārdharatre mokṣaścānte śākyaputreṇa dṛṣṭaḥ//
maunnaṁ bhoyagaṁ bhuccā manunnaṁ sayaṇāsanam/
muṇannammi agārammi maṇunnaṁ jñayaya muṇi
Sad. DS. p. 37

268. *'surāghaṭasahasreṇa māṁsabhūtaudanena ca/*
yakṣe tvāṁ prīyatāṁ devī puriṁpunarupāgatā/
Vāl. Rāmā, Ayodhyākāṇḍa, Canto 52, Verse 89

269. *'vīrapāṇavatpatrapuṭapātradṛśyā'*
CR. *Araṇyakāṇḍa*, p. 244

270. Ibid, p. 246
271. Ibid. p. 19
272. *'vīrapānavatpatrapuṭapātra'*
CR. *Araṇyakāṇḍa*, p. 244

273. *'tāmbulīnāṁ dalaistatra racitāpānabhūmayaḥ/*
nārikelāsavaṁ yodhāḥ śātravaṁ ca papuryaśaḥ//
Raghu, 4.42

274. CR. *Sundarakāṇḍa*, p. 430.
275. *'bhikṣāmaṭantaṁ durgatavargaṁ nirghṛṇā kadācidapi kamalānālo'.* CR. Araṇyakāṇḍa. p. 245
276. *'śaśodararomamṛdhkambalasya ca'* Ibid.
277. *'kālāgarudhūmasya ca kāmiraṇgarāgasy'*
Ibid, p. 245

278. CR. *Kiṣkindhākāṇḍa.*
279. Ibid, *Ayodhyākāṇḍa*, p. 270
280. Ibid, *Bālakāṇḍa*, p. 98
281. Ibid, p. 34
282. Ibid. p. 31
283. Ibid, *Ayodhyākāṇḍa*, p. 139
284. Ibid, *Sundarakāṇḍa*, p. 423
285. Ibid, *Bālakāṇḍa*, p. 26
286. Ibid, *Yuddhakāṇḍa*, p. 493
287. *'cūḍāmoṇiṁ...lohitavatpāṭalapaṭaṁ saṇdhyā rāgabandhuraṁ kaṁdharamiva dadarśa daśakandharam'*
Ibid, p. 478

288. *ānītacūḍāmaṇisaṁnidhānādaviḥpromodena raghūdvahena/*
tatrānuyuktaḥ pavanātmajanmā vijñapayāmāsakṛtapranāmaḥ//
CR. Sundarakāṇḍa, Verse. 73

Chapter VI

ALLUSIONS

The author of the *Campūrāmāyaṅa* is conversant with Vedic, Epic and Purāṅic lores. This is evidenced by his reference to such allusions as of Lord Indra violating the wife of sage Gautama, the emergence of the river Gaṅgā, the allusion of Viśvāmitra and Triśaṅku, the epic allusions of the sage Jahnu ascending to the position of Gaṅgā's father, Vātāpi assuming the form of the goat and Śibi's self sacrifice for a dove, divine demsel Ghṛtācī Rambhā and Mohinī.

(a) Ahalyā

Ahalyā was a princess of the Puru dynasty and wife of Maharṣi Gautama. Ahalyā was turned into stone by the curse of her husband Gautama. The *Rāmāyaṅa* narrates that the beautiful wife of Gautama was violated by lusty Indra for which the angry sage cursed her to be a stone.[1] This allusion or legend is retold by Bhoja.

When Viśvāmitra was leading Rāma and Lakṣmaṅa to the palace of Janaka they came across an āśrama on their way giving a description of that āśrama Viśvāmitra told the princes that it was the āśrama of sage Gautama.[2] He said that Indra on one occasion, fell in love with Gautama's beautiful wife Ahalyā. At that time the sage was out of the āśrama. Indra entered the āśrama in the disguise of the sage himself and violated the lady. But before Indra could get out Gautama returned to the āśrama. He cursed both Indra and Ahalyā. Ahalyā was to turned into a stone by the curse.[3] But being sympathatic for her the sage said that she would be restored to her original state when she would be touched by the feet of Rāma in the Tretāyuga.[4] The story occurs in the *Rāmāyaṅa*[5] In the *Campūrāmāyaṅa*, Rāma touched the stone with his foot and brought her back to her original form.[6] Ahalyā and Gautama lived in the same āśrama again for another long period.

(b) Gaṅgā

Gaṅgā is a holy river of India, Gaṅgā emerged from the fingers of Viṣṅu's feet.[7] Bhagīratha brought down Gaṅgā to the earth. King Sagara of the Solar dynasty had sixty thousand sons and Sagara performed on aśvamedha yajña and his sons went round the earth with the sacrificial horse.[8] When they reached the sea-shore the sacrificial horse disappeared due to the trick played by Indra on them. The sons of Sagara dug the earth and reached pātāla where they found the horse tied near sage Kapila who was engrossed in meditation. The sons of Sagara thought that it was Kapila who had stolen the horse. They enraged the sage by their rashness and haughty action. The sage burnt them down to ashes.[9] Aṁśumān, the grandson of Sagara reached pātāla after that incident. He appeased Kapila with pleasing words and the latter returned the sacrificial horse to him, Kapila also told him that the sons of Sagara would be liberated by bringing Gaṅgā to the earth.[10] Bhagīratha, the prince of the Solar Dynasty performed austere penances.[11] He succeeded in brining down Gaṅgā. Gaṅgā was so proud of her extraordinary might that she fell upon the head of Lord Śiva while descending with the motive of washing him away.[12] The haughty Gaṅgā wanted to carry down Śiva also to Pātāla. Śiva blocked her passage inside his matted hairs for many years.[13] Bhagīratha pleased Śiva by means of rigid tapasyā and brought her to the earth. The waters of the river fell into Bindusaras, and flowed in the form of seven tributaries.[14] The legend incidentally narrated in the *Rāmāyaṅa* has been retold by Bhoja in the Bālakāṅḍa of his work.[15]

The river Gaṅgā reached the āśrama of the sage Jahnu where haughty Gaṅgā flooded the āśrama. The sage was angry at her behaviour and drank her. This time also

Bhagīratha succeeded in appeasing the sage who released her for which she is called Jāhnavī also. Gaṅgā finally, followed Bhagīratha to Pātāla and liberated his ancestors reduced to ashes by the curse of Kapila.[16]

(c) Viśvāmitra

The story of Viśvāmitra's extraordinary achievements are narrated by Bhoja in the Bālakāṅḍa of the *Campūrāmāyaṅa.* Viśvāmitra was a Kṣatriya. On one occasion he went to the hermitage of Vasiṣṭha and became his guest. He was surprised to see the miraculous power of Vasiṣṭha. 'Kāmadhenu' a cow possessing the capacity of granting any wish. The king was greedy of having the cow as his property. He tried to allure Vasiṣṭha by fabulous offers to part with 'Kāmadhenu' to which Vasiṣṭha did not agree. Finally, Vīśvāmitra tried to apply force. Thus, the quarrel began between the king and the sage. Understanding the intention of Vasiṣṭha, Kāmadhenu produced from her body thousands of warriors who fought with Viśvāmitra and defeated him.[17] Finally, the kng admitted that the power of a Brāhmaṅa hermit was the real power. He left his kingdom and performed severe penances by means of which he amassed immense divine powers.[18] The Viśvāmitra Vasiṣṭha legend is found in the Purāṅa also.

The king Triśaṅku of the Solar dynasty wanted to reach heaven with the mortal body. Vasiṣṭha discouraged his misadvanture. But Viśvāmitra come to his help.[19] He began to perform a sacrifice to lift up the king bodily to heaven.[20] Triśaṇku began to rise towards heaven.

When Indra interrupted him. He did not allow Triśaṅku to enter bodily into heaven. Viśvāmitra by means of his power of penance created an artificial heaven and established Triśaṅku in the new svarga.[21]

Hariścandra was a great legendry king of India. The suffering of Hariścandra in the hands of Viśvāmitra are wellknown in Indian society. The name of Hariścandra is linked with the Śunaḥśepa legend also which has been narrated briefly by Bhoja in his *Campūrāmāyaṅa.* King Hariścandra l.ad a son named Rohitaśva by the grace of Varuṅa. It was the original agreement of Hariścandra with Varuṅa that when a son would be born it would be sacrificed in honour of Varuṅa by the king. But the king refused to keep his promise when his son Rohitaśva was born. Finally, Varuṅa was adament on his stand, Hariścandra somehow collected a Brāhmaṅa boy named Śunaḥśepa who was a son a Ajigarta against a fat sum. Śunaḥśepa was to be sacrificed for Varuṅa instead of Rohitaśva.[22] When Śunaḥśepa was brought to the place, Viśvāmitra arrived on the spot. He sympathised with Śunaḥśepa and asked the king to release the boy and gave a warning that if the boy was not released, the sacrifice would be hempered. Viśvāmitra taught Śunaḥśepa the way to release himself from the hand of Varuṅa. According to his advice, Śunaḥśepa recited Varuṅamantras and saved his life.[23]

Incidentally, Bhojarāja refers to the death of the sons of Vasiṣṭha who were cursed by Viśvāmitra. In the *Mahābhārata*, however, it has been said that Viśvāmitra killed Vāmadeva and other sons of Vasiṣṭha with the help of king Kalmāṣapāda who became a demon under a curse of Viśvāmitra.[24]

(d) Cūlimuni

The legend of Cūlimuni occurs in the Bālakāṅḍa of Vālmīki's *Rāmāyaṅa*. The legend is retold by Bhojarāja in his *Campūrāmāyaṅa*.[25]

According to the *Rāmāyaṅa* once Somadā a Gandharva lady attended the sage Cūli. Cūli was so pleased with her, that he give her a boon to have a son. The son was born ater sometime who was later on named Brahmadatta.[26]

Bhojarāja does not refer to this legend but he informs us that Kuśanābha had one hundred daughters whose bodies become bent under the curse of Vāyu (Wind god). Later on, they were married to king Brahmadatta. Brahmadatta removed their physical deformity.[27]

(e) Jahnu

We have already referred to the Jahnu-Gaṅgā legend found in the *Rāmāyaṇa* of Vālmīki.[28] It has been discussed by us that Jahnu was a powerful sage. Gaṅgā tried to submerge his āśrama. Jahnu drank up the river. But later on, he released her at the entreaty of Bhagīratha through his ear. From that incident Gaṅgā earned the name 'Jāhnavī'.[29]

(f) Śibi

Śibi is a legendary king who earned a high reputation for his spirit of self-sacrifice for the welfare of others. Gods tried to test the genuiness of his character. The legendary episode of Śibi's self-sacrifice for a dove is found in the *Mahābhārata.*[30] The same episode reappears in the *Campūrāmāyaṇa.*[31]

It is narrated in the *Mahābhārata* that on one occasion Indra and Agni with an intention to test the character of Śibi assumed different forms. Agni assumed the form of a dove and Indra of a hawk. The hawk persuded the dove to the court of Śibi. The dove took refuge in the lap of the king and the latter tried to protect him from the greed of the hawk. After a great deal of bargaining, the hawk agreed to leave the dove if Śibi was ready to offer his own flesh of the weight of the dove. The king agreed to this proposal. But he found that every time he cut his flesh, it was less in weight than that of the dove. Then the dove appeared in his real form and divulged the identity of himself and the hawk. Gods were greatly pleased with the extraordinary spirit of the sacrifice of the king. They blessed him and told him that a son named Kapotaroma would be born to the king.[32]

(g) Vātāpi and Ilvala

The story of the wicked demons Vātāpi and Ilvala is narrated in the Vanaparva of the *Mahābhārata.*[33] There is a reference to the Vātāpi and Ilvala allusion in the *Campūrāmāyaṇa* also in the passage – 'Vanyairgajairajagarāḥ piśitāśanebhyo vātāpidānavadaśāmupadeśayanti'.[34] Ilvala and Vātāpi were two wicked Asuras. Vātāpi could elude people by assuming different forms. These Asuras considered Brāhmaṅas as their enemies. The elder brother Ilvala converted the younger brother Vātāpi into a goat as soon as Brāhmaṅas visited his house. Then he killed the false goat and prepared a sumptuous dish for his guest, when the guests herdly finished their meal Ilvala would call aloud Vātāpi to come out. Vātāpi came out of the stomach of the guest who naturally died. In this way, Ilvala killed many Brāhmaṅas. One day Agastya came to his place. He consumed Vātāpi by means of his uncommon spritual power.[35]

(h) Ghṛtāci

Ghṛtācī was an exceptionally beautiful Apsaras who revelled in disturbing the peace of the sages and becoming mother of children by them. Gṛtāchī succeeded in breaking the penance of the sages like Kuśanābha, Vyāsa and Bharadvāja. She occupied a very prominent position among celestial damsel.

There is a casual reference to Ghṛtācī who was the wife of king Kuśanābha in the *Campūrāmāyaṅa.* She begot one hundred daughters.[36] Ghṛtācī was an exceptionally beautiful Apsaras who could entice even the great sage Vyāsa. The description of Vyāsa falling in love with this enchanting damsel is narrated in the *Devibhāgavata.*[37]

The Adīparva of the Mahābhārata describes how once sage Bharadvāja also fell in her love.[38] Bhojarāja intelligently avoids any description of Ghṛtācī's character. He simply states that she was the wife of Kuśanābha and says that Ghṛtācī gave birth to one hundred daughters.[39]

(i) Rambhā

Rambhā was one of the most beautiful fairies. Rambhā was the daughter of Kāśyapa and Prabhā. Once Indra was afraid of the rigorous tapasyā being performed by sage

Viśvāmitra. He deputed Rambhā to disturb the meditation of the sage. The story of Rambhā is found in the *Rāmāyaṅa*[40] of Vālmīki. Bhoja refers to the episode of Rambhā and Viśvāmitra very briefly.[41]

(j) Mohinī

Bhoja narrates briefly the story of Lord Viṣṅu assuming the form of a beautiful divine damsel Mohinī at the time of churming the ocean by gods and demons. Mohinī, by means of her extraordinary beauty befooled the demons and misguided them. Demons were served with wine while gods were served with nectar arising from the Milky Ocean (Kṣīra samudra).[42] The story is narrated in the Bhāgavata Purāṅa and some purāṅic sources.[43]

References

1. Vāl. Rāmā. Bālakāṅḍa, Canto 48-49
2. '....*Mithilāṁpratiprasthitaḥ pratapasāmuttamasya Gautamasyāśrāmṁ pradarśya taddārānuṣaktāṁ kathāmitthamakathayat.*'

   CR. *Bālakāṅḍa*, p. 84
3. '*atrāgamadgautamadharmadārānnāryajuṣṭena pathā mahendraḥ/ sa ca krudhā nivṛṣaṅaṁ vṛṣāṅaṁ bhāryāmadṛśāṁ ca muniścakāra..*

   Ibid, Verse 90.
4. *Vanametadgate Rāme śāpānmuktā bhavisyasi/ ityuktvā Gautamaḥ patnīṁ himādriṁ tapase yayau//*

   Ibid, Verse 91.
5. Vāl. Rāmā. Bālakāṅḍa, Canto, 48-49
6. (a) '*tadenāmenaso muktāṁ pratigṛhṅātu gautamaḥ/ iti tasyāśraṁ bheje sākaṁ rāmeṅa kauśikaḥ//*

   (b) *duḥkhe sukhe ca raja ava babhūva hetu stādṛgvidhe mahati Gautamadharmapatnyāḥ/*

   yasmādguṅena rajasā vikṛtiṁ gatā sā Rāmasya pādarajasā prakṛtiṁ prapede//

   CR. Bālakāṅḍa, Verses 93, 94
7. 'bhavadviṣṅupādāṅguṣṭhanirgatasya hi jalasyaitanmāhātmyam'

   VP. 4.14.30

8. (a) *'asmañjaṁ sutaṁlebhe vaidarbhī keśinī tayoḥ/*
ṣaṣṭiṁ putrasasrānāṁ sumatiśca yaviyasi//

(b) *'asamañjasacāritramasamañjampohya saḥ/*
ārabdhahayamedhaḥ sannamuncat turaṅgamm//
CR. Bālakāṅḍa, Verses 66, 67.

9. *'ta ate tapasā dīpte tamaḥstomapramāthini/*
kāpile jvalane vīrā lebhire śalabhopamām//
Ibid, Verse 70

10. *'asamañjasutaṁ pautramaṁśumantamathābravīt/*
saptiṁ hṛtvā samādhattāṁ saptatantuṁ bhavāniti//

soapi gatvā bilaṁ tatra dṛṣṭvā bhasmīkṛtānpitṛṛṅ/
sāśrustebhoañjaliṁ ditsuścarallebhe turaṅgamm//

mātulo garuḍasteṣāmenaṁ tatrivamabravīt/
gaṅgāmihānyāyuṣmanneṣāmeṣā gatiḥ parā//
Ibid, Verses 71-73

11. *'tato gokarṅamāsādya tapasyati Bhagīrathe/*
devo devapagāṁ vohumanvamaṁsta dayānidhiḥ//
Ibid, Verse 77.

12. *'avalepabharākrāntā suralokataraṅginī/*
papāta pārvatīkāntajatākāntāragahvare// Ibid, Verse 82

13. Ibid, Verse 83.

14. *'Gaṅgā saptākṛtirjātā nyapatdhara mūrdhani/*
tena stutyā prasannena kṣiptā Bindusarasyapi//
Ibid, Verse 85

15. Vāl. Rāmā. Bālkāṅḍa, Canto. 35-44.

16. (a) *'saiṣā Bhāgīrathī jahnoḥ satrakṣetraṁ samāvṛṅot/*
tāṁ sa pitvā tataḥ śānto jahau srotreṅa vartmanā//
(b) *tayā tatinyā jahnavyā prāpayatridivaṁ pitṛṛṅ/*
Bhagīrathḥ puraṁ prāpa paripūrṅamanorathaḥ//
CR. Bālakāṅḍa, Verses 87, 88

17. *'tiṣṭhan kṣatrārhavṛttau munirgamadsāvāśramṁ*
brahmasūno-
rātithyaṁ tatra labdhvā niravadhi surabheḥ
Prābhavādityavetya/
sā tena prārthitābhūttadanu munivare nābhyupete cakarṣa
krośantīṁ tāṁ tayaiva pracuravalajuṣā kāndiśikoba bhūva//
Ibid, Verse. 95

18. *'bahuśastadvalacakitasya tapobalādhigatavividhāyudha*
nigamasya bhūyoapisurabhinimittaṁ samārabdasama-
rasya
divyāstraparamparāṁ brahmadaṅḍena
nirundhannarudndhatījāniravatasthe.'

'tatoayaṁ jātavyaikaḥ kṣātrāttejasaḥ paraṁ brāhmameva maho mahīya iti niścitya tatsidhaye dakṣiṅasyāṁ diśi tīvarataraṁ tapaścacāra'

Ibid, p. 89

19. *'atha sāvitraḥ kṣatriyastriśaṅkuḥ saśarīraḥ svargasidhimabhyarthayamāno vasiṣṭhena prtyākhyāta -stasya putrairmahodayādibhirnirbandhakupitairdatta caṅḍālabhāvastamenaṁ śaraṅamabhajat'*

Ibid, p. 90

20. 'asāvapi tanmonorathaparipūrtaye kratumekaṁ Prākramat.'

Ibid,

21. *'apātayatsvargamupāśrayantaṁ saṁjātamanyuḥ śatamanyuranam/ tatoavalambyāsya niyogaśaṅkuṁ lebhe Triśaṅkurgagane pratiṣṭhāṁ//*

Ibid, Verse 97.

gagane tānyanekāni vaiśvanarapathābahiḥ/
naksatrāṅi muniśreṣṭha teṣu jyotishṣu jājvalan//
avākiśarāstriśaṅkuśca tiṣṭhatvamarasaṁnibhaḥ/
anuyāsyanti caitāni jyotiṁṣi nṛpasattamm/

Vāl, Rāmā. Bālakāṅḍa, 60 Verses 31, 32

'saśarīraṁ tadā taṁ vai divamāropayatprabhuḥ/
viśvāmitraprasādena Triśaṅkurdivi rājate//

Bra. Purāṅa, p. 134, Verses 112, 114.

22. *'...ambarīṣyayajñapaśuvināśaprāyaścittārthaṁ bahvibhigorbhiḥ krītvā narapaśutāṁ nīyamānastāvad-ṛcīkasya madhyamaputraḥ Śunaḥśepaḥ śaraṅamyācata.*

CR. Bālakāṅḍa, p. 92

Vāl, Rāmā. Bālakāṅḍa, Canto 61, Verses 5-24

23. *'ayaṁ bhagavānnijatanayavinimayena rakṣitumenamun-mukhaḥ parāṅmukhebhyastebhyo haviṣyandādibhyaḥ śāpena vasiṣṭhaputradaśāṁ datvā gāthādvayaprītabhyā mindropendrabhyāmmbariṣaṁ Śunaḥśepaṁ ca paripūrṅa-monorathau kārayāmāsa.*

CR. Bālakāṅḍa, p. 93

Vāl, Rāmā. Bālakāṅḍa, Canto 62.

24. *'antardhāya tatotmānaṁ Viśvāmitroapibhārata/*
tāvbhvāticakrāma cikīrṣannātmanaḥ priyam//
sa tu śaptastadā tena śaktinā saktina vainṛpottamaḥ/
jagāma śaraṅaṁ śaktiṁ prāsadayitumarhayan//
tasya bhāvaṁ viditvā sa nṛpateḥ kurusattama/
viśvāmitrastato rakṣa ādideśa nṛpaṁprati//
śāpāttasya tu viprarṣerviśvāmitrasya cājñayā.
rākṣasaḥ kiṁkaro nāma viveśa nṛpatiṁ tadā//

Vasiṣṭho ghātitāñcchurtvā Viśvāmitrena tānsutān/
dhārayāmāsa taṁ śokaṁ mahādririva medinīm//
Mbh. Ādiparva, Ch. 176, Verses 18-21, 43.

25. *'atha viditavṛttāntena kuśanābhena tena kṣamā meva pratikriyāṁ manyamānena cūlisūnava saumadeyāya rājñe brahmadattāya dattāstāḥ Prakṛtisthā vabhūvuḥ'.*
CR. Bālakāṅḍa, p. 64

26. *'atasminnevakāle tu cūlināma mahādyutiḥ/*
urdharetāḥ śubhācāro brāhaṁ tapaupāgamat//
tapasyantamṛṣiṁ tatra gandharvī paryupāsate/
somadā nāma bhadraṁ te urmilātanayātada//
parituṣtaṁ muniṁ jñatvā gandharvī madhurasvaram/
uvāca paramaprītā vākyajña vākyakovidam//
lakṣmyā samudito brāhyā brahmabhūto mahātapāḥ/
brāhmeṅetapasā yuktaṁ putramicchami dhārmikam/
apatiścāsmi bhadraṁ te bhāryā cāsmi na kasyacit/
brāhmaṅopagatāyāśca dātumarhasi me sutam//
tasyāḥ prasanno bramarṣirdadau brāhmamanuttamm
brahmadatta iti khyātaṁ mānasaṁ cūlinaḥ sūtam//
Vāl, Rāmā. Bālakāṅḍa, Ċanto 33, Verses 11-13, 16-18

27. CR. Bālakāṅḍa, p. 64

28. Vāl, Rāmā. Bālakāṅḍa, Canto 43-44
Bra. Puraṅa, Ch. 97
Mbh. Vanaparva Ch. 109, Verses1-19

29. (a) *'saiṣā bhāgīrathī jahnoḥ satrakṣetraṁ samavṛṅot/*
tāṁ sa pītvā tataḥ śānto jahau śrotreṅa vartmanā//

(b) *tayā taṭinyā jāhnavyā prapayatridivampitṛṛṅ/*
bhagīrathaḥ puraṁ prāpa paripurṅa monorathaḥ//
CR. Bālakāṅḍa, Verses 87, 88

30. *'devānāṁ kathā sañjātā mahītalaṁ gatvā mahīpatiṁ*
śibimausīnaraṁ sadhvenaṁ śibiṁ jijñasyam iti/
evaṁ bho ityuktā agnīdrāvupatiṣthetām//
agniḥ kopatarupeṅa taṁabhyadhāvadāmisārtha mindraḥ syenarupeṅa/
atha kapoto rājñao divyāsanāsīnasyotsaṅgaṁ nyapatat//
atha puruhito rājānamabravīt/
vasu dadātu antavān pārthivoasya niṣkṛtiṁ
kuryāt ghoraṁ kopatasya nipātamāhuḥ//
atha kapoto rājānambravīt/
prāṅarakṣārthaṁ śyenādbhitobhavantaṁ prānārthī
prapadye aṅgairiṅgāni prapyārthī munirbhūtvā prāṅāṁstvāṁ prapadye//
Mbh. Vanaparva, Ch. 197. Verses 1-6

31. *'kiṁ nāgataste śravasāḥ sakāśamaridamaḥ satyagirāṁ purogaḥ//*
śyenāmiṣībhūtakapotapotajīvātave śastranikṛttagātraḥ//
CR. Ayodhyākāṅḍa, Verse 17

32. *'vaiśānaroahaṁ jvalano dhūmaketu*
rathaiva śyeno vajrahastaḥ śacīpatiḥ/
sādhu jñatuṁ tvāmṛṣabhaṁ sauratheya
nau jjñāsayā tvatsakāśaṁ prapannau

atāsāṁ prajānāṁ pālayitā yaśasvī
surasīrnamatha saṁato bhṛśam/
atasmāt pārśvāt puruṣo janiṣyati
kapotarometi ca tasya nāma//"
Mbh, Vanaparva, Ch. 197, Verses 25, 27.

'kiṁ nāgataste śravasoḥ sakāśamariṁdamaḥ
satyagirāṁ purogaḥ/
śyenāmiṣībhūtakapotapotadjīvātave śastranikṛttagātraḥ//
CR. Ayodhyākāṅḍa, Verse 17.

33. *'Ilvalastānviditvā tu maharṣisahitānnṛpān/*
upasthitānsahāmātyo viṣayānte hyapūjayat//
teṣāṁ tatoasuraśreṣṭhasatvātithyamakarottadā/
susaṁskṛtena kauravya bhrātrā vātāpinā yadā//
tatorājarṣayaḥ sarve viṣannā gatacetasaḥ/
vātāpiṁ saṁskṛtaṁ dṛṣṭvā meṣabhūtaṁ mahāsuram//
athābravīdagastyastānrājarṣinṛisattamaḥ/
Viṣādo vo na kartavya hyahaṁ bhokṣye mahāsuram//
dhuryāsanamathāsadya niṣasāda mahārṣiḥ/
taṁ paryavesaddaityendra ilvala prahasanniva//
agastya ava kṛtsnaṁ tu vātāpiṁ bubhuje tataḥ/
bhuktavatyasurohvānmakarottasya celvalaḥ//
tatovāyuḥ prādurbhūddhastasya mahātmanaḥ/
śabdena mahatā tāta garjanniva yathā ghanaḥ//
vātāpe niṣkramasveti punaḥ punaruvāca ha/
taṁ prahasthābravīdrajannagastyo munisattamaḥ//
kuto niṣkramituṁ śakto mayā jīrṅastu soasuraḥ/
ilvalastu viṣaṅṅobhūdṛstvā jīrṅaṁ mahāsuram//
Mbh. Vanaparva, Ch. 99 Verses 1-9.

34. CR. Araṅyakāṅḍa, Verse 10.
35. Mbh. Vanaparva, Ch. 99
36. 'kuśanābhastu ghṛtācyāṁ kanyāśatamajandyat'
CR. Bālakāṅḍa, p. 63

37. DB, 1st skanda.
38. *'maharṣibhirbharadvājo havirdhāne caranpurā//*
dadarśāpsarasaṁ sākṣādghṛtācīmāplutāmṛṣiḥ/
rupayauvanasaṁpannāṁ madadṛptaṁ madālasām

tasyāḥ punaraṁaditīra vasanaṁ paryavartat/
vyapakṛṣṭāmbarāṁdṛṣṭvā tāmṛṣiścakame tataḥ//
tatra saṁsaktamanaso bharadvājasya dhīmataḥ/
tato asya retaścaskanda tadṛṣirdronaādadhe//
tataḥ sambhavaddroṅaḥ kalaśe tasyadhīmataḥ/
adhyagīṣṭa sa vedāṁśca vedāṅgāni ca sarvaśaḥ//
Mbh. Ādiparva, Ch. 130, Verses 34-38

39. CR. Bālakāṅḍa, p. 63
40. *'Surakāryamidaṁ rambhe kartavyaṁ sumahatvayā/*
lobhanaṁ kauśikasyeha kāmamohasamanvitam//
ayaṁ surapate ghoro viśvāmitro mahāmuniḥ/
krodhamutsrakṣyate ghoraṁ mayi deva na saṁśayaḥ//
atha tasya ca śabdena gītenāpratimena ca/
darśanena ca rambhāyā muniḥ saṁdehamāgataḥ//
sahasrakṣya tatsarvaṁ vijñāya munipuṁgavaḥ/
rambhāṁ krodhasamāviṣṭaḥ śaśapakusikatmajah//
tasya śāpena mahatā rambhā śailī tadābhavat/
vacaḥ śrutvā ca kandarpo maharṣeh sa ca nirgataḥ//
Vāl. Rāmā. Bālakāṅḍa, Canto 64, Verses. 1, 3, 10, 11, 15
41. *'tatra jambhariprahitāṁ rambhāṁ śaili bhaveti*
śaptvā pūrvaśyāṁ diśinirastaniḥśvāsaṁ
tapaścaratyamuṣminnūṣmanā
taporudvignitāmarasakhastāmarasāsanaḥ
sannidhāya jtendriyatvād brahmarṣirasi
vasiṣṭhoapyevaṁ vyāharatu bhavantamityābhāṣat'
CR. Bālakāṅḍa, p. 95.
42. *'purā khalu surāsurānāṁ sudhānimittaṁ, mithovirodhe*
pravṛtte māyāṁ viśvamohinīṁ viśvarupaḥ pradarśya
daiteyanidhanaṁ śatadhārapāṅināṁ kārayāmāsa'.
CR. Bālakāṅḍa, p. 82
43. *'iti svān pratyaṣedhana vai daiteyā jātamatsarāḥ/*
duravalāḥ pravalān rājan,' gṛhītakalasān muhuḥ//
atasmisnntare viṣṅoh sarvopāyavidīśvaraḥ/
yoṣidrupamanirddeśyaṁ dadhāra paramādbhutam//
Bhā 8th Skandha, Ch. 8, 41,42.

Chapter VII

CONCLUSION

We have already discussed the salient features of the *Campūrāmāyaṅa* of Bhoja and Lakṣmaṅasūri. We have divided the thesis into seven chapters. The first chapter is the introduction while the last one is naturally the concluding chapter. We shall present the findings of our study in the present chapter.

We have laid great emphasis on the personality of Bhoja in the introduction. Bhoja was a profound scholar in different subjects and a prolific writer also. Our intention is to show that Bhoja was a man of extraordinary character. No Sanskrit writer has succeeded in claiming himself as authority on so many subjects of varied interests ranging from Sanskrit poetics to Astrology, Medicine and Śaiva philosophy.

A critical study of the *Campūrāmāyaṅa* is not enough to give an adequate assessment of the profound scholarship of Bhoja. We have presented a critical analysis of all the available works of Bhoja in our introduction in order to give an idea of Bhoja's scholarly abilities. Bhoja was an administrator, a writer, a lover of learning and a great scholar. But much is not known about him except from his works. Even the 'Bhojaprabandha'[1] of Ballālasena is not a scientific biography of the king. The author presents many concented stories about the kings. Bhoja's greatness is reflected in his writings.

The Epic of Vālmīki is a voluminous work. The author makes every effort to describe all the things both small and great in an adequately poetical language. For Bhoja and

Lakṣmaṅasūri it was never possible to a write out a Campū Kāvya of the dimension of the *Rāmāyaṅa.* Such an Epic Campū is not desired by readers also. Bhoja lays down the Rāma story within a reasonable frame-work of a standard Campū. The Rāma story is well-known in the Indian society since very ancient times. Bhoja tries to give a new touch to the Rāma story. He drastically cuts the Epic story to size. Though the author makes the Epic theme an interesting one by applying his literary skill and genious, the original theme has lost much of his charm. In the new clothing Bhoja tries to present all the minor episodes of the *Rāmāyaṅa* in his Campū Kāvya which was probably not necessary. He could concentrate his mind on the important episodes necessary for enhancing the beauty of the Rāma-story. But the presents himself in the *Campūrāmāyaṅa* as a loyal followers of Vālmīki[2]. Though the *Campūrāmāyaṅa* is an attractive literary composition, it must be admitted that it has never reached the height of the Epic of the great sage Vālmīki. No Sanskrit work has been able to excel the most excellent poem of the great Indian poet whose work will never cease to dominate the minds of readers all over the world. The motive of Bhoja and also Lakṣmaṅasūri was not to Challenge the supremacy of Vālmīki, but their aim was to sing the greatness of Rāma through an enjoyble literary medium. This was particularly necessary, because Rāma could establish himself in the society as an incarnation of Lord Viṣṅu.[3]

The greatness of a writer does not depend so much upon the theme, but the mode of his presentation is more important for the readers. Bhoja says in the beginning that a Campū Kāvya should be a mixture of prose and melodious verses.[4] He maintains a constant vigil on what he says in the beginning. He maintains a lucid and musical style throughout his work.[5] He sometimes presents some episode such as the emergence of the river Gaṅgā in poems.[6] Within a limited dimension which saves time and helps readers to avoid monotomy.

Bhoja is an entirely different person in the *Campūrāmāyaṅa.* When we read the *Campūrāmāyaṅa* it is difficult for us to believe that the same person is an author of many technical works like the *Samarāṅganasūtradhāra* and the *Yuktikalpataru.*

The Rāma-story of the *Campūrāmāyaṅa* displays two distinct trends. It delineates the heroic sentiment through the heroic exploits of Rāmacandra.

At the sametime it is a devotional literary work dedicated to Lord Viṣṅu within a sweet melodious literary grab. That Bhoja was a perfect devotee of Viṣṅu can be understood from the following verse of the *Campūrāmāyaṅa* :

> *'Narāyaṅāya nalināyatalocanāya nāmāvaśeṣitam-*
> *ahābalivaibhavāya/*
> *nanācarācaravidhāyakajanmadeśanābhīpuṭāya*
> *puruṣāya namaḥ parasmai//*[7]

A devotional poem is bound to be sectarian in character atleast to a certain degree. But Bhoja presents the Rāma story in such and attractive language that the sectarian motive is effectively covered by the literary beauties of the poem.[8]

Though the Aṅgi Rasa or the principal sentiment of the *Campūrāmāyaṅa* is Vīra or rather Yuddhavīra, Bhoja excels in delineating other Rasas also and particularly the Karuṅarasa or the tragic sentiment. It is clear from the lamentation of Tāra in the Kiṣkindhākāṅḍa which is presented in the form of poems which can easily penetrate into the hearts of readers.[9] Bhoja is also a master in delineating Bhayānakarasa or the sentiment of Fear. The description of Tāḍakā as found in the verse ;

> *Hṛtvādreḥ śikharāṅi tāni paritaḥ kṣiptvā*
> *hasitvā krudhā*
> *kṛtvā hastavighaṭṭanaṁ tata itaḥ sthitvā*
> *naṭitvā muhuḥ/*
> *siktvā kṣamāsṛjā srajāntrakṛtayā baddhvā*
> *kacānkhecarān*
> *dagdhvāgneḥ sadṛśā dṛśāniśicarā rundhanti*
> *randhraṁ divaḥ//*[10]

is an excellent example of Bhayānakarasa in the *Campūrāmāyaṅa.* In the verse Vīra Rasa or the heroic sentiment occupies a secondary position to Bhayānakarasa which keeps the readers in a state of thrill. The poet, however, does not lay much emphasis on presenting Śṛṅgārarasa or Hāsyarasa in his work. He probably thinks that these sentiments are not compatible with the theme of the work.

The writer is proficient in the art of presenting different characters. In this connection we can instantly point out to the character of Rāma which is portrayed in a glowing manner.[11]

Lakṣmaṅasūri also cleverly handless the Epic characters. The story of the purity of Sītā being tested through the fire ordeal in the Rāmāyaṅa.[12] is presented in such a manner by him that the readers do not find in it the scope to turn over the most thrilling situation.

The character of Hanūmān[13] and that of Tārā[14] are two most illuminating characters in the *Campūrāmāyaṅa.* However, the character of Rāvaṅa the villain is pale compared to that of the hero and other characters like Hanūmān. In the *Rāmāyaṅa*, Rāvaṅ's exploits are described in an elaborate manner.[15] In the Bālakāṅḍa of the *Campūrāmāyaṅa* also the terror created by Rāvaṅa is described by the gods before Lord Viṣṅu.[16] We learn from the '*Śiśupālavadha*'[17] also that Rāvaṅa caused the turmoil in the divine city of Amarāvatī. However, Rāvaṅa stands nowhere before Rāma in the *Rāmāyaṅa* as the hero of the Epic possesses superior fighting skill and might.[18] In the Epic Rāvaṅa steals away Sītā. Though he fights a fierce battle with Rāma, he is overpowered by his adversary. In the *Campūrāmāyaṅa*, Rāvaṅa plays a less important role than Rāma and Hanūmān.

Like Vālmīki Bhoja also presents many excellent images.[19] Vālmīki refers to Gaṅgā as 'phenanirmalahāsinī' Gaṅgā which is a new image of the poet imposed upon the river.[20] But Bhoja goes a step forward in presenting imagery. Thus, in the ayodhyākāṅḍa, it is said that when Daśaratha proposed to the courtiers that Rāma should be installed on the throne, they were so delighted that they remarked in the following way—

devethiteapi tanayaṁ tava Rāmabhadraṁ lokaḥ
svayaṁ bhojatu nāma kimatra citram/
candraṁ vinā yadupalambhanahetubhūtaṁ,
kṣirodamāśrayati kiṁ triṣitaścakoraḥ//[21]

In this verse they frankly speak to the king that while people can enjoy the beauty of the rising moon in the sky they never rush to the milky ocean in search of the luminous moon.

The social life depicted by Bhoja is mainly confined to the Epic days. We do not gather much material to study the socio-cultural life of the contemporary society of Bhoja which had undergone a significant change since the Epic of Vālmīki.

In the course of the gradual evolution of the Campū Kāvya we see that many Campūs were written in the mechanical way. In this connection we can refer to the *Ānandavṛndāvanacampū* of Kavikarṅapūra, in which 'yamakas' dominate the entire fibre of the story. We can refer to the passage 'jyaṁ ca kumudvatī mudvati bhavatyurdhamiti mahat kautukaṁ kau tu kam na rañjayati, jayati caidaṁ... paricāyayāmāsa.[22] Which contain 'yamakas' profusely that can create boredom in the minds of the readers. Even the *Nalacampū* of Trivikramabhaṭṭa bears to a great extent an artificial character. This has been particularly noticed in the description of the Vindhya mountain.[23] The *Campūrāmāyaṅa*, on the other hand possesses very little artificiality. The poet has paid single-minded devotion to working out an attractive Campū Kāvya which is easily intelligible to readers at the same time.

References

1. Bhoja Pra. jīvandhara vidyāsāgars, 1872, 1883 also Vāsudeva Panshikar, NSP, Bombay, 1921.
2. (a) *Vālmīkigītaragupuṁgavakīrtilaśaistṛptiṁkaromi kathamapyadhunā budhānām/*

Gaṅgājalairbhūbi Bhagīrathayatnalabdhaiḥ kiṁ tarpaṇaṁ na vidadhāti naraḥ pitṝṇam//

(b) *atha sarasijayonerājñayā rāmavṛttaṁ karabadarasamānaṁ prekṣya dṛṣṭayā pratīcyā/ Śubhamatanuta kāvyaṁ svādu rāmāyaṇākhyaṁ madhumayabhaṇitīnāṁ mārgadarśi maharṣiḥ//*

CR. Bālakāṇḍa, Verse 4, 8

3. *'kiṁtu sarasijāsanaśāsanampyamodhīkurvannurvītale putrīyataḥ sutrāmamitrasya daśarathasya monorathamapi pūrayitumādṛtamanuṣaveṣaḥ sannahameva taṁ haniṣyāmiti vyāhṛtyāntaradhāt'*

Ibid, p 32

4. *Gadyānubandharasamiśritapadyasūkti hṛdyāhivādya-kalayā Kaliteva gītiḥ/ tasmāddadhātu kavimārgajuṣāṁ sukhāya campūprabandha racanāṁ rasanā madiyā//*

Ibid, Verse 3.

5. *'tatra kaṁcana krauñca mithunādeakaṁ pañcaśaravidhyamapi Vyādhenānuviddhaṁ nidhyāyato baddhānukampasya bhagavato vālmīkervadanāravindaccha-ndomayi kācidevaṁ niḥsasāra sarasvatī/'*

Ibid, p. 6

6. Ibid, Verses 63-88
7. Ibid, Verse 16
8. *'Rāmākarṣaṇabhagnakārmukabhubā dvānena rodorudhā dṛptakṣatrayaśaḥsitacchadakule jīmūtanādayitam/ vīraśrīprathamapraveśasamaye puṇyāhaghoṣāyitaṁ sītāyāḥ kila mānase pariṇaye māṅgalyatūryāyitam//*

Ibid, Verse 104.

9. *nāhaṁ suketutanayā na ca saptasālī vāli na ca tribhuvanaprathitaprabhāvaḥ/ tārāsmi vajrahṛdayā viśkikhairbhedyā dhvanī kathaṁ bhavasi rāghava! māmaviddhvā//*

Ibid, Kiṣkindhākāṇḍa, Verse 18.

10. Ibid, Bālakāṇḍa, Verse 48.
11. 'Rāmastadākarṇya pramuditahṛdayaḥ kṛtāñjalirenāṁ prati vyajijñapat'

(a) *bhīto bhūbharataḥ kimambā Bharataḥ kimvā Vanātpāvanat trastoahaṁ sagarānvavayakakudastātah kutaḥ śocati/ divyāyaḥ saritonivāpakaraṇalladhvīṁ pratinjñamimā māvābhyāmbhipūrayiṣyati na cetputri kathaṁ syādayam//*

(b) *vanabhubi tanumātrātranāmājñapitaṁ me*
sakelabhuvanabhāraḥ sthāpito vatsamurdhni//
tadiha sukaratāyamavayostatkirtāyām
mayi patati garīyanamba te pakṣapātaḥ//

(c) *tataḥ svavācā vyavahṛtya hṛdyaṁ vatsābhiṣekotsava maṅgalaṁ me/*
praṅāmasaṁjñasyamayārpitasya kiṁ purṅapātrasya na pātramāsīt//

Ibid, Ayodhyākāṅḍa, Verse 24-26

12. *adhomukhaṁ sthitaṁ Rāmaṁ tataḥ kṛtvā pradakṣiṅam/*
upāvartata vaidehī dīpyamānaṅ hutāśnam//
praṅamya daivatebhyaśca brāhmaṅebhyaśca maithilī/
badhvāñjaliputā cedamubācāgnisamīpataḥ//
yathā me hṛdayaṁ nityaṁ nāpasarpati rāghavāt/
tathālokasya sākṣi māṁ sarvataḥ pātu pāvakaḥ
yathā māṁ śudhacāritrāṁ duṣṭāṁ jānāti Rāghavaḥ/
tathālokasya sākṣi māṁ sarvataḥ pātu pāvakaḥ//
avamuktvā tu vaidehī parikramya hutāśanam/
viveśa jvalanaṁ dīptaṁ niḥśaṅkenāntarātmanā//
janaśca sumahāṁṣtatra bālavṛdhasamākulaḥ/
dadarśa maithilīṁ diptaṁ praviśantīṁ hutāśanam//
sā taptanavahemābhā taptakāñcanabhuṣanā/
papāta jvalanaṁ dīptaṁ sarvalokasya saṁnidhau//
dadrśustāṁ viśālākṣīṁ patantīṁ havyavāhanam/
sītāṁ sarvāṅi rupāṅi rukmavedinibhāṁ tadā//
dadṛśustāṁ mahābhāgāṁ praviśantīṁ hutāśnam/
ṛṣayo devagandharvā yajñe pūrṅahūtīmiva//
pracukruśuḥ striyaḥ sarvāstāṁ dṛṣṭvā havyavāhane/
patantīṁ saṁskṛtāṁ mantrirvasordhārāmivādhvare//
dadṛśustāṁ trayo lokā devagandharva dānavāḥ/
śaptāṁ patantīṁ niraye tridivāddevatāmiva//
tasyāmagniṁ viśantyaṁ tu hāheti vipulaḥ svanaḥ/
rakṣasāṁ vānarāṅāṁ ca sambabhūvābhutopamaḥ//

Vāl. Rāmā. Yuddhakāṅḍa, Canto 117, 23-34

'anantaramarundhatīva pavitracāritranidheradhidevatā patidevateyamanādipuṁsoapi parasya matyardharmena pratyāyanāya nāyakasya puraḥ puraṁdaramukhān barhirmukhānpuraskṛtya bhagavantamaravindāsanamin-dukaleva punarude ṣyantī tapanamiva dahanamanujagāhe//

(a) *prāvikṣadaciṣi paraṁ nijaśudhihetordevī viśudhacaritā*
ahṁściraṁ hi yadapāvanavastusaṅgātyaktaḥ svayaṁ tadamunā damunā babhuva/

(b) *viśudhaśīlāmanalena saṅgādvidehajāṁ tatra vilokya sītām/*
prahāṁ punaḥ pratyuṣasīva pūṣā ptyagrahītsoagrasaro raghūṅāṁ//

CR. Yuddhakāṅḍa, pp. 552-554.

13. *Kascidasti samastavānarapatiḥ sugrīva iti/*
tena brātṛbhāyādṛṣyamūkamūpāśritena yuvābhyāṁ
samṁ sakhyamicchatā preṣitaṁ Hanūmadabhidhānaṁ
vikṣurupacchannaṁ Vānaramīmaṁ janamāñjaneyaṁ
prabhañjanasaṁjataṁ jānītamiti/
tatastadīyaṁ vacanamākaṁya kaṁayugalasudhāvarṣi
devarṣipratimo dāśarathistamupāśliṣya taddarśitena
pathā viracitabhuvanasaukhyaṁ sakhyaṁ
tapanatanayena sākamagnisākṣikamakarot//

CR. Kiṣkindhākāṅḍa, pp. 300-301

14. *kṣitipatitanayānāṁ hanta garbheścarāṅāṁ*
kimuniravadhi maugdhyaṁ śaurjyavajjanasidhvam//
mama hṛdi nirapāye vartamāne kapīndre
raghuvara ! yadmuṣmai tiṣṭhase cāpapāṅiḥ//

Ibid, Verse 19

15. *tataḥ pravṛttaṁ sukrūraṁ Rāmarāvaṅayostadā/*
sumahaddirathaṁ yuddaṁ sarvalokabhayābaham//
torākṣasasainyaṁ ca hariṅāṁ ca mahadbalam/
pragṛhītapraharaṅaṁ niśceṣṭaṁ samavartat//
samprayuddhau tu tau dṛṣṭvā balavannararākṣasau/
vyākṣiptahṛdayāḥ sarveparaṁ vismayamāgatāḥ/

Vāl. Rāmā Yuddhakāṅḍa, Canto. 107, 1-3

16. *'tadanuhavirāharaṅāya dharaṅau kṛtāvataraṅāḥ*
sarve gīrvāṅagaṅāḥ śatamukhapramukhāścaturmukhā
ya daśamukhapratāpagrīṣmoṣmasaṁploṣaṅamāvedya
tena saha śaraṅamiti śāṅgadhanvānaṁ manvānā
nānāvidhaprastutastutayaḥ kṣīrāmburāśimāseduḥ/'

CR. Bālakāṅḍa, p. 16

17. *vinodamicchannatha darpajanmano raṅeṅa Kaṅḍavāstridaśaiḥ samṁ punaḥ/*
sa Rāvaṅo nāma nikāmabhīṣanaṁ babhūba rakṣaḥ kṣatarakṣanaṁ divaḥ//
prabhurbubhūṣurbhuvanatrayasya yaḥ śiroatirāgaddasamṁ cikartiṣuḥ/
atarkayadvighnamiveṣtasāhasaḥ prasādamicchāsadṛśaṁ pinākinaḥ//
samutkṣipan yaḥ pṛthivībṛtāṁ varaṁ barapradānasya cakāra śulinaḥ/
trasattuṣāradrisutāsasaṁbhramsvayaṁ grahāśleṣa sukhena niṣkrayam//

purīmavaṣkanda lunohi nandanaṁ musāṅa ratnāni harāmarāṅganāḥ/
bigṛhya cakre namucidviṣā vasī yaḥ ithyamasvā sthyamaharddivaṁ divaḥ//
aśaknuvan sohumadhīralocanaḥ sahasraraśmeriva yasya darśanam/
praviśya hemādriguhāgṛhantaraṁ ināya vibhyaddivasāni kauśikaḥ//

Śiśu. 1/48-53

18. *tataḥ krodhāddaśagrīvaḥ śaransaṁdhāyavīryavan/*
mumuca dhvajamuddiśya rāghavasya rathesthitam//
tumulaṁ trāsajananaṁ bhīmṁ bhimapratisvanam/
tadvarṣambhavadyudhe naikaśastramayaṁ mahat//
Rāvaṅoapi tataḥ krudho rathastho rākṣaseśvaraḥ/
godāmusalavarṣeṅa rāmṁ pratyardyadraṅe//

Vāl. Rāmā. Yuddhakāṅḍa, Canto 107/8, 19, 63.

19. *taraṅgākṛstamātaṅḍaturaṅgāyasitāruṅa/*
fenacchannasvamātaṅgamārganavyagravāsavā

CR. Bālakāṅḍa, Verse 79.

20. *jalāghātattahāsogrāṁ phenanirmalahāsinīm/*
kvacidvenīkṛtajalāṁ kvacidāvartaśobhitām//

Vāl, Rāmā. Ayodhyākāṅḍa, Canto. 50/16

21. CR. Ayodhyākāṅḍa, Verse 6.
22. AVC, 392-393.
23. *'avamasau krīḍitānanekapāmarān girīn grāmāṁścha bahutaṁgopaśobhitāḥ saritaḥ sīmnaśca vyūhapatrarathān pathaḥ pādapāṁśca laṅghayan, sālasahitaḥ purīrnāriśca sevamānaḥ pacyamānagodhumaśyāmalāḥ ksetrabhuvo bhillapalliśca pariharan, vidhavāḥ śatrusīmantiniratavīścatikrąman, parivārīni bandhukulāni sarāṁṣi ca bahumānayan, nāticirena ravirathaturaṅgaparihṛtaviṣamaśiraḥ iśikharasahasra mjasrammaragaṅa gandharvasidharudhaskandha madhyaṁ vindhyācelamanusasāra'.*

NC. 5, p. 275

BIBLIOGRAPHY

(A) Original Sanskrit Works

Abhijñanaśakuntalam of Kālidāsa : Ed. by Ramendra Mohan Bose, Modern Book Agency, Pvt. Ltd., 10 Baṇkiṁ Chatterjī Street, Calcutta 12, 4th edn., 1963.

Abhilaṣitāthācintāmoṇi (Mānasollāsa) of Someśvara : (i) Gos. 28, 48, 138., 3 Vols. 1925, 1939, 1961. (ii) Vol. 1. (Chs. 1-3), Mysore Oriental Library Series 69, 1926.

Abhinavabhāratī of Abhinavagupta (Commentary on the 'Nāṭyaśāstra') : Gos. Vol. 1, 1st edn. 1926, 2nd edn. 1956, Vol. II. 1934, Vol. III, 1954.

Agnipurāṇa : Ānandāśrama Sanskrit Series No. 41, Poona, 1900

Aitareya Brāhmaṇa : Ānandaśrama Sanskrit granthāvaliḥ No. 2. 32, 1977

Alaṁkāraśekhara of Keśavamiśra : Ādyar Lirary Series No. 70. 1949 also Śrīveṇkaṭeśvara Oriental Institute, Tirupati.

Alaṁkārasarvasva of Ruyyaka : (i) With Jayaratha's commentary, KM. 35, 1939.
(ii) With Samudrabandhana's Commentary, TSS. 40, 1926.
(iii) With Vidyāchakravartīn's Commentary, Meharchānd Lachhmandāss, Delhi.1963

Amarakoṣa of Amarasiṁha : (i) Tīkā Sarvasva of Sarvānanda Trivandrum Sanskrit Series. 38, 43, 51, 52, 1914, 1915, 1917.
(ii) Poona Oriental Series No. 43,1913
(iii) Padacandrikā by Rāyamukuta, Calcutta Sanskrit College, 2 vols, 1966, 1973

Ānandavṛndāvana Campū of Kavikarṇapūra : Ed. by Manīndra Nāth Guha, Published by Śrī Śrī Haridās Śāstrī Śrī Gadādhar Gaurīhari Press, Kaliydāḥ, Vṛndāvan.

Aṣṭādhyāyi of Pāṇinī, Vol. I, II. : Ed. by Candra Vasu, Motilal Bānārasīdāss, Delhi

Aśvavaidyaka with an appendix containing the text of Nakula's 'Aśvacikitsita' : Ed. by Umesh Chandra Gupta, Govt. Sanskrit College, Calcutta, 1st. edn. 1887. The Asiatic Society of Bengal. 1887.

Bhāgavata Campū of Abhinava Kālidāsa : Gopal Narayan Co., Booksellers, Kālbādevī, Bombay, 1926

Bhaṭṭikāvya of Bhaṭṭī : With Commentary of Jayamaṇgala by Ed. by Vāsudeva Lakṣmaṇśāstrī Paṇśīkar, NSP, Bombay, 8th edn. 1934.

Bhāvaprakāśa of Bhāvamiśra : Ed. by

(i) Kavirāj Śrī Devendranāth Sengupta and Kavirāj Śrī Upendranāth Sengupta, C. K. Sen and Co. Ltd. 27 No. Kulutolā street, Calcutta.

(ii) Kāsī Sanskrit Granthamālā No. 130 Edited with the 'Vidyotini' Hindi Commentary, Notes and Appendix by Sri Brahmaśāṇkara Miśra and Sri Rupalājī Vaiśya, Chawkhambā Sanskrit Series Office, Vārānasī—1, 5th edn. 1969.

Bhojaprabandha of Ballālasena : Ed. by

(i) Jīvanānda Vidyāsagar, Calcutta, 1872, 1883

(ii) Vāsudedeva Lakṣmaṇ śāstrī paṇśīkar, NSP. Bombay, 1921.

Brahmāṇḍpurāṇa :

Ed. by Prof. J. L. Śāstrī, Motilal Bānārasidāss, 1st edn. 1973

Brahmasūtraśāṇkarabhāsya : with the Commentaries Bhāsyaratnaprabhā of Govindānanda Vāmatī of Vāsaspatimiśra, Nyāyanirṇaya of Ānandagiri, Ed. by J. L. Śāstrī, Motilal Bānārasīdāss, 1st. edn., 1980, 2nd edn. 1988.

Brahmasūtrabhāsyanirṇayaḥ of Vādarāyaṇa : Ed. by Ciddhānananda purī, Kāsī Śrī Rāmkṛṣṇa-sevāśram, 1943

Bṛhatsaṁhitā of Varāhmihira : Chawkhambā Vidyā Bhavan, Vārānasi, 1977

Campū Bhāratam of Anantabhaṭṭa : Chawkhambā Vidyābhavan, Vārānasī, 1957.

Campūrāmāyaṇa (R) of Bhoja :

(i) With Commentary of Rāmacandra Budhendra, Ed. By Vāsudeva Lakṣmaṇśāstrī Paṇśīkar, NSP, Bombay, 1917, Reprinted 1982, Chawkhambā Sanskrit Sansthān

(ii) Pt. Rāmnāth Tripāthī Chaukhambā Amarbharatī Prakāśan, Vārānasī, 1st edn. 1979.

(iii) Jīvanānanda Bhaṭṭācārya, Calcutta, 1st edn. 1878, and 2nd edn. 1880

(iv) V. Śaṇkar Śāstrī and T. V. Ratnam Āyyar, Madras Oriental Press.

(v) Rāmacandra Miśra, Chaukhambā Vidyābhavan, 1st edn. 1956, 2nd edn., 1971

(vi) T. V. Tattvācāryd, Madras Vivekānanda Press 1888.

Cāṇakyarājanīti of Cāṇakya : Ed. by L. Sternbach, Ādyar, 1963.

Cārucaryā of Bhoja : Ed. by

(i) B. Rama Rao, Dakṣiṇ Bhāratī Press, Hyderabad, 1st. edn. 1971.

(ii) Veturiśaṇkar Śāstrī (In telegu script) Muktyāl ārṣarasāyanśālā, 1957.

Carakasaṁhitā of Caraka : Ed. by Rājeśvara Dutta Śāstrī, Yadunanda Upādhya, Gaṇgā Sāhāya Pāṇḍeya, Chaukhambā Vidyā Bhavan, Vārānasī – 1961.

Caturvargacintāmoṇi of Hemadri : Ed. by Pt. Yogeśvara Bhaṭṭācārya, Pt. Kāmakhyānāth Tarkaratna, Asiatic Society Bengal.

Caurapañcāśikā of Bilhana : KM. 13

Chandamañjarī of Gaṇgādāsa : Ed. by Pt. Ananta Rām Śāstrī Haridās Sanskrit granthamālā, No. 115, Vanāras

Cikitsātilaka of Śrī Nivās Śāstrī : Ed. by S. Veṇkata Subrahmaṇya Śāstrī, Govt. Oriental Manuscript Library, Madras, 1958.

Citracampū (An alligorical work on the life of the king Citrasena of Bengal) : Ed. by – Rāmcaraṇ Chakravartī, Vanāras, 1940.

Colacampū of Virupākṣa : Madras Govt. Oriental Series no. 12, Tanjore Sarasvatī Mahal Series No. 55, Madras.

Daśakumāracarita of Daṇḍin : Ed. by Tārā Candra Śarmā, Haridās Sanskrit Series, 92, Chawkhambā Sanskrit Series Office Vanāras, 3rd edn. 1965.

Daśarupaka of Dhanañjaya : Ed. by –
(i) Dr. Baijnāth Pāṇḍeya, Motilal Bānārasīdāss, 1st edn. 1979.
(ii) J. K. Rājavaidya Śāstrī Gondal, Kathiawar, 1942.

Dhvanyāloka of Ānandavardhana :
(i) With Locana of Abhinavagupta, KM No. 25, 1928
(ii) With Locana, Kaumudī of Uttuṇgodaya and Upalocana of Kuppusvāmīśāstrī, KSRI, Madras, 1944.

Gaṅgāvataraṇacampū of Śaṇskara Dikṣita : India Office Catalogue, 7, 4041/114.

Gopāla Campū of Jīva Goswamī : Ed. by – Śyāmādas, Vṛndāvan Harināma Saṁkṛttana.

Hanūmatvijayacampū or (Mārutivijayacampū) of Raghūnātha Kavi : Tanjore catalogue

Harṣacarita of Bāṇabhaṭṭa : Ed. by
(i) Vāsudeva Lakṣmaṇ Śāstrī Panṣīdāss, NSP, Bombay, 1937
(ii) P. V. Kāne, Motilal Bānārasīdāss, 1st edn. 1964, 2nd edn. 1987.

Isādidaśopaniṣad : With Śāṇkarabhāsya, Motilal Bānārasīdāss, 1st edn. 1964, 2nd edn. 1987.

Jātakamālā of Āryaśūra : Ed. by – Śūryanārāya Chaudhurī Motilal Bānārasīdāss.

Jīvandharacampū of Samarapuṁgava Dikṣita : Ed. by – T. S. Kuppuswāmī Śāstrī, Tanjore, 1905.

Kālamādhavakārikā of Mādhavācārya : Ed. by Śaṇkara Śāstrī, Ānandāśrama Sanskrit Series No. 119. Poonā 1942.

Kāmandakīyanītisāra of Kāmandaka : Trivāndrum Sanṣkrit Series, No. 14, 1912.

Kathāsaritsāgara of Somadeva : Ed. by Pt. Kedārnāth Śarmā Sārasvat, Vihār Rāstrabhāsā Pariṣad, Patnā, 1st edn. 1960.

Kāvyadarśa of Daṇḍin : With Commentary's by Tarunavācaspati and the Hṛdayamgama by M. Raṇgāchārya, Madras, 1910.

Kāvyalaṁkārasūtravṛtti of Vāmana : Ed. by Pt. Kedārnāth śarmā Chaukhambā Amarbhāratī, Prakāśan, Venāras, 2nd Ed. 1979.

Kāvyānuśāsana of Hemacandra : With his own Commentary Viveka K. M. No. 70, 1901, ed. by Pārik and Kūlkārṇī, Bombay, 1964.

Kāvyānuśāsana of Vāgbhaṭa : With his own Commentary, KM. No. 43, 1915.

Kāvyaprakāśa of Mammata : Ed. by –

(i) Narendra Candra Vedāntatīrtha, Calcutta Sanskrit Granthamāla VI. Matropolitan Printing and Publishing House, Calcutta, 1936.

(ii) Govt. Oriental Library Series No. 60

(iii) Trivāndrum Sanskrit Series, No. 88, 100, 1926, 1930.

Kumārasambhavam of Kālidāsa : Ed. by –

(i) M. R. Kale, Motilal Bānārasīdāss.

(ii) With Mallinātha's Commentary, with commentary of Aruṇgiri nātha and Nārāyaṇa, Trivandrum Sanskrit Series, No. 36

Kūrmapurāṇa : Ed. by Pt. Rāmśarmāācārya, Sanskrit Saṁsthān Khājākutub Vedanagar, 1970.

Madālasācampū of Trivikramabhaṭṭa : Poonā, 1882

Madanarekhāākhyāyikācampū of Jñanabharasūri : Ed. by– Bechards Doshī, L. D. Institute of Indology, Ahmedābād, 1973.

Mādhavacampū : Ed. by Ciranjīva Bhaṭṭācārya, 1871.

Mahābhārata of Vyāsa (Ādi, Sabhā, Vana, Anuśāsana, Karṇa, Udyoga, Bhīṣmaparva and Śāntiparva) : Ed by Pt. Rāmacandra Śāstrīkinjawadekar, Chitraśālā Press, 1026, Sadāshivpeth, Poonā City.

Mandāramarandacampū of Kṛṣṇa Kavi : N. S. P. Bombay, KM. 52, 2nd edn. 1924.

Manusmṛti : Ed. by – Prof. J. L. Shāstrī, Motilal Bānārasīdāss, 1st edn. 1983.

Mārgasahāyacampū of Navanīta : Descriptive Catalogue, Madras, No. 12336

Meghadūta of Kālidāsa : With commentary of Mallinātha, Ed. by – M. R. Kāle, Motilal Bānārasīdāss.

Naiṣadhacarita of Śrīharṣa : Ed. by Mahāmohopādhya –

Pt. Śivadatta and Nārāraṇ Rām Ācharya, NSP, Bombay, 1942.

Nalacampū of Trivikramabhaṭṭa : KSS. No. 98, Ed. By – Kaliāśpati Tripāthī, Chaukhambā Sanskrit Saṇsthān, Vārānasī, 3rd edn. 1976.

Nāmamālikā of Bhoja : Ed. By Ekanāth Dattātreya Kūlkārṇī and Vāsudeo Dāmodar Gokhle, Deccan College Post Graduate and Research Iṇstitute, Poonā, 1st edn. 1955.

Nāradapurāṇa, Part I : Ed by – Śrī Rāma Śarmā ācārya, Sanskrit Saṇsthān Khājā – Kutub (Vedanagar) Bereli 1984.

Nāṭyaśāstra of Bharata : Ed. by –
(i) Rām Kṛṣṇa Kavi, GOS, No. LXVII, Oriental Institute, Baradā, 1934.
(ii) KSS No. 60, Chawkhambā Sanskrit Series Office, Vidyāvilās Press, Vānāras, 1929.

Navasāhasāṁkacarit of Padmagupta : Ed. by –
(i) Vāman Śāstrī Istampurkār, Bombay Sanskrit Series, No. 53, Bombay. 1895
(ii) Jitendra Candra Bharatīyā Śāstrī, Part I, Chaukhambā Vidyābhavan, Sanskrit Granthamālā, No. 66, Vānāras, 1961

Nīlakaṇṭhavijayacampū of Nīlakaṇṭha Dikṣhita : With Vibudhānanda's Commentary of Mahādevasūri, Sanskrit education society, Madras, 1st edn. 1941, 2nd edn. 1958, 3rd edn. 1972.

Nṛsiṁhacampū of keśavabhaṭṭa : Ed. by Dr. Sūryakānta Śāstrī, Chaukhambā Vidyābhavan, Vidyāvilās Press, Vārānasī, 1st edn. Saṁvat, 2016 (1959)

Pañcatantra of Viṣṇuśarmā : (i) Ed. by Dr. Jhannes Hertel, The Hārvārd University Press, 1915
(ii) M. R. Kāle, Motilāl Bānārasīdāss.

Pārijātaharaṇacampū of Śeṣakṛṣna : KM. No. 14, NSP, Bombay, 1926

Pārijātamañjarī (Nāṭaka) : Ed. by E. Hultzsch, Bombay Education Society, Press, 1915.

Prabandhacintāmoṇi of Merutuṇgācārya : Ed. by Durgasaṇkar Kevalrām Śāstrī, Bombay, 1932.

Prabhāvakacarita of Candraprabhasūri : NSP, Bombay, 1909

Prākṛtprakāśa of Vararuci : Ed. by – Śrīkānt Pāṇḍeya, Sāhitya Bhāndar, North Subhāṣ bāzār, Merath-2 1st edn. 1981.

Ragūvaṁśa of Kālidāsa : Ed. by Kṛṣna Rāo Mahādeva Jogalkar, NSP, Bombay, 1934.

Ṛgveda with Commentary of Sāyana Vaidika Śaṁśodhana, Maṇḍla, Poonā, 1951.

Ṛgveda Saṁhitā : Ed. by Lakṣmaṇsarup, Motilāl Bānārasīdāss, Oriental Publishers, 1943

Rājamārtaṇḍa (Medicine) of Bhoja :

(i) Jādavjī Tricumji Ācārya, Āyurvedīya granthamālā No. 45, 1st edn. 1912, 2nd edn. 1924.

(ii) With Hindi Commentary by Pāvanīprasād Śarmā, Ed. by Brahma Śaṇkar Miśra, Chawkhambā Vidyābhavan, Vārānasī, 1966.

Rājamārtaṇḍa (Astrology) of Bhoja : Ed. by – Kṣemarāj Śrīkṛṣnadās, 1953.

Rājamārtaṇḍa of Bhoja (With the Commentary of Patañjali Yogasūtra) : Ed. by Nyāyācārya Kāvya, Pt. Dhvandhīrāj Śāstrī Kāsī Sanskrit Series, Haridās Sanskrit granthamālā, No. 83,Venāras 1930.

Rājataraṇginī of Kalhana : Ed. by Pāṇḍa Ramtej Śāstrī Pandit Pustakālaya Kāsī, 1960.

Rāmāyaṇa of Vālmīki : Ed. by –

(i) Vāsudeva Lakṣmaṇ Śāstrī, Panśīkar, NSP, Bombay, 1930.

(ii) Pañcānan Tarkaratna, 3 Vols, Calcutta, 1908.

(ii) Bālākāṇḍa and Ayodhyākāṇḍa critically edited by GOH, Bhaṭṭ and P. L. Vaidya, Oriental Institute, Borodā, 1960, 1962.

Śabdakalpadruma I, II, III, V : Rādhakānta Deva, Reprint, 1961

Śabdānuśāsana of Hemacandra, Part I : Ed by Śrī Ānandabodhinīvṛttikārah ācāryaśrī candra Sagarasūrivargaḥ published by Śrī Ṛṣabhdevjī Chaganīrāmajīpetī sansthā, T. Daherakhidakī, Khārākuā, Ujjain (Mālava), Vikramasaṁvat – 2007, Munshī Rām Manoharlāl, Oriental and Foreign Book Sellers, Naisarak, Delhi- 6.

Ṣaḍdarśanasamuccaya of Haribhadrasūri : With Commentaries of Tarkarahasya dīpikā of

Guṇaratnasūri an and Avacūrṇī, Ed. by Dr. Mahendra Kumārjain, Nyāyācārya, with the introduction of Pt. Dalasukh Mālavanīya, Bhāratīya jñanapīṭha publication, 1969.

Sāhityadarpaṇa of Viśvanātha : Ed. by Satyavrata Singh, Vidyābhavan Sanskrit Granthamāla, No. 29. Chawkhambā Vidyābhavan, Vanāras, 5th edn. 1979.

Śālihotra of Bhoja : Ed. by Ekanāth Dattātriya Kūlkārṇī Deccan College Post Graduate and Research Institute, Poonā, 1st Edn. 1953.

Samarāṅgaṇasūtradhāra of Bhoja : Gos. No. 25, Originally Edited by T. Ganapati Śāstrī revised edited by Vāsuevacaraṇ Agraval. Oriental Institute, Baroda, 1966.

Sāṁkhyakārikā of Iśvarakṛṣna : With Commentary of Yuktidīpikā, Calcutta, 1938, 1948.

Saṁkṣiptasāra of Kramadīśvara : Ed. by Jivanānanda Vidyāsāgara. Sanskrit College, Calcutta.

Sarasvatīkaṇṭhābharaṇa of Bhoja : Ed by –

(i) Kedār nāth Śarmā and Vāsudeva Śarmā, NSP, Bombay, 1934.

(ii) Ānundo Rām Barooah, with notes and extracts from old Commentaries, 1st edn. 1884, Calcutta.

(iii) Ratneśvara Miśra, Chawkhambā Orientaliā, Vānārasī-1976.

Sarvadaśanasaṁgraha of Mādhavācārya : Ed. by Dr. Umā Saṇkar Śarmā Ṛṣi, Chawkhambā Vidyābhavan, Vārānasī, 3rd edn. 1984.

Siṁhāsandvātriṁśatputtalikā : Calcutta, 1931, 1948

Śiśupālavadha of Māgha : With the Commentary of Mallinātha Ed. by – Pt. Haragovinda Śāstri, Vidyābhavan Sanskrit granthamālā, No. 8.

Śrādhaviveka of Śūlapāṇi : Ed. by – Śrīkṛṣṇa Tarkālaṁkāra, by Chandīcaran Smṛtibhuṣan, Calcutta Sanskrit College, Press, 1920.

Śrīmad, Bhāgavat: Ed. by Dhanañjaya Das and Nirmal Das, Vinodvihārī Chakravartī 1346. Baṇgābda, Calcutta.

Śrinivāsacampū of Veṇkaṭadhvāri : Gopāl Nārāyaṇ Company, Bombay.

Śṛṅgāraprakāśa of Bhoja : Ed. by Dr. V. Rāghavan, 3rd revised enlarged Edn. Vasanta Press. The theosophical society, Ādyar, Madras, 1978.

Sṛṅgāramañjarī of Bhoja : Singhi Jain Series, 30, 1959.

Śukranīti of Śukra : Ed. by Gaṅgā Prasād Śastrī, 1941.

Sūktimuktāvalī of Bhagadatta Jalhana : Oriental Institute Boroda.

Taittīreyasaṁhitā Ānandāśrama Sanskrit Granthavalīḥ, Vols. 1-V, 1940-1946.

Tattvaguṇārśacampū of Annayācārya : Descriptive Catalogue Madras, No. 12295

Tattvaprakāśa of Bhoja

(i) With Tātparyadīpikā vṛtti and Hindi translation, Commentary by Kumāradeva and Aghoraśivācārya.

(ii) Kāmeśvaranāth miśra, Chawkhambā Orientalia, Vārānasī, 2nd edn. 1976.

(iii) T. Gaṇapati Śāstrī, TSS, No. 68, 1st edn. 1920.

Ūnādisūtra of Bhoja : Madras University Sanskrit Series, No. 7, Part 6. The Ūnādisūtras in various recensions. The Ūnādisūtra of Bhoja with the Vṛtti of Dandanātha Nārāyana, Ed. by T. R. Chintāmoṇi, University of Madras.

Upaniṣadsaṁgrah : Ed. by Prof. J. L. Śāstrī, Motilāl Bānārasīdāss.

Uttararāmacarita of Bhavabhūti : Ed. by – G. K. Bhāt, The Popular publishing House, Tower Road, Surat, 2nd edn. Oct. 1965.

Varadāmbikāpariṇayacampū of Tirumalambā : Ed. by – Sūryakānta Śāstrī, Vānāras.

Varāha purāṇa : Ed. by Pt. Rāmji Śarmā Ācārya, Sanskrit Sansthān, Khājākutub, Vedanagar, Bereli (U.P.)

Vidvanmodataranginīcampū of Cirañjīva Bhaṭṭācārya : Śrī Veṇkaṭaḍeśwara Press, Bombay, 1928.

Vikramāṇkadevacarite of Bilhana :

(i) BSS 14, 1875

(ii) Princess of Wales, Sarasvatī Bhavan texts Series, No. 82, 1945.

Vikramāṇkabhudayānī (A Historical Campū of Someśvara of Kalyāṇa) : Muruli nagar Boroda, Oriental Institute, 1966.

Viṣṇupurāṇa, I, II : Ed. by–
(i) Pt. Rāmjī Śarmā Ācārya, Sanskrit Sansthān, Khājākutub, Vedanagar, Bereli (U.P.)
(ii) Veṇkaṭeśvar Press, Bombay, 1912.
(iii) Dr. Śrī Śrī Jīvanyāyatīrtha, Navabhārat Publishers, 72, Mahātmā Gāndhī Road, Calcutta 9.

Viśvaguṇadarśacampū of Veṇkaṭadhvāri : NSP. Bombay 1923.

Yajñavalkyasmṛti : Ed. by Jagannāth Śāstrī, Chaukhambā Sanskrit Series Office, Vidya Vilās Press, North Gopal Mandir, Vānāras, 1930.

Yātrāprabandhacampū of Samarapuṁgava Dīkṣita : KM. No. 90 NSP, Bombay, 1936

Yuktikalpataru of Bhoja : Ed. by Pt. Iśvar Candra Śāstrī Calcutta Oriental Series No., 1st edn., 1911.

(B) Modern Works

Agraval, H. R. : '*A short history of Sanskrit literature*' Munshī Rām Monoharlāl, Oriental publishers and Book Sellers, Naisarak, Delhi- 6.

Ali, Salim, : *The book of Indian Birds*, 11th edn. Bombay Nutural History Society, Oxford University Press.

Altekar, A. S. : '*Education in Ancient India*'. Nanda Kishore and Brothers.

Altekar, A. S. '*The Position of Woman in Hindu Civilization*', Motilal Bānārasīdāss, Delhi.

Apte, V.S. : '*Sanskrit English Dictionary*', Vol. II, (Kho-bha), Motilal Banarasidass, Delhi.

Aufrecht, Simon Theodor : 'Catalogus Caṭalogorum', Vol. I, II, III.

Aufrecht, Simon Theodor. '*Catalogue Codicum Manuscriptorum Sansriticorum post vedicorum.*'

Benīprasād : 'The State of Ancient India' The Indian Press Ltd. Allahabad, 1928.

Bhāgavatī Kāmākhyācaran : '*Sanskrit Sāhityar Jiliṇani*' Granthapīth, Pānbāzār, Guwahati, 1st edn., 1973, 2nd edn. 1988.

Bharadvaja, K. '*A Philosophical study of the Concept of Viṣṇu in the Purāṇas*', Pitambar publishing Co. Delhi, 1st edn. 1981.

Borooah, Anundo, Ram, : *'Ancient Goegraphy of India'* Publication Board Assam, Gauhati 3.

Bulche, C. : 'Ram, : 'Rāma Kathā utpati Aura Vikāśa', Hindi Parisad, Viśvavidyālaya, Prayāge, 1950.

Candrasekharan, K. : *'Sanskrit literature'*, Motilal Bānārasīdāss, Delhi.

Dalal, C. D. : *'A Catalogus of Manuscripts in the Jain Bhandars at jeasalmere'*, Central Library, Boroda – 1923, Gos, No. XXI.

Das, S. K. : *'Educational system of Ancient Hindus'*, Calcutta 1930.

Dasgupta, S. N. and De, S. K. : *'A History of Sanskrit Literature'*, Classical Period, Vol. I, University of Calcutta, 1975.

De, S. K., : *'History of Sanskrit Poetics'* Motilāl Bānārasīdāss, Delhi.,

Deshmukh, P. S. : *'The Origin and Development of Religion in Vedic Literature'*, Oxford University Press, 1933.

Dharma, P. C. *'The Rāmāyaṇa Polity'*, Madras - 1941

Duff, M.C. : 'The Chronology of Indian History' (From the earliest times to the beginning of the Sixteen century) Cosmopublication, Delhi, 6, 1st edn. 1972.

Dutta, A. C. 'A Class Book of Botany' (for degree), Oxford University Press, 8th edn, 1975.

Cutta, N. K. : *'Origin and Growth of Caste in India'*, The Book Company Ltd. Calcutta. 1931.

Frank, Whaling : *'The rise of the religious significance of Rāma'*, Motilal Bānārasīdāss, 1st edn. Delhi 1980.

Ghosa, R. C. *'The Literary remains of Dr. Bhāudājī'* Rama and friend Publishers Calcutta, 1888.

Ghoshal, U.N. : *'Studies in Indian History and Culture'*, Orient Longmans, 1957.

Gowen, H. H. : *'A History of Indian Literature'*, (From Vedic time to present day), Seema Publication,

Hopkins, E. W. *'Epic mythology'*, Strassburg, 1915.

Israey, Samuel : *'Indian Wildlife'* (the great adventure Series) APA Productions.

Iyer, T. Paramasiva : *'Rāmāyaṇa and Laṇkā'*, Part I, II, Bangalore City, 1940.

Jayal, Shakambare : *'The Status of Woman in the Epics'* Motilal Bānārasīdāss, 1966

Kāne, P. V. : *'History of Sanskrit Poetics'* Motilal Bānārasīdāss, Delhi, 1966

Kāne, P. V. *'History of Dharmaśāstra'*, Vol. I, II, III,. Govt. Ori. Series, Class B, No. 6, Poona 1930-41

Keith, A. B. : *'History of Sanskrit Literature'* Oxford University Press, London, 1st edn. 1920.

Khan, Banjamin : *'The Concept of Dharma in the Vālmīki Rāmāyaṇa'*, Munshī Rām Monoharlāl, 1965.

Krishnamachariar, M. 'History of Classical Sanskrit Literature', Tirumalai Tirupati Devasthanamas Press, Madras, 1937.

Law, Bimala Churan : *'Historical Geography of Ancient India'*, Cosmos Publication, Delhi

Macdonell, A. A. : *'History of Sanskrit Literature'*, London, 1905

Mainkar, T. G. : *'Writings and Speech of Dr. Bhāudajī Lad (1824-1874)'* University of Bombay, 1974

Majumdar, R. C. : *The History and Culture of Indian People* (The struggle for empire), Bhāratīya Vidyābhavan, Bombay, 1st edn. 1957.

Mani, Vettam : *Purāṇic Encyclopaedia*, A Comprehensive Dictionary with special Reference to the Epic and Purāṇic Literature, Motilāl Bānārasīdāss, Delhi 1st edn. 1975, Reprint, 1979, 1984, 1989.

Miśra, Hari Rām : *'Theory of Rasa in Sanskrit Drama'* Vindhyacal Prakasan, Vanaras, 1967.

Monier Williams M. *'The Sanskrit English Dictionary'* Oxford University Press, London 1951.

Mookherji, H. : *'Plant groups'* New Central Book Agency, 8/1, Centamoni Das Lane, Calcutta, 7th edn. 1967.

Mookherji R. K. : *'Ancient Indian Education'*, Macmillan and Company Ltd., London, 1951.

Navelkar, N. R. : *'A New Approach to the Rāmāyaṇa'*, Jabalpur.

Oliver, S. Egbert : *'American Literature' 1890-1965*, Euasia Publishing House Pvt. Ltd. Ram Nagar, New Delhi 1991.

Omprokaśh : *'Food and Drinks in Ancient India'*, Munshī Rām Monoharlāl, Delhi 6, 1961.

Pāṇḍey Rājavalī : *'Hindu Saṇskāras'*, Vikram Publication, Vānāras, 1949.

Pāṇḍey Candraśekhar : *Sanskrit Sāhitya Ki Ruprekhā*, Chawkhambā Vidyābhavan, Vānāras, Vārānasī 1965.

Rāmaswāmī, K. S. *'Studies in Rāmayaṇa'*, 1st edn., 1944, Borada.

Raṇgenāthan, M. K. : 'A Mahodaya art Souvenir of Theertha and Varṇa from the immortal Bhoja's Royal House of the Eleventh Century', B. N. K. Press, Madras, 1948.

Saṇkaran, A. : *'Some Aspects of Literary Crictícism in Sanskrit', University*, University of Madras, 1929.

Śāstrī Śrīnivāsa, V. S. : *'Literatures on the Rāmāyaṇa'* Madras Sanskrit Academy, 1961

Śāstrī, P. P. S. : *'Catalogue of Manuscript in the Palace Library'*, Tanjore.

Śharmā, Ramashraya : *'A Socio Political Study of the Vālmīki Rāmāyaṇa'*, Motilal Bānārasīdāss, Delhi 1986.

Shukla, D. N. : *'Hindu Science of Architecture and Town Planning with special reference to Bhoja's Samarāṅgaṇasūtradhāra'*, Motilal Bānārasīdāss, Delhi.

Triparthī, Chavināth : *'Campū Kāvya kā Ālocanatmaka Evam Aitihāsika Adhyana'*, Chaukhmba Vidyābhavan, Bānārasī 1965.

Vaidya, C. V. : *'Epic India'*, Bombay Book Depot, Bombay 1933.

Våradāchari, V. : *'History of Sanskrit Literature'* Rām Nārayaṇ Lāl Beṇīprasād, Allāhabad, 2nd edn., 1960.

Vyās, S. N. : *'India in the Rāmāyaṇa Age'*, Tatmā Rām and Sons, Delhi-1967.

Weber, A. : *'The History of Indian Literature'* Chawkhamba Sanskrit Series, Vol. XIII, Vānaras – 1961

Winternitz, M. : *'A History of Indian Literature'*, Vol. I, III, Motilāl Bānārasīdāss, Delhi, 1987.

Wurni, Alois, *'Characters portrayals in the Rāmāyaṇa of Vālmīki'*, Ajanta Publications, Delhi 1st edn. 1976.

W. J. Wilkins, : *'Hindu Mythology', (Vedic and Purāṇic)*, Delhi Book Store, Naisarak, Delhi 6, 1st edn. 1972.

Sources for the collection of the Campūkāvyas :

1. Descriptive catalogue of Sanskrit : Manuscripts of Govt. Oriental Library, Madras, (DC. Madras) Ed. by S. Kuppuswāmī Śāstrī.
2. Treenal Catalogue of Sanskrit Manuscripts, Govt. Oriental MSS Library, Mādras, Vol. I–V (TC).
3. India Office Catalogue of Sanskrit Manuscripts (India. Off. Cata.).
4. A descriptive Catalogue of Sanskrit Manuscripts in the Sarasvatī Mahal Library, Tanjore, Vol. VII, Kāvyas (Tanj. Cata.) Ed. by P. P. S. Shąstrī.
5. Notice of the Sanskrit Manuscripts. Ed. by Rajendra Lāl Mitra, Vol. I, and II, Calcutta.
6. Catalogue of Sanskrit Manuscripts in Ādyar Library, (Ādyar Skt. Mss. Cata.)
7. Reports on Sanskrit Manuscripts in S. India by E. Hultzsch, Madras, 1905 (HR)

Journals and Magazines

Epigraphica Indica, Calcutta, (Epi, Ind.)

Indian Historical quarterly, Vol. L, No. I, Calcutta (IHQ)

Chakravartī, Chintaharan, Traditions about Vānāras and Rākṣasas'.

Prince of Walse Sarasvatī Bhavan Studies, Vols. IV, V. Ray, Manṁathanāth. (i) Food and drinks in the Rāmāyaṇic Age.
(ii) In estimate of the Civilization of the Vānāras as depicted in the Rāmāyaṇa.

The Journal of Sanskrit Academy, Osmania, University, Vol. VII, 1985, Ed. by. Rāmachandran, p.

'*Bhojas grammatical work 'Sarasvatīkaṇṭhābharaṇa' A general perspective with special reference to Strīpratyayas.*

INDEX